Teaching for Excellence

Honors Pedagogies revealed

Doceren om te excelleren
Pijlers van honors didactiek

(met een samenvatting in het Nederlands)

Proefschrift

ter verkrijging van de graad van doctor
aan de Universiteit Utrecht op gezag
van de rector magnificus, prof.dr. G.J. van der Zwaan,
ingevolge het besluit van het college voor promoties
in het openbaar te verdedigen op vrijdag
21 december 2012 des ochtends te 10.30 uur

Marca Valérie Christien Wolfensberger

Geboren te Genève, Zwitserland

Promotor:
Prof.dr. R.J.F.M. van der Vaart

Teaching for Excellence

Marca V. C. Wolfensberger

Teaching for Excellence

Honors Pedagogies revealed

Waxmann 2012

Münster / New York / München / Berlin

Bibliographic information published by die Deutsche Nationalbibliothek
Die Deutsche Nationalbibliothek lists this publication in the
Deutsche Nationalbibliografie; detailed bibliographic data
are available on the internet at http://dnb.d-nb.de.

ISBN 978-3-8309-2823-2

© Waxmann Verlag GmbH, 2012
Postfach 8603, 48046 Münster, Germany
Waxmann Publishing Co.
P. O. Box 1318, New York, NY 10028, U. S. A.

www.waxmann.com
info@waxmann.com

Cover Design: Christian Averbeck, Münster
Cover Picture: © Fotoliall – Fotolia.com
Print: Hubert & Co., Göttingen
Maps and figures: Margot Stoete and Ton Markus, University Utrecht
Printed on age-resistant paper, acid-free as per ISO 9706

Printed in Germany

Table of contents

List of tables

List of figures

1   Introduction

1.1   Research problem and research questions

There is definitely something 'special' about working with honors students, though it may be difficult to pinpoint. Honors programs in higher education are designed for gifted and motivated students who are willing and able to do more than a regular program can offer, certainly in terms of academic challenge but often in their broader personal development as well (Clark & Zubizarreta 2008; Hébert & McBee 2007). One of the common mantras among honors programs and colleges dedicated to the mission of deeper, more meaningful and transformative learning experiences for high-ability students is, that honors emphasizes more depth, more connected and applied learning, more space for creative endeavors, more attention to students' individual passions and interests. Also, honors courses are presumably designed to improve students' cognitive capacity while strengthening their interpersonal and intrapersonal abilities (see, for example, Draper, Hazelton, McNamara & Kahn 1999). As a result of such priorities in honors teaching and learning, a pivotal role in honors education is played by the teacher, who, as a catalyst to talent development, is said to have a crucial impact on student achievement (Hattie 2009). Others add that the teachers' pivotal role is especially evident with high achievers (e.g., Baldwin, Vialle & Clarke 2002; Croft 2003; Renzulli 1968, 2008). Consequently, regarding honors programs for undergraduate students, teachers claim that rather than assigning extra coursework, they provide a 'different' focus, with more openness, risk-taking and challenge than found in regular classes, in order to elicit the degree of excellence which is implied by typical honors goals and strategies (Clark & Zubizarreta 2008; Friedman & Jenkins-Friedman 1986). From the early days of honors education onwards, practitioners and authors have stressed that honors education requires 'other' content and 'different' methods (Pennock 1953). The key to a successful honors program is said *"not* [to be] *the intelligence of the student or the subject matter of the course, but the attitude and approach of the instructor"* (National Collegiate Honors Council 2012).

But what exactly are the characteristics of honors pedagogy, and what are the teaching strategies that are particularly relevant to and successful in honors education? In spite of the substantial body of literature about the practice of honors education, largely referring to the United States, very little systematic and empirical research has been done on honors pedagogy. The lack of research on teaching strategies for honors in higher education is particularly striking, as acknowledged by various experts in the field (Achterberg 2005; Cosgrove 2004; Rinn & Plucker 2004; Shepherd & Shepherd 1996). It is the purpose of this study to contribute to a better understanding of honors pedagogies, focusing not just on what might distinguish honors teaching and learning from standard expectations and methodologies but also on how honors pedagogy offers both instructors and students an opportunity to fundamentally rethink their philosophy of education. The first goal is to conceptualize teaching approaches for honors education on the basis of a survey of literature from various domains (honors, giftedness, motivational theory). The second goal is to ascertain empirically what experienced honors teachers actually say they do in their honors classes (teaching strategies), in what ways this differs from how they teach regular classes, and how these practices relate to their deeper attitudes and beliefs with regard to teaching and students.

Most of what is currently known about honors education originates from studies conducted in the United States, where honors education has by far the longest tradition. The prime focus of the present study is also on honors teaching in the United States, though narrowed to the undergraduate level in higher education. As a researcher who is active in the development of honors programs in Dutch higher education, the author is alert to lessons that can be learned from the American practice for European honors education. In this context it is important to know to what extent American and Dutch honors teachers have similar or different approaches and dispositions in their honors teaching. Cultural differences, distinctive educational systems, and diverse priorities play a role in defining both the shared and unique perspectives on honors education in both countries. Therefore, a baseline comparison will be made between American and Dutch honors teachers with respect to their teaching strategies and their underlying attitudes and beliefs about (honors) teaching and students.

In summary, the central research question of this study may be phrased as follows: What are the key components of honors pedagogy and how do these translate into honors teaching practice?

1.2 Honors education

1.2.1 United States

The roots of honors education go back to the early 1920s when Frank Aydelotte (1880-1956), as President of Swarthmore College, settled on honors programs as a way to reconcile equal opportunity with academic rigor. His goal was to instill motivated and talented students with confidence and ambition (Aydelotte 1941). Once his Swarthmore honors program was in place, Aydelotte took it on the road. Of course Aydelotte was not single-handedly responsible for all the developments, but by 1940 he had helped establish honors programs on about one hundred campuses (Schaeper & Schaeper 1998). Today about half of the approximately 4000 universities and colleges in the United States have an official strategy of honors education for selected undergraduate students, such as an honors program, honors courses or an honors college (see, for example, Cummings 1994; Digby 2005; Long 2002). Some 850 institutions are members of the National Collegiate Honors Council (NCHC), a nation-wide professional association of undergraduate honors programs. NCHC was established in 1966 to assist in creating and enhancing opportunities for exceptionally able undergraduates. Member institutions are diverse in terms of scale, scope and ranking; they include research universities and community colleges and public as well as private institutions (England 2010).

One of the reasons to create and promote an honors program or honors college is the fierce competition among colleges and universities for the best students (Long 2002; Sederberg 2008). This is certainly the case at many public universities, as they attempt to attract gifted and motivated students who might otherwise attend prestigious private institutions (England 2010). Honors programs are attractive for talented prospective students, since such programs have the reputation of being relatively inexpensive, high-quality college options. Honors education features for instance special courses, seminars, colloquia, experiential learning opportunities, undergraduate research opportunities, capstone courses. Honors programs may offer additional resources and opportunities to selected students in the form of special scholarships, separate seminars and small classes, higher quality of interaction and content of the classes, personal attention from faculty and academic freedom (Clark & Zubizarreta 2008; Long 2002; Robinson 1997). Often there are additional advantages such as personal advising or mentorship, enhanced student services (e.g., help with grants and information about internships), networking possibilities and facilities such as an honors lounge, housing or prescheduling (Long 2002; Robinson 1997).

Honors requirements constitute a substantial portion of the participants' undergraduate work, typically 20% to 25% of the total course work and certainly no less than 15% (Digby 2005). Fully developed honors programs generally consist of at least two components. One is often called a university honors program or 'general honors' and is targeted at general-education requirements. The other comprises a set of disciplinary honors programs organized at departmental level, also called 'departmental honors'. Participation in general honors is not always compulsory for admission to disciplinary honors.

1.2.2 Outside the United States

Honors education is not restricted to the United States; it has diffused into other, mostly Anglo-Saxon, countries. The organizational structure of honors programs and honors colleges varies widely around the globe. In Canada, for instance, honors programs are generally limited to the departmental level within higher education (England 2010). An honors undergraduate degree in Australia can be an embedded program, but is commonly an add-on year (3+1 model). The honors program then consists of a separate year of study following the bachelor's degree and is seen as a pathway to research-oriented graduate study (Kiley, Boud, Manathunga & Cantwell 2011; Zeegers & Barron 2009). Also in other parts of the world, in a number of Asian or Middle-Eastern countries for example, special programs for gifted students have been developed. For instance in China some key universities have honors programs, mainly focusing on science and technology; specific teachers are assigned to honors students as individual tutors (Kitagaki & Li 2008). Therefore, phenomena related to excellence may take distinct forms in different cultural settings.

Honors programs made their first appearance in Northwestern Europe in the early 1990s. The Netherlands was then in the vanguard of a "*quiet revolution of excellence*" (Van den Doel 2007); Denmark and Germany followed. The first honors programs in the Netherlands were mainly aimed at graduate students (Wolfensberger, Van Eijl & Pilot 2004). However, the Bologna transition (implementation of the bachelor-master structure) throughout the Dutch higher education system resulted in a radical shift of honors to the undergraduate level. Most higher education institutions in the Netherlands now have honors courses, programs or colleges. The Dutch government, through substantial national incentive programs, has stimulated the rapid diffusion of honors in the Netherlands (Commissie Ruim Baan voor Talent 2007; Sirius Programma 2012).

The Dutch programs show similarities to those in the United States, such as featuring special courses, experiential learning or undergraduate research opportunities or a focus on reflection and academic depth, despite the obvious cultural and other contextual differences (Van Eijl, Pilot & Wolfensberger 2010). Dutch research universities and universities of applied sciences mainly offer mono-disciplinary degree programs, quite unlike the American context, where the liberal arts and sciences tradition is strong. And whereas the faculty in an American honors setting is mainly drawn from the arts and sciences with an accent on humanities, this is less the case in the Netherlands, where honors education has developed fairly equally across the life sciences, natural sciences, social sciences and humanities (Wolfensberger, De Jong & Drayer 2012). Many early honors programs in the Netherlands were added to the course load of a regular BA/BSc program, whereas in the United States honors credits mostly replace regular credits. And there is a huge difference between Dutch and American higher education in terms of fees, admissions and selection.

1.2.3 Debates about honors

Concerns about elitism and about diverting resources to talented students have been discussed widely ever since honors education started in the early 1920s. Issues such as equal access, social class and admissions have made honors a subject of debate throughout society (Bastedo & Gumport 2003; Brown 2001, 2002; Weiner 2009). Long (2002) reported that "*institutions are under pressure of state legislature and public not to abandon the mission of providing postsecondary options for students of all ability levels*" (p. 13) while they are also trying to attract high-ability students by offering honors programs and by other means. In Northwestern Europe the issue of equal access to higher education is even higher on the political agenda than in the United States. A factor further complicating the acceptance of honors in Europe is the widespread distrust of 'excellence' (Lambert & Butler 2006). Until recently in the Netherlands, special programs to support weaker students were generally accepted, whereas 'high potential programs' (honors) were considered inappropriate in a democracy where all students should be treated equally – a stance that still prevails in many European countries. This view was reinforced by the commonly held belief that gifted students will succeed anyway, even without support (although research suggests that these students achieve greater success with specialized assistance; see, for example, Park & Oliver 2009). In the Netherlands and in several European countries the acceptance of special 'talent' or 'excellence' programs, also in higher education, is currently gaining ground. But the debates about equity versus excellence, open access versus selectivity, and about the allocation of scarce resources are still taking place. Finding an acceptable balance in these matters is not an easy task (Bastedo & Gumport 2003; Hrabowski 2009; Rinn & Cobane 2009).

Another type of debate concerns transparency, legitimacy and assessment in honors programs. National or international benchmarking of honors programs is virtually non-existent (Zeegers & Barron 2009). As more public or private funds are spent on honors programs, more questions will be asked about the added value, output and proven indicators of their success. The pressure for accountability may raise difficult issues, particularly if the programs are required to 'prove' their value by standard measures such as GPA, grades, credits, study success and career indicators. Honors education is about much more than grades and cannot be reduced to what is measurable in a conventional way (Carnicom & Snyder 2010; Lanier 2008; Otero & Spurrier 2005; Wolfensberger et al. 2012).

1.3 Conceptual issues

Although honors education may be organized in various ways, its philosophy is basically the same in all cases (Austin 1991; Sederberg 2008). The terms for the various forms of organization – honors colleges, honors programs, honors courses – are used interchangeably in this study. The term honors class is reserved for direct teacher-student interaction in either formal classroom settings or as structured interaction in extracurricular activities.

The focus of this study is on teaching honors classes. All the things that teachers actually do in (honors) classes, such as encouraging students, giving feedback, explaining subject matter, et cetera, will be loosely defined as teaching strategies. It is a conscious choice to define teaching strategies very broadly, since both the literature and our research data suggest that (honors) teaching is not just about formal didactic activities (for example, giving feedback) but equally about teacher behavior that reflects upon the person and personality (for example, being friendly, accessible or enthusiastic). As will be shown, experienced honors teachers apply these strategies as part of a more inclusive approach: trying to create the conditions conducive to optimal learning for their honors students. One example of such conditions, as will be discussed at length in chapter 2, is a sense of community among and with honors students. The creation of such fundamental conditions will be labeled teaching approaches. At an even deeper level, teachers will have certain beliefs, attitudes, and dispositions with regard to teaching, academic study and students. At this level, we will use the notion of teaching 'orientation'.

It is not the purpose of this study to analyze or critically assess qualities ascribed to honors learning outcomes ('academic excellence' for instance) and to honors students (such as talented, gifted or intrinsically motivated). However, such words will be used quite often in the text of this study, both in the survey of the literature and in the reporting of interview outcomes. The author acknowledges that the concept of 'excellence' is difficult to define. As Trost (2002) points out "... *excellence is not a scientifically underpinned term, and a unanimously accepted definition does not exist (...) the small common* denominator of all definitions is achievement far above average. Consequently, excellence can be observed in all domains of human performance" (p. 317). In this study, the term refers to academic excellence in higher education: above average academic achievement as one of the desirable practices and outcomes of honors education.

As with the term 'excellence', there is no consensus about the exact meaning of student characteristics in honors, such as 'talented' or 'gifted' (see, for example, Gagné 1995; Mönks, Heller & Passow 2002; Sternberg & Davidson 2005). The notion of giftedness will be discussed at some length in chapter 2. The words talent and gifted in this study are used in the same manner and are in line with Gagné (1995) who has defined talent as follows: "... *talent is high performance due to systematically developed abilities (or skills) and knowledge in at least one field of human activity [higher education – MW], to a degree that places a student's achievements within at least the upper 15% of student-peers who are active in that field or fields. The key to developing expertise then is purposeful and meaningful engagement*" (p. 109). Honors programs select students on the basis of their talent, high performance or ability (for example, on the basis of grades earned in previous education), but will also take students' motivation into account. 'Motivation' is another concept that is omnipresent in honors literature.

Various studies have shown that students who consistently demonstrate high levels of accomplishment have equally high levels of intrinsic motivation (Niemiec & Ryan 2009; Renzulli 1986; Robinson 1996; Ryan & Deci 2000). Honors students seem to be more intrinsically motivated than regular students (Clark 2008; Gerrity, Lawrence & Sedlacek 1993; Rinn 2005; Wolfensberger 2004). Intrinsic motivation is, according to Ryan & Deci (2000): "*the inherent tendency to seek out novelty and challenges, to extend and exercise one's capacities, to explore, and to learn ... and refers to doing an activity for the inherent satisfaction*" (p. 70). Again, it is not the purpose of this study to analyze or critically assess aspects of motivation in honors settings. However, motivational theory will be used in chapter 2 for the sake of validating honors teaching approaches.

1.4   Relevance of this study

This study will contribute to a better academic understanding of honors teaching approaches and strategies and also to the practice of honors education. From an academic point of view, it is the ambition of the author to fill an important gap in the honors literature by providing an evidence-based overview of the approaches and strategies appropriate to honors teaching. As already indicated, studies about such approaches and strategies are rare. Most of the research on honors education has focused on program descriptions and rationales (Long & Lange 2002), effects of honors programs on students' achievements and student retention (Cosgrove 2004; Shushok 2002; Tsui 1999), and on characteristics of honors students themselves (Clark 2002; Gerrity et al. 1993; Mathiasen 1985; Rinn 2007). The attempt undertaken in this study to fill the knowledge gap about honors teaching approaches and strategies involves two steps: (a) developing a conceptual framework for honors pedagogy on the basis of a multiple-perspective literature survey, and (b) gathering data about honors teaching practices through a rather large-scale questionnaire among American and Dutch honors teachers and a substantial number of in-depth interviews with American honors teachers.

At a practical level, the results of this study among experienced teachers of honors students may reveal a convincing honors pedagogy showing how to 'teach and motivate' honors students. The wording 'knowledge-based society', 'excellence' and 'high achievement' is omnipresent in the current political and educational discourse (Bok 2008; Rijksoverheid 2011; Rostan & Vaira 2011; Veerman et al. 2010). This implies that research about factors that foster strong performance among college students is becoming even more critical (Garcia & Pintrich 1996; Mooij & Fettelaar 2010). The results of this study are primarily about teaching as a means to foster such strong performance in an honors setting. But at another level, the results of this study may also show how teachers can help students – all students, either in honors classes or in regular classes – to get the most out of their college years. After all, it is very well possible that teachers do use their honors experience for the enrichment of regular, non-honors teaching (Dennison 2008; Renzulli 2005; Wolfensberger, Van Eijl & Pilot 2004).

Another aspect of the practical relevance of this study is specific to the European context. Honors programs are a relatively new phenomenon in European higher education. As more students and teachers become involved in honors programs, it becomes increasingly important to invest specifically in faculty development for honors. This study may be helpful in the design of professionalization courses for honors teachers; it may equip them with knowledge of honors teaching approaches and strategies and thereby encourage excellence in both students and teachers.

1.5   About this study

Chapter 2 gives a survey of the academic literature, with the purpose of designing a framework of teaching approaches and teaching strategies for honors education. Three different strands of academic writing will be explored: honors literature, publications about giftedness, and studies about motivation, specifically self-determination theory. The reasons for selecting these bodies of literature will be discussed. The chapter also contains a brief survey of studies pertaining to the exploration of the attitudes and beliefs of (honors) teachers, which serve as context variables for their honors teaching.

Chapter 3 explains the methods employed in the empirical part of this study. Data were gathered by conducting a questionnaire survey among honors teachers in the United States and in the Netherlands and by holding in-depth interviews with American honors teachers. All aspects of the methodology – instrument design, data collection, and processing and analysis of data – will be explained in detail, first for the questionnaire and then for the interviews.

Chapter 4 focuses on the American honors teachers who participated in the survey and were interviewed. Who are these teachers? What are their attitudes and beliefs with regard to university teaching in general and honors teaching in particular? The chapter combines questionnaire data and interviews; the aim of the chapter is to provide background and contextual information that allows for a better understanding of teaching approaches and strategies in honors classes. These teaching approaches and strategies are the subject of chapter 5. Again, questionnaire data and interview results will be presented in combination. This chapter will show that the framework for honors pedagogy, as developed in chapter 2, indeed describes what American honors teachers say they do in their classes. The comparison of their teaching strategies in honors classes with those in regular classes adds more depth to the analysis. The interviews add substantial detail, context, depth and perspective.

In chapter 6 the focus shifts to the Dutch honors teachers who filled in exactly the same questionnaire as the American teachers. The results will show that the developed framework of honors pedagogy is also a good descriptor of Dutch honors teaching practice, although there is some difference in attitudes and beliefs and in concrete teaching practices between the Dutch and American contexts. The chapter also offers a systematic comparison of core findings in these two contexts and thereby provides the baseline needed to reflect on the transferability of U.S. honors practices to the Dutch (or European) context. Chapter 7, finally, provides the outcomes, continues with the limitations of this study and discusses the implications. The chapter closes with avenues of further research of honors education.

2 Honors teaching and the honors teacher, a literature survey

2.1 Introduction

This chapter will lay a conceptual and theoretical foundation for the empirical part of this study, which will be presented in chapters 3-6: an investigation of the teaching strategies that university teachers employ in honors education and of their attitudes and beliefs towards (honors) teaching and (honors) students. The literature survey underpinning this chapter consists of two parts.

Section 2.2 will focus on honors teaching strategies. There is a long tradition of honors teaching in the United States and an extensive body of literature about honors education (see for instance Andrews 2011; Holman 2007; Rinn 2006). Empirical publications about honors teaching strategies, based on substantial sets of data, are very rare, however (Achterberg 2004; Holman & Banning 2012; Rinn & Plucker 2004). Most studies about honors are based on case studies describing honors practices in one particular university or program (Cosgrove 2004; Fuiks & Gillison 2002; Holman & Banning 2012). Their narrow scope may give a good impression of the mainstream and uncontested strategies in honors practice. It will become evident in the course of section 2.2.1 that the teaching strategies that are generally seen as essential in honors education fall into three broad categories:

- Teaching strategies that create rapport and connectedness between teachers and students and among students; and that create a learning community (key word: community).
- Teaching strategies that enhance the depth and scope of students' academic knowledge, understanding and skills (key word: academic competence).

- Teaching strategies that give students space for experimentation, risk-taking, personal initiatives and pursuit of their interests (key word: freedom).

It might be argued that such teaching strategies are derived from practice (as described in the honors literature) and that there is no empirical evidence that they are actually effective in evoking excellence among honors students. There is substantial evidence, however, of the effectiveness of such teaching strategies to be drawn from empirical work on the teaching of gifted children or students. This domain of research mainly focuses on pre-university contexts: the 'gifted' in secondary or primary schools. In section 2.2.2 the focus will turn to this field of research to provide an empirical underpinning of the three above-mentioned categories of honors teaching strategies. The extensive literature review included also sixteen review papers and handbooks. Section 2.2.3 will offer further theoretical validation of the importance of the three dimensions (community, academic competence, freedom) from the perspective of motivational and self-determinational theory.

Through conducting this literature review a synthesis of the existing work regarding teaching approaches appropriate for honors was made. It was an inductive step to distill three theoretical dimensions from the most prominent themes in the honors literature. It was then with a deductive approach that giftedness research and motivation & self-determination theory was studied. The same phrases were used as labels for the three most important teaching approaches, to operationalize them as teaching strategies (Teddlie & Tashakkori 2009).

Section 2.3 will focus on the honors teacher. Teaching strategies do not exist in isolation. The teaching strategies that an honors teacher is inclined to use will depend on her or his deeper values, attitudes and beliefs with regard to university teaching and to university students. On the basis of intuition or personal experience one might guess that honors teachers like to teach, that they are motivated to help students get the most out of their education, and that they are generally student-centered in their approach. Such informed guesses are an insufficient basis, however, for the research design that will be described in chapter 3. Section 2.3 will therefore explore some of the academic work on teachers' conceptions of teaching (2.3.1), their motivation and self-determination (2.3.2) and their perception of students (2.3.3), giving specific attention to the relevance of these factors for honors teaching.

The results of the literature survey, both about honors teaching and about the honors teacher, will be used as input for the research design that will be set forth in chapter 3.

2.2   Honors teaching

2.2.1   Practice: literature about honors teaching

Frank Aydelotte (1880-1956) is generally seen as one of the founding fathers of honors programs in U.S. higher education. He became president of Swarthmore College, Pennsylvania, in 1921. One of his innovations there was the creation of honors education, in which he combined local teaching traditions with some practices that he had experienced in the UK as a Rhodes Scholar at Oxford University. Swarthmore honors became a source of inspiration for later initiatives elsewhere in the country (Cohen 1966; Guzy 2003; Schaeper & Schaeper 1998). Some of the key strategies of the Swarthmore honors program are still advocated today: active learning; faculty and students acting on an equal footing; communal questioning and learning; the tutorial system and interdisciplinary, challenging and independent work (Clark & Zubizarreta 2008; Guzy 2003; Haynes 2006; Hébert & McBee 2007; Mack 1996; Swarthmore College Faculty 1941). Admission to the Swarthmore program was based on intellectual achievement and personality characteristics (Guzy 2003). Faculty members were required to be sufficiently qualified to give able students the best intellectual leadership (Swarthmore College Faculty 1941). The aim of the Swarthmore honors initiative was to inspire in students 'a love affair with learning' (Cohen 1966). Since Aydelotte's days, there has been an explosion of honors programs in U.S. higher education: in the early 21st century, about half of all public and private colleges and universities in the U.S.A. had some form of honors program (Achterberg 2005). And most of these still strive, in Swarthmore's tradition, to offer experiences that integrate the epistemological, interpersonal and intrapersonal dimensions of learning and that make honors students aware of being part of an integrated, cohesive community (Clark & Zubizarreta 2008; Draper et al. 1999; Haynes 2006).

Despite the proliferation in the number of honors programs, research on how to teach gifted learners at college level is still largely uncharted territory (Achterberg 2005; Andrews 2011; Cosgrove 2004; Long & Lange 2002; Rinn 2007; Rinn & Plucker 2004; Robinson 1997; Scager et al. 2012; Shushok 2002). One telling fact is that Holman (2007), in her bibliography of honors research in the U.S.A. (with a grand total of 882 references), included only one PhD dissertation about honors faculty and their teaching strategies (Spangler 1985), out of a total number of 132 PhD dissertations about honors (see also Holman & Banning 2012). As noted in the introduction to this chapter, most of the publications that touch upon honors teaching are descriptive and based on case material. Yet the descriptive literature does give insight into the mainstream teaching practices in honors. The following discussion will relate this body of literature to the three categories of community, academic competence and freedom.

Community

The themes of community and connectedness are ubiquitous in the honors literature (Graffam 2006; Haynes 2006). Suggestions are often made on what honors teachers do or should do in order to create connections and a sense of community. It is claimed that this community fosters strong performance and offers the possibility to stimulate discussions (Robinson 1997). Many authors advocate a type of honors community that includes interactive teaching and learning and (peer) feedback combined with commitment to students and a teaching style that strives for critical and significant learning (Clark & Zubizarreta 2008; Cohen 1966; Fuiks & Gillison 2002; Swarthmore College Faculty 1941). According to Zubizarreta (2008a), it is both essential and characteristic for honors teachers to use their ability to create connectedness and so generate an honors community inside and outside the classroom.

Some authors highlight the importance of teacher commitment, noting their willingness to help students, their readiness to be accessible to them and their desire to take responsibility for the students' educational experience while encouraging the students' own sense of responsibility, both for themselves and for their community (see, for example, Draper et al. 1999; Haynes 2006; Strong 2008). Draper et al. (1999) also stress shared responsibility in and for the honors classroom: *"No one can 'hide' in an honors class; each person is active and engaged"* (p. 6). Many of the publications make claims about what teachers should do within and for the honors community: establish rapport with students and know them by name; give feedback to honors students as if they were junior colleagues; show an interest in students' interests, wishes and personal goals; try to understand the complex intellectual make-up of honors students in order to give meaningful feedback (see, for example, Clark & Zubizarreta 2008; Fuiks & Clark 2002; Kezar 2001; Park 2005). Although small classes are prevalent in honors, it is unclear whether class size is tied to *"the kinds of special academic experiences that come from classroom environments that encourage and support closer relationships among students and between professors and students"* (Zubizarreta 2008b, p. 147).

According to Kaczvinsky (2007) an honors community may be the best opportunity for academically gifted students to develop friendships and form social bonds while also satisfying their intellectual interest, in a way that cannot be realized in regular classroom settings. Rinn & Plucker (2004) stress that through connectedness and community, honors teachers and students can create a constructive atmosphere of academic rigor.

Academic competence

Honors programs typically offer enhanced academic challenges (Hébert & McBee 2007). This meets the needs of honors students who are, according to Kaczvinsky (2007), academically confident and more intellectually interested, quicker, more engaged and more open to new ideas than regular students. Mack (1996) believes that honors teachers should support and challenge students *"to think broadly as well as narrowly, generally as well as professionally"* (p. 38). This means that honors students should develop both their logical and analytical skills and their ability to think across disciplinary borders (Mack 1996). In honors education, *"… depth and intensity are extended, concepts (versus procedures) are emphasized, and the breadth is often interdisciplinary"* (Robinson 1997, p. 229).

The goal of enhancing academic competence is sometimes organized through a thoughtfully sequenced and connected set of courses that result in desired learning outcomes (Draper et al. 1999; Haynes 2006; Wolfensberger & Van Gorp 2008); sometimes there are only limited options to choose from. The setting generally involves small-scale classes and more intensive contact with faculty than common in regular classes (Draper et al. 1999). The general picture sketched by the honors literature is that enhancing academic competence involves critical and reflective thinking (for instance, Corley & Zubizarreta 2012; Taylor 2002), the crossing of disciplinary boundaries (for instance Bennett 2009; Lòpez-Chávez & Shepherd 2010), and a stronger focus on research compared to standard undergraduate programs (for instance, Cambia & Engel 2004). According to Guzy (2003) most honors programs have an optional or required thesis or senior project assignment.

Many authors discuss the qualifications and teaching strategies that teachers need in order to strengthen the academic competence of honors students. Most importantly, they need scholarship (mastery of their academic discipline or specialization) and intellectual rigor, combined with a willingness to collaborate and engage in team-teaching while crossing academic boundaries (Clark & Zubizarreta 2008). Honors teachers need to explore the interrelationships between traditional fields of study, look for cutting-edge research and discuss this in their classes, and teach different points of view (Austin 1986; Friedman & Jenkins-Friedman 1986; Wolfensberger 2008). Teachers should have the skill to provide opportunities for accelerated learning, with a focus on fundamental content, and to create authentic learning tasks (Gross & Van Vliet 2005). They should also have the classroom management skills to create multiple perspectives, for instance by grouping or coupling students for work on research papers in such a way that they bring different points of view and expertise to the task (Draper et al. 1999).

Freedom

In their 1941 publication, the honors faculty of Swarthmore College made some astute observations about freedom versus structure. They believed that honors education requires teachers to challenge students and to grant them the responsibility and room for their own choices. Such conditions would provide a stimulus powerful enough to sustain the student's interest while ensuring enough supervision to keep them from getting lost in their ideas and research. The teacher should offer guidance so the student can find her or his own affinities and learn to select sources. Above all, the teacher should be at hand as an interested and competent coach to oversee the students' intellectual performance, to veto unpromising ideas, and to give positive reinforcement of their achievements. Swarthmore honors teachers referred to honors capstones and independent study projects as crucial elements that support

27

freedom within learning because they place educational emphasis on self-engendered activity of the mind (Swarthmore College Faculty 1941).

The issue of 'freedom' – within bounds and with guidance and support – is an important concern in the literature on honors teaching strategies. Many honors projects are accomplished through independent study with guidance and support from a faculty member: *"an experience designed to give the student a sort of apprenticeship with a scholar in the student's field of interest"* (Robinson 1997, p. 229). The pursuit of freedom entails empowering students to make their own decisions about their subject matter, planning and study environment while acknowledging their level of maturity. Teachers are therefore engaging students in a critically reflective process that helps them understand, integrate, apply, and develop the metacognitive habits and skills associated with higher-order learning (Corley & Zubizarreta 2012; Haynes 2006). In their role as guide or supervisor, teachers serve as role models, respecting the students' wishes, conscious of when to refer them to other experts, knowing *"when to wait and when effectively to interrupt, to erupt, to explode"* (Cohen 1966, p. 41).

According to Haynes (2006), development and learning among honors students is enhanced when teachers are attuned to their developmental needs and patterns. Thus, to facilitate the freedom to explore, faculty members need to spend time with honors students getting to know them, to respect their interest and to observe their abilities (Kezar 2001). This falls into the category of community, discussed earlier.

"Honors faculty take risks in their teaching and use their honors classroom as a learning laboratory – giving students more autonomy, experimenting with new techniques, bringing in ideas which may not have been used in a particular discipline before, encouraging students to become involved in their communities" (Fuiks & Gillison 2002, p. 102). In this way, honors classes with a degree of freedom may become spaces of experimentation, where students and teachers are co-creators of honors education.

There is no single model for teaching an honors course. But the general components of an honors environment come across very clearly in the literature. Draper et al. (1999) describe these in the following statement about the honors program in which they teach: *"Within the program there is a general belief that students will work up to their potential if they are challenged to do so. Secondly there is a belief that students can rebound academically. And thirdly, there is the belief that students must have a sense of belonging in their school."* (p. 12). These three points relate respectively to freedom, academic competence and community. The same key components were already present at Swarthmore's honors college: community in its scale and close teacher-student interaction; academic competence in its ambition; freedom in the fundamental conviction that honors students should explore areas of their personal intellectual interest. The literature survey about honors teaching has confirmed the key importance of these three characteristics. Teachers can employ a mosaic of strategies and actions to create community, academic competence and (bounded) freedom. Basically, according to Schuman (2005), honors teachers love serving as *"matchmakers between the discipline about which they are passionate and students of whom they are fond (...) they have some brains, some skills and are in love with teaching"* (p. 33). Little systematic evidence, however, is available on actual teaching strategies in honors education. Our attempt to fill this gap forms the core of the empirical work presented in chapters 3-6. But we shall first take a closer look at the categories of community, academic competence and freedom. Now we shall explore empirical work (2.2.2) and theoretical studies (2.2.3) that could shed light on the relevance of these categories for enhancing excellence.

2.2.2 Empirical underpinning: research about teaching gifted students

There is a large body of academic literature, with a strong embedding in empirical research, about learners who are generally labeled as 'gifted'. Broadly speaking, the field called 'gifted research' deals with topics such as the (combination of) characteristics of learners typically seen as gifted and the context variables that have an impact on their learning. As this section will show, research about gifted learners provides evidence of the importance of learning environments that foster a sense of community, stimulate academic competence and offer a degree of freedom to the learner. Research on gifted learners also gives some clues about which teaching strategies promote the intellectual and social development of gifted learners.

As mentioned in the introduction to this chapter, the vast majority of studies about gifted learners deal with pre-university age levels: secondary school children and primary school children (Sternberg 2002). There is no reason to assume, however, that insights into gifted learners and their learning needs or about the teaching approaches that are effective with them would be irrelevant to gifted university students. In fact, many of the outcomes of the literature about (teaching) gifted learners reflect the practices, principles and intuitions found in the honors literature (section 2.2.1).

Only a relatively small part of the research about gifted learners treats teaching strategies, as various review articles about the field indicate (Dai, Swanson & Cheng, 2011; Heller, Mönks, Sternberg & Subotnik 2002; Ziegler & Raul, 2000). In the International Handbook of Giftedness and Talent (Heller et al. 2002), for instance, which was prepared by one hundred researchers from 24 countries, the focus is on student characteristics and student learning outcomes but not on teachers. The topic of fostering talent in higher education has received scant attention (Heller et al. 2002). Some researchers do examine teachers' perceptions of gifted learners, but such studies are the exception (see, for example, Chan 2011; Leikin 2011).

The literature reveals that gifted students, as a group, have different characteristics than regular students in the same age range and that they need distinct learning opportunities (Olszewski-Kubilius 2003; Sternberg & Davidson 2005). Some authors note that gifted students have above-average scores for ability, persistence, commitment, motivation and creativity (Gagné 1995; Heller, Perleth & Lim 2005; Renzulli 2003, 2008; Sternberg 2001). However, as others emphasize, they will not succeed without specialized assistance (Colangelo & Davis 2003; Gagné 1995; Gross 2003; Karnes & Bean 2001; Leikin 2011; Park & Oliver 2009; Rogers 2007). It is therefore suggested that teachers of academically talented students should acquire special 'giftedness expertise' that teachers of regular students do not require (Croft 2003).

There is a considerable amount of data to support the idea that for the gifted child nothing matters more in school than the teacher, who should meet some of the following criteria: empathy, high tolerance of ambiguity, democratic attitude (Sisk 1987). In the 1960s, Bishop (1968) studied more than 200 successful teachers of gifted students and concluded that these teachers have several characteristics in common: expertise in the area being taught, a high level of intelligence, maturity, experience and the will to strive for high levels of achievement. Feldhusen (1997) explored the competencies and characteristics of successful teachers of gifted students and described the most important qualities of these teachers. Among these are skills in teaching, problem solving and creativity, interaction with students, conducting of student-directed activities, facilitation of independent research and appropriate motivational techniques. Some other studies identify the desirable characteristics of teachers of gifted students as enthusiasm, general knowledge, expertise and intellectual interest, achievement orientation, skills in teaching, ability to recognize individual differences or ability to connect with students (Graffam 2006; Hultgren and Seeley 1982; Mills 2003). Mills (2003) reports that teachers who are considered to be successful in working with gifted students are open and flexible, have a preference for intuitive processing, value logical analysis and prefer abstract themes and concepts. Also they have a strong background and interest in their academic discipline. Baldwin et al. (2002) and Park & Oliver (2009), finally, stress the importance of three teacher variables that have an important impact on the effectiveness of teaching gifted students: knowledge of gifted students that engenders effective teacher-student relationships; subject-matter content knowledge and pedagogical content knowledge; an inclination towards independent work as a learning strategy.

This broad range of teacher characteristics and teaching strategies, suggested by numerous studies, may be effective with gifted students, as largely proven in empirical research, but this does not mean that such characteristics and strategies are not effective or less effective in regular courses and with regular pupils or students. Croft (2003) noted how challenging it is to determine which characteristics and competences are unique to effective teachers of the gifted. Nevertheless, the field of giftedness research does provide ample evidence for the relevance of the three broad categories identified earlier (community, academic competence, freedom – see section 2.2.1) for the learning process of gifted young people.

Community

Research suggests that a safe learning community is of particular importance to gifted students, an environment where they feel free to take initiative (Stopper 2000; Vialle & Tischler 2004). Various studies highlight the importance of the teacher's ability to engender social coherence in such learning communities (VanTassel-Baska 2002). Talent is best fostered in a supportive context, within communities (both in and outside the school) that offer frameworks for development and resources for support, inspiration and sustenance (Sosniak 2003). Freeman (1999) showed that a teacher's connectedness with gifted learners is essential. Gaining insight into the student's goals, and knowing how well a student is performing, would allow the teacher to set appropriate objectives. It is only when the teacher is sufficiently in tune with the student that she/he can provide relevant feedback, engender peer-feedback and teach a student how to use self-evaluation (Freeman 1999). Freeman also pointed out that gifted learners need help in developing their learning tactics, even though they have better strategies for self-regulation than non-gifted learners.

Moreover, teachers should be role models. Gifted learners are often inspired by figures of authority who exhibit wisdom and promote positive values of civic engagement (Lockwood & Kunda 1997; Pleiss & Feldhusen 1995; Renzulli 2003, 2008; Sternberg 2001, 2003). Other qualities of outstanding teachers of gifted students include enthusiasm, empathy and openness, all qualities needed to create community (Whitlock & DuCette 1989). This claim is in line with empirical findings suggesting that teachers need particular qualities to implement inclusive education, such as commitment, the ability to support and establish rapport with students and a positive attitude (Cheung & Hui 2011).

Academic competence

Compared to regular programs, the gifted curriculum promotes accelerated learning, depth, creativity, complexity and challenge (see, for example, Rogers 2007; Shore, Cornell, Robinson & Ward 1991; VanTassel-Baska 2002; Vialle 2001). In a review of empirical studies, Reis & Renzulli (2010) report that the use of strategies such as enrichment, differentiation, acceleration and curriculum enhancement corresponds to higher achievement by talented students. Teachers should therefore be enrichment specialists, offering an ever-growing range of opportunities within the student's chosen area of specialization (Renzulli & Purcell 1996). Teachers who differentiate and compact curricular content provide more challenge to their students (Reis & Renzulli 2010).

Generally speaking, the literature suggests that teachers should make sure that learning tasks are demanding and challenging without becoming undoable (given the age level and the schooling level of the learners involved). Learning environments with high demands elicit students' development because complex learning is supported (Renzulli 1986). Many studies reflect this point, for instance both Anderson & Krathwohl (2001) and Vialle & Tischler (2004) found that teachers who incorporate multiple perspectives and interdisciplinary material encourage a higher level of thinking and creativity. Hansen & Feldhusen (1994) analyzed the teaching practices of trained teachers of gifted learners and found that they put greater emphasis on higher-level thinking skills and discussion but less on grades and lecturing than did untrained teachers. Discussion involves articulation and reflection, which helps learners transform their (learning) experience into abstract knowledge. Through the focus on higher order thinking tasks, discussion and reflection, the teacher (mentor) embraces the Vygotskian notion (Cole, John-Steiner, Scribner & Souberman 1978) of the zone of proximal development. This approach helps the mentee push the boundaries of knowledge and skill while the teachers provide systematic feedback and support, facilitating analysis and reflection (Gruber & Mandl 2002).

The fact that teaching the academically talented should be challenging, difficult and rigorous implies a need for scholarly teachers (Leikin 2011). To be successful with gifted learners, teachers must have advanced competency in their domain of academic specialization, the ability to apply knowledge to solve real-life problems, high energy, a passion for their discipline and the ability to convey this passion (Leikin 2011; Mills 2003). Dixon et al. (2004) say that teachers of academically gifted students do not need to teach them to think (critically), but should rather teach their students that thinking must not be taken lightly.

Freedom

Gifted learners are significantly more likely to prefer independent study, independent projects and self-instructional materials to all other forms of instructional delivery (Jeter & Chauvin 1982; Rogers 2002, 2007). Offering and monitoring a challenging degree of freedom increases students' self-regulation and is thus an important element of pedagogical strategies within gifted education (Freeman 1999; Gentry, Rizza & Owen 2002; Park & Oliver 2009). While many methods are advocated, several stand out in this regard: student-initiated learning, ability-peer tutoring, guided dialogue and reflection leading to metacognition (Freeman 1999; VanTassel-Baska 2002). Csikszentmihaly, Rathunde & Whalen (1997) note the importance of balancing fun with challenge and thereby motivating students to persist in developing their talents.

Gruber & Mandl (2002) comment that to effectively support the development of gifted learners, teachers should be not only authentic but also able to introduce active learning processes and projects relevant to daily life. As Sternberg & Grigorenko (2007) counseled, students should not only be allowed to work independently and choose and plan their own topics but also see that they are making progress. This illustrates the intimate relationship between offering freedom and providing structured feedback and support. VanTassel-Baska & Stambaugh (2005) claim that educators for the academically gifted need to take flexible approaches to content and give students some choice: *"Without the use of some form of flexibility within the curriculum, adjusting for the needs of gifted students in the regular classroom is an impossible task"* (p. 216).

2.2.3 Theoretical validation: motivational theory

The previous sections showed that honors literature and research on giftedness provide strong evidence of the importance of the three (intertwined) approaches to honors teaching set forth earlier: creating a sense of community, enhancing academic competence and offering a certain degree of freedom to the student. It is interesting, though not surprising, that motivational theory underpins the key role of these same three approaches in high performance and (intellectual) growth. An important direction in current theorizing on human motivation is self-determination theory, a school of thought and empirical work in which Deci and Ryan are the most prominent scholars (see for example: Deci & Ryan 1985, 1991, 1995, 2002; Ryan & Deci 2000). Intrinsic motivation is essential in fuelling one's self-determination. The complex links between intrinsic and extrinsic motives will not be discussed here.

Deci and Ryan have convincingly shown in their work that there are three essential psychological needs or conditions that motivate a person: psychological relatedness, competence (increasing mastery of any field, skill or routine and the inherent satisfaction and confidence that come with increasing mastery) and autonomy. If these needs are not fulfilled, self-motivation and self-determination will become problematic. Psychological relatedness resonates with the notion of a sense of community. Autonomy is clearly related to (a certain degree of) freedom: I am doing it because I want to.

Self-determination theory was not specifically developed with honors teaching in mind. It claims to be universal, as it is about innate psychological needs, and would thus apply to any context. But intrinsic motivation is a key notion in all honors literature and practice. Honors students are by definition – and by selection – academically gifted and highly motivated (Kaczvinsky 2007). Honors environments are generally described as stimulating and motivating for both teachers and students (Clark & Zubizarreta 2008). Intrinsic motivation is clearly connected to high levels of academic performance (Eccles & Wigfield 2002; Ryan & Deci 2000). Rea (2000) claims that "… *the more often that students are optimally motivated to use their talents, the more committed they become to the development of these talents*" (p. 188). Intrinsic motivation produces optimal achievement, as also evidenced by Csikszentmihalyi's concept of flow (Csikszentmihalyi 1996; Hoekman, McCormick & Gross 1999). A considerable amount of research has explored how the degree to which teachers support their students' intrinsic motivation is positively associated with the students' performance (Gottfried & Gottfried 2004; Pelletier, Séquin-Lévesque & Legault 2002; Philips & Lindsay 2006; Ryan & Deci 2000; Taylor, Ntoumanis & Smith 2009).

In order to sustain students' intrinsic motivation, it is important to encourage their sense of community. Self-determination theory – which takes the work of Ryan and Deci as its starting point – defines 'relatedness' as a sense of belonging, a connection to significant others. This aspect of the theory presupposes a degree of social coherence, or community, in the classroom. Applying that theory, several authors have identified the relationship between teacher and student as crucial to effective teaching (for an overview, see Vialle 2004). Others have noted the role of intrinsic motivation in the creation of relatedness and community; as several studies indicate, teachers are influenced by their perceptions of students' motivation and behavior (Pelletier et al. 2002; Taylor et al. 2009). Alumni also report that the sense of belonging in honors classes has helped them to sustain their motivation: "… *the pleasure of community, having been understood and cared about, having been welcomed and respected within their classroom settings*" (Moore & Kuol 2007, p 140).

Students' intrinsic motivation appears to be low when they experience teachers as cold and uncaring, uninterested in their work or failing to respond to requests for access (Anderson, Manoogian & Reznick 1976; Ryan

& Grolnick 1986). Cotton & Wilson (2006) report that the quality of contact between faculty and students has greater influence than its frequency and that student-faculty interaction is an important determinant of students' learning outcomes. In a learning community, with good interpersonal relationships and a sufficient level of trust, feedback is an important instrument for sustained intrinsic motivation. Research shows that positive and relevant feedback creates a more stimulating and motivating environment for both teachers and students (Corbalan, Kester & Van Merriënboer 2009; Levesque, Zuehlke, Stanek & Ryan 2004).

According to self-determination theory, a person's perception of autonomy and competence should closely interact in order to enhance wellbeing (Levesque et al. 2004; Vansteenkiste, Lens & Deci 2006). Teachers need to inspire in students a desire for competence, that is, to *"experience satisfaction in exercising and extending one's capabilities. Naturally, people seem to seek out challenges that are optimal for their level of development"* (Levesque et al. 2004, p.68). A teacher can promote competence in honors students by giving them challenging assignments (Sansone & Harackiewicz 2000). Teachers can extend the boundaries of knowledge and skills because, according to the taxonomies of Bloom and Anderson, motivated and gifted students have greater metacognition, allowing them to evaluate and process information more quickly (Anderson & Krathwohl 2001).

Learning environments with a degree of freedom are autonomy-supportive contexts that provide choice and opportunity for self-direction and a minimal amount of pressured evaluations, imposed goals and demands (Levesque et al. 2004; Ryan & Deci 2000; Vansteenkiste et al. 2012). Autonomy refers to the students' basic need to experience their behavior as self-endorsed or volitional. Such environments *"offer greater positive, nondemeaning, informational feedback and a context in which the other person's perspective is considered"* (Levesque et al. 2004, p. 69; see also Reeve, Bolt & Chai 1999). It is typically within autonomy-supportive conditions that the striving for competence is most fully expressed (Levesque et al. 2004; Niemiec & Ryan 2009). Various studies indicate that a direct way to improve performance is to increase students' autonomous academic motivation by, for example, providing choices during learning activities (Fortier, Vallerand & Guay 1995; Niemiec & Ryan 2009; Zuckerman, Porac, Lathin, Smith & Deci 1978). Autonomy-supportive teachers listen more, encourage student initiative, ask questions about the students' wants and offer empathic perspective-taking statements (Reeve et al. 1999). By referring students to experts when necessary or by allowing their input into the decision-making process, the teacher makes it clear that she or he is aware of the students' perspectives (Garcia & Pintrich 1996). Respecting the autonomy of students and offering them freedom of choice sustains and fuels their intrinsic motivation; and intrinsically motivated (honors) students have a need for autonomy. Autonomy/freedom is more, though, than just lifting the usual constraints of a structured learning environment, such as deadlines, pre-set goals, or fixed assignments. Autonomy is not the opposite of structure. Martens & Boekaerts (2007) observe that autonomy-supportive conditions are mostly described as what they are not: not pressured, not goal-oriented, there are no deadlines.

All in all, the rich academic literature about self-determination theory in relation to (higher) education suggests that autonomy/freedom, relatedness/community and academic competence are crucial to sustain and strengthen the strong intrinsic motivation of honors students and to achieve high-quality outcomes in honors programs.

2.2.4 Conclusions

Three teaching approaches stand out as essential in honors teaching: creating community, enhancing academic competence, and offering freedom. These are dominant themes in the academic literature about honors practice. We have seen that the field of giftedness research offers empirical evidence for the importance of these approaches. Self-determination theory suggests that the three approaches set the essential conditions (relatedness, competence, autonomy) for supporting students' intrinsic motivation and thereby for their high achievement.

The three teaching approaches may therefore be considered as the pillars of honors pedagogy. Honors literature, giftedness research and motivational research (in education) offer many suggestions for concrete teaching strategies that are vital to creating community, enhancing academic competence, or offering a certain degree of freedom to students. These suggestions were presented throughout the previous sections (2.2.1 to 2.2.3).

Figure 2.1 – Teaching approaches in honors education and related teaching strategies

Creating community	• Interaction, (peer) feedback, active learning • Encouragement, joy, inspiration • Availability, interest in students, commitment
Enhancing academic competence	• Multi- and interdisciplinary thinking, multiple perspectives • Scholarly teaching, academic depth, involvement in research • Challenging learning tasks, difficulty, acceleration
Offering freedom	• Flexibility, allow for self-regulation, openness • Innovative teaching, experimentation, fun • Professionalism, novice relationship, challenge

The clusters of teaching strategies that we encountered in the literature are depicted in figure 2.1. There is clearly some overlap and connection between groups of teaching strategies and even between the three key approaches. There is also variation in the nature of the teaching strategies: to be inspiring is of a different and less instrumental order than to set challenging learning tasks. But the literature survey shows that honors teaching is not just about choosing the most appropriate instruments from the didactic toolbox. Sincere involvement of the teacher as a person and as a member of the learning community is at least as important. That is why the groups of teaching strategies were deliberately defined loosely and inclusively.

Regarding the creation of a sense of community and connectedness in honors classes, one strong cluster of strategies is about interactivity: these include active learning and interactive teaching strategies with a focus on feedback. We also encountered many suggestions related to enthusiasm: the teachers should inspire and encourage students and share the joy of learning within the honors community. A third cluster is about concrete and practical engagement in the honors community: a teacher should be available and approachable, show sincere interest in the students and their aspirations and generally be committed to the learning community.

With regard to the enhancement of academic competence, many authors (particularly in the honors literature) stress the importance of promoting and stimulating multi- and interdisciplinary thinking, discussing the connections between various fields of study, connecting theory to practice and showing multiple perspectives. Thinking in terms of breadth and connections is clearly seen as one domain of academic competence. Another cluster of strategies that promote competence is depth: depth of knowledge, analytical thinking, and engaging students in research. A third cluster of teaching strategies, related to the previous two but somewhat different in focus, is about setting difficult or challenging learning tasks relative to the honors students' level of ability. The difficulty may lie in the quantity or speed of processing new information (acceleration) or in its contextual or conceptual complexity (this is clearly linked to the previous strategies of breadth and depth).

The third approach, offering freedom, primarily requires a strategy of flexibility, which means offering choice and allowing students to self-regulate their study to a certain extent. This is not the same as taking an experimental approach to teaching: to try something new and allow for innovation and co-creation with the students. After all, the open and flexible classroom might become a routine. Second, authors have stressed that reflective, innovative and experimental teaching strategies are vital to the honors class. A third dimension of offering freedom, finally, is the strategy of setting demanding and challenging tasks, which may be very specific in terms of the required outcomes, whereby students have to make many decisions freely and independently: how to organize their (group) work, when to consult their teacher and with what questions, what to read, how to design the research process, et cetera. This is the freedom (and responsibility) that comes with 'professional' tasks.

2.3 Honors teachers

2.3.1 Conceptions of teaching

Not only in honors classes but overall, teachers are inclined to employ approaches, strategies and forms of behavior that fit their dispositions, attitudes and beliefs about a number of things: the nature and value of teaching at a university; their motivation to teach and self-determination; their ideas and perception of (honors) students. Teaching approaches and strategies cannot be seen in isolation, factors of personal context are important. Thus, we shall now move to a brief discussion of the teachers' characteristics and dispositions that will be included in the research design (chapter 3). The following sections concern conceptions of teaching, motivation and self-determination, and perception of (honors) students, respectively.

The teaching practices of (university) teachers are influenced by their deeper perceptions and understandings of teaching in higher education: by their conceptions of learning and teaching (Biggs & Tang 2007; Denessen 1999; Dewey 1921; Entwistle 1991; Kember & Gow 1994; Kember & Kwan 2000; Pajares 1992; Pratt 1992; Trigwell, Prosser & Tayler 1994; Trigwell, Prosser & Waterhouse 1999). Also in research studies into faculty development attention has been paid to changes in teachers' conceptions and behavior (Postareff, Lindblom-Ylänne & Nevgi 2007; Stes, Coertjens & Van Petegem 2010) Pratt (1992) defined conceptions as follows: "*Conceptions are specific meanings attached to phenomena which then mediate our response to situations involving those phenomena. We form conceptions of virtually every aspect of our perceived world, and in so doing, use those abstract representations to delimit something from, and relate it to, other aspects of our world. We view the world through the lenses of our conceptions, interpreting and acting in accordance with our understanding of the world*" (p. 204). In everyday language, one might also speak of (basic or fundamental) orientations instead of conceptions. But in his review of teaching conceptions among university teachers, Kember (1997) suggested that 'orientations' are of a broader and more generalized level of categorization, as encompassing two or more conceptions (p. 257).

Teachers are not of one mind; they will think and feel differently about education. However, as Kember's review of teaching conceptions (1997) demonstrated, researchers largely agree that conceptions of teaching in higher education fall into two broad orientations towards teaching: a 'teacher-content' orientation and a 'student-learning' orientation (Bunting 1985; Denessen 1999; Kember 1997; Kember & Kwan 2000; Light & Calkins 2008; Prosser & Trigwell 1999). This does not imply that there are (only) two types of teachers; such a simplification would be a caricature. Between the polar opposites, teachers can occupy many different positions, and these may change with the context and over time (Light & Calkins 2008).

In general, honors teachers might be expected to be student-learning oriented rather than teacher-content oriented. This suggestion will be evaluated below. Following Denessen (1999), both orientations will be discussed in light of teachers' ideas about three key aspects: educational goals, the pedagogical relation between teacher and student and instructional emphasis.

Teacher-content orientation

The teacher-content orientation applies to (university) teachers with a content-centered teaching approach. Teachers with this orientation perceive teaching essentially as organizing, presenting and testing a certain body of their own academic content knowledge. The educational goal associated with this orientation is for students to acquire the information needed for further study and/or a good career (Gibbs & Coffey 2004; Kember 1997; Light & Calkins 2008). To that end the teacher, who is a scholarly expert with a passion for her or his domain of knowledge and research, provides the students with sound academic knowledge, preferably in a well-structured manner. Teachers with this orientation will consider the pedagogical relation to be disciplined and hierarchical. Their attention will be directed towards the class as a whole, ensuring that all students meet the same learning goals, rather than tailored to the needs of individual students (Kember & Kwan 2000). While individual differences may be acknowledged, there will be limited room for individual choice. Instructional emphasis in this orientation is on the products of education, such as achievement and grades (Denessen 1999; Light & Calkins 2008). The teacher determines what should be learned and will be inclined to give frequent tests. All students are supposed to meet the same externally imposed standards, and preferably at the same time. If these teachers do accommodate students' individual characteristics, they teach to their students' strengths rather than challenging them, or cater to their weaknesses instead of addressing them (Kember & Kwan 2000).

Teachers with this orientation may have difficulty offering freedom to honors students and creating a sense of community, although they may be excellent coaches or supervisors in a small-scale research environment. They may do well in enhancing academic competence, since this aspect is closely aligned with their personal drive and perception of what university is all about.

Student-learning orientation

The second one, the student-learning orientation, with its learning-centered teaching approach, applies to those teachers who regard teaching as facilitating students' personal construction of knowledge and their personal development (Light, Cox & Calkins 2009; Denessen 1999). Their stance on educational goals is that students should seek understanding and not be satisfied with reproducing course content. Student-learning oriented teachers are more likely to encourage students to adopt a deep learning approach (Trigwell et al. 1999). Its key features are to understand the concepts and make flexible use of knowledge as well as to enhance one's personal growth and adjustment. Deeper learning approaches are related to higher-quality learning outcomes (Trigwell et al. 1999). Concerning pedagogical relations, the keyword in this orientation is 'involvement'. Teachers with a learning-centered teaching approach want to know more about and deal with individual students in order to meet their academic and sometimes more personal (pastoral) needs (Kember & Kwan 2000). Teachers with a student-learning orientation adjust according to students' characteristics and encourage students to discover and construct knowledge complementary to their strengths and to broaden their experience base (Kember & Kwan 2000). The instructional emphasis in this orientation is on the educational process. Denessen (1999) noted that student-oriented attitudes emphasize the formative impact of the school, the active participation of students within the classroom and the school and both independent and cooperative learning. Teachers with a learning-centered teaching approach are *"more inclined to recognize the need to motivate students as an intrinsic part of their role as a teacher"* (Kember & Kwan 2000 p. 476).

This brief characterization of the student-learning orientation suggests that teachers with a strong inclination towards this orientation may be well-equipped to employ the three teaching approaches identified within honors pedagogy: create a sense of community, enhance academic competence, and offer a degree of freedom. Their approach to academic competence – stressing deep learning – may be more effective than the content-driven approach of teachers with a teacher-content orientation. Research by Gibbs & Coffey (2004) has shown that students who take a deep approach to learning have *"... superior learning outcomes, particularly in terms of understanding and developing new and more sophisticated conceptions of the subject"* (p. 89). Teachers with a student-learning orientation will certainly be able to create conditions for community and freedom. Thus, it is reasonable to expect that honors teachers will predominantly have a student-learning orientation. But again, people do not fall into binary categories. Keeping this in mind and thereby avoiding stereotyping, teaching orientation items in the survey will be included (chapter 3).

42

2.3.2 Motivation and self-determination

The author is not aware of any systematic research about teachers' motivation for honors teaching in higher education. Research suggests, however, that motivational characteristics of teachers do have an important impact on their teaching approaches and teaching strategies (Deci, Vallerand, Pelletier & Ryan 1991; Pelletier et al. 2002).

For instance, the more self-determined teachers are in their work, the more they support autonomy for their students (Deci et al. 1991; Pelletier et al. 2002). Teachers' motivation and self-determination can therefore induce certain forms of interpersonal behavior and may also affect their ability to create a learning community (Pelletier et al. 2002). So the teacher's motivation influences the teaching approaches and strategies that she or he adopts.

Deci et al. (1991) state that the highest quality of conceptual learning seems to occur under the same motivational conditions that promote personal growth and adjustment. Teachers can create these conditions when they themselves are motivated and self-determining, in other words by being role models. Indeed, according to Deci et al. (1991), teachers' behavior – specifically, the degree to which they support students' autonomy rather than trying to place boundaries on their learning – has an important effect on students' motivation, sense of self-determination and therefore on their learning outcomes. For instance, providing students with the opportunity to participate in the decision-making process regarding educational activities creates a deeper learning experience and beneficial adjustment outcomes.

It is also suggested that there is a reciprocal relationship between student motivation and teacher motivation. In other words, teachers who are enthusiastic about the students will stimulate their motivation and vice versa (Pelletier et al. 2002). According to the same study, positive student engagement is associated with more teacher engagement. Deci et al. (1991) claim that students who are highly motivated and autonomous may elicit greater support for their autonomy from their teachers.

It is important for honors teachers to have a sense of self-determination and freedom in how they organize their classes. It may happen that teachers do not feel confident enough to set the classroom conditions and formats themselves and together with their students, or they may actually be constrained by departmental or university rules. Rules and procedures about grading, deadlines, scheduling, course outlines and the like may undermine intrinsic motivation and beneficial learning in an honors setting (Deci et al. 1991). A factor related to the feeling of self-determination is the amount of pressure and control that departments exert on their faculty members. Various studies show that putting teachers under such pressure will make them more controlling towards their students (Deci et al. 1991). As Pelletier et al. (2002) put it: *'pressure from above and pressure from below'*.

For all these reasons, teachers' sense of self-determination is an important factor in establishing appropriate learning approaches and strategies for honors students. Teachers with a strong sense of self-determination will find ways to reconcile formal requirements with productive learning conditions. Teachers supporting those basic needs – relatedness, competence and autonomy – create a positive and safe learning environment (Doornenbal 2007). And clearly their motivation to teach (honors) has multiple direct and indirect effects on the success of their (honors) classes. It was also shown that the success of specific honors approaches – creating a sense of community and offering students freedom – depends to some extent on the intrinsic motivation of the teacher. The empirical part of this study will highlight teacher motivation and self-determination as important context variables for honors teaching practices.

2.3.3 Perception of (honors) students

As a final component of the dispositions, attitudes and beliefs of honors teachers, we now turn briefly to the teachers' perceptions and expectations of students. It has been shown that variation in such perceptions and expectations leads to different approaches to teaching and teaching strategies (Rosenthal & Jacobson 1992; Rubie-Davies 2010). Rosenthal's 'Pygmalion experiment' asserted that when teachers expected their students to perform at high levels, they did. Rosenthal & Jacobson (1992) called this a 'self-fulfilling prophecy effect', suggesting that when teachers believe in their students' abilities and expect an eagerness to learn, they interact with them in such a way that the students' academic development is promoted.

Students have to apply for admission to honors courses. Admission generally requires high SAT scores, strong GPAs and proven motivation. It may be expected that teachers see honors students as gifted, motivated and having great learning potential, which may influence their teaching (Copenhaver &

Intyre 1992; Guzy 2008). Stake (2002) found that the teachers' conceptualization of student achievement greatly influences the students' planning and the teachers' instructional strategy and assessment. Moreover, as already mentioned, the perception that teachers have of the intrinsic motivation of their students may set in motion productive types of interpersonal behavior towards the students (Pelletier et al. 2002). Expectations clearly have an impact on the approaches and strategies that teachers put into practice in their honors classes. Also this fact will be taken into account in the empirical part of this study.

2.3.4 Conclusions

Three aspects of university teachers' dispositions, attitudes and beliefs were briefly discussed on the previous pages: their conception of learning, their motivation and self-determination, and their perception of (honors) students. Research shows that each of these aspects influences which teaching practices a teacher will be inclined to like or dislike, to employ or maybe to reject.

Figure 2.2 – The honors teacher and honors teaching approaches – key components

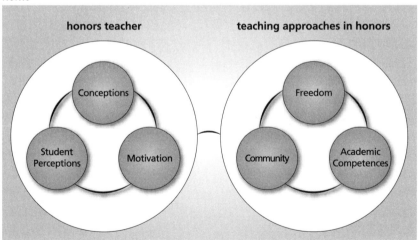

Although the research on these three aspects hardly touches upon the specific context of honors teaching, the author hopes to have substantiated that these factors are highly relevant to the honors teaching approaches set forth earlier, namely creating community, enhancing academic competence, and offering a certain amount of freedom to students. This relationship is visualized in figure 2.2. This figure shows the contours of what will be taken into account in the next chapters. Of course, other factors have an impact on teacher behavior in honors classes, such as the level of their domain expertise and the degree to which they have gone through professional training in (honors) teaching. Such factors, although relevant and important, will not be considered here.

All components of figure 2.2 will play a role in the research design (chapter 3), although the focus is on the three teaching approaches and the related teaching strategies of honors teachers.

3 Methods

3.1 Introduction

In line with the theory as set forth in chapter 2, it is expected that teachers take a different approach for honors courses than for regular courses. The literature survey showed that there are three broad dimensions of teaching approaches, for which such differences may be expected: creating community, stimulating both depth and breadth in academic competences, and offering a certain amount of freedom. Thus, the research question may be refined as follows:

To what extent do honors teachers approach their teaching differently – with regard to creating community, enhancing academic competence and offering freedom – with honors students compared to regular students, and what are the beliefs, attitudes and expectations on which they base such differences in their approach?

This study uses a mixed methodology (Cresswell 2009; Tashakkori & Creswell 2007), combining questionnaires among and interviews with honors teachers. As explained in the introductory chapter, this methodology was applied for honors teachers in the United States, resulting in a rich data set that allows factual conclusions, but also contextualization, elaboration with detail, and interpretation. The goal was to become acquainted with the way experienced honors teachers comprehend honors teaching and then to revisit the theory discussed in chapter 2 in light of that insight. Dutch honors teachers were only asked to fill in the questionnaire. Given the recent growth of honors programs in the Netherlands, this study seeks to make a baseline comparison (between U.S. and Dutch teachers) of teaching approaches for honors versus non-honors. The results will show whether Dutch teachers' approaches and attitudes towards honors are fundamentally similar or rather different compared to their American colleagues. This is an important point when considering to what extent lessons can be learned from American practices in a European (in this case Dutch) context, which is clearly different, both culturally and institutionally.

American and Dutch university honors teachers filled in exactly the same questionnaire. Section 3.2 discusses the design of this questionnaire, the set-up of the actual survey and the methods used for the analysis of the resulting data. Section 3.3 explains similar aspects for the interviews conducted among American honors teachers: interview design, data collection, and methods of analysis.

The chapters that focus on American honors teachers (4 and 5) will combine quantitative and qualitative data. Chapter 6, where the focus is on Dutch honors teachers, is based on questionnaire data only but offers a comparative perspective (Dutch and American teachers).

3.2 Questionnaire

3.2.1 Design process

Before the questionnaire was designed, there had been a preparation phase with orientation meetings in the United States and in the Netherlands. This contact allowed the author to find out what language and concepts the honors teachers use when they speak about their honors classes and honors teaching. This was important for the phrasing of the questionnaire items. In the United States the orientation meetings took place in 2003-2004, with teachers at eight honors programs or colleges: De Paul University, Louisiana State University Baton Rouge, Loyola University, New Orleans University, North Central College Chicago, Northeastern Illinois University, Southern University Baton Rouge and Tulane University. It was interesting to notice that in the experience and perception of the teachers, the primary difference between honors and regular classes is in the students. They were hesitant to admit that they would use different or more sophisticated teaching strategies with honors students, or devote more time to them, since in their opinion all students (honors and non-honors) should be treated equally. Nevertheless, they gave plenty of examples of differences in classroom approaches, but the issue was sensitive. A major benefit of this dialogue was the realization that the survey should not include any items that might suggest preference for honors teaching (over teaching regular classes). Orientation meetings in the Netherlands took place in 2003-2005, with teachers of four (then) recently developed honors programs or colleges, at the universities of Amsterdam, Groningen, Leiden and Utrecht. They all acknowledged and had experienced that teaching an honors class is 'different' from teaching a regular class. For the Dutch teachers, high academic achievement and personal development were the main goals and ingredients of honors education. Notions like involvement in research, the teaching of deep and fundamental conceptual knowledge, or exploring knowledge frontiers were often used by Dutch honors teachers. This helped us in phrasing some of the questionnaire items.

After the actual development of the questionnaire (see 3.2.2 to 3.2.4), three Dutch and two American experts assessed its design and phrasing. The experts were asked to comment on the questionnaire to ensure coherence, relevance and clarity. The experts were from different disciplines and were experienced in honors research and honors teaching. They pointed out the importance of including comparative statements (as opposed to preference statements) between honors and regular programs (as, for instance, '*I teach my honors students more fundamental content knowledge than my regular students*'), in line with the findings from U.S. orientation visits. They made some very valuable suggestions about the sequence of items and about phrasing, particularly in cases where words might be understood differently in the U.S. context compared to the Dutch context. They also commented that control questions should be included to ensure that all respondents would have sufficient relevant and recent hands-on experience in honors teaching.

After this expert assessment, the questionnaire was piloted both in the United States and in the Netherlands. Six American and six Dutch university teachers were asked to fill in the questionnaire. They communicated their suggestions to the author, which led to some changes in the questionnaire. Among their suggestions was the idea to allow for multiple answers to some of the questions. For instance, honors faculty from the United States indicated that many of the teachers of honors programs also have a function as honors director, supervisor or coordinator. Such multiple answers were facilitated in the final version of the questionnaire.

The questionnaire design will be explained in more detail in 3.2.2 to 3.2.4. Section 3.2.2 deals with the (personal) background data included in the survey. Section 3.2.3 explains how the insights gained in chapter 2, about honors pedagogy, were operationalized into the questionnaire. Section 3.2.4, finally, will clarify how the contextual items that were included in the questionnaire can shed light on the respondents' teaching conception and relevant attitudes.

3.2.2 Background data

The first part of the questionnaire contains fourteen multiple-choice questions and one open-ended question on factual background data such as gender, age and working situation (see appendix 1 for the complete questionnaire). In order to obtain background information about the working situation, teachers were asked to indicate the department and type of honors program in which they are active.

The name of their institution was not requested; however, teachers could give their e-mail address if they wished to receive a summary of the results. As class size can matter (Fenollar, Róman & Cuestas 2007; Zubizarreta 2008b), teachers were asked to indicate the average group sizes of the honors and regular classes they teach. As the number of years of teaching experience is said to have an influence (Brekelmans, Wubbels & Van Tartwijk 2005), another question dealt with the length of experience the respondents have in teaching honors classes as well as regular classes. It was also requested that respondents had been 'recently involved' in honors, which was defined as teaching at least one group of honors students or assessing honors work during the last two years.

3.2.3 Teaching strategies

Part 2 of the questionnaire applies to the teaching approaches and related teaching strategies of university teachers in honors versus non-honors settings. The structure of this part of the questionnaire consists of two different sets of statements (see appendix 1).

Figure 3.1 – Honors teaching approaches, teaching strategies and comparative questionnaire items

	Comparative items in questionnaire (honors versus regular)
Creating community	
• Interaction, (peer) feedback, active learning	19, 22
• Encouragement, joy, inspiration	28, 41, 42
• Availability, interest in students, commitment	26, 33, 34, 39, 40
Enhancing academic competence	
• Multi- and interdisciplinary thinking, multiple perspectives	17, 20
• Scholarly teaching, academic depth, involvement in research	16, 18
• Challenging learning tasks, difficulty, acceleration	21, 23, 29, 30
Offering freedom	
• Flexibility, allow for self-regulation, openness	27, 31
• Innovative teaching, experimentation, fun	36, 43
• Professionalism, novice relationship, challenge	35, 38

The first set (items 16 to 43) consists of a series of 28 statements (on a five-point Likert scale with its anchors defined as 1 = completely disagree, 5 = completely agree) about teaching with a focus on possible differences between honors teaching and non-honors teaching. Twenty-four statements elaborate on one of the three teaching approaches identified in chapter 2 (creating community, enhancing academic competence, offering freedom). Figure 3.1 shows which item relates to which cluster of key words (teaching strategies) identified in chapter 2. Five statements, including one that overlaps with the 24 just mentioned, relate to attitudes and beliefs and will be discussed in section 3.2.4 (items 24, 25, 32, 37, 43).

The 24 statements are mostly comparative in the sense that they compare teaching strategies or other forms of classroom behavior between honors classes/students and regular classes/students. Eighteen statements make a straightforward comparison, as for example '*My approach to honors education has more active teaching and learning methods than my approaches in regular class*'. In the other six items the comparison is either split up in two separate statements (33 and 34) or more implicit. All statements are cast in the first person singular: respondents are supposed to refer to their personal practices.

Most of the words in the comparative items have a clear relationship to one specific teaching approach. '*Different points of view*' (statement 20), for example, clearly relates to the teaching strategy of introducing '*multiple perspectives*', which is part of the approach to enhance academic competence. In some cases, however, the relationships between words in the statement in teaching strategies and approaches may be less clear. '*Challenge*' or '*challenging*', for example, may relate to enhancing academic competence (whereby challenging means academically complex or difficult), but also to offering freedom (through open-ended assignments or a project posing the challenge of self-regulation). In the case of this particular example, the word '*challenge*' was only used in an item related to academic competence ('*Challenging assignments*', 29).

The second set of statements in this part of the questionnaire (items 44-47) requires the respondents to choose from a list of characteristics and qualities of teachers they consider most important for teaching in an honors program (44, 46) and for teaching in a regular program (45, 47). The format is a combination of multiple choice and ranking: we refer to the items here as ranking items. Respondents are asked to think about (teacher qualities for) honors teaching and regular teaching separately, not comparatively. Items 44 and 45 are not cast in the first person singular; respondents should choose qualities (for honors and non-honors education) they find important for any teacher, not particularly for themselves.

Content-wise, the options to choose from in items 44 and 45 overlap to a large extent with the earlier comparative statements (16-43). The added value is that the results may confirm findings from the earlier items by presenting similar questions with different framing (not comparative and not in the first person singular). Respondents choose the three qualities from a list of ten that they consider '*especially important for a teacher*' in honors education and in regular education, for example, '*Makes connections with other areas of study*' or '*appreciate questions and remarks*' .

Items 46 and 47 are again cast in the first person singular: respondents should reflect on their own personal qualities and decide which of those make them particularly suitable to teach honors and non-honors classes. They must choose five statements (both for their honors teaching and for their regular teaching) from a list of seventeen. An extra eighteenth line was added ('*other, namely...*'). The seventeen statements are not about specific teaching strategies; rather, they deal with underlying dispositions, such as '*I explain well*', '*I am friendly*', '*I inspire students*' or '*I give useful feedback*'.

Again, all statements are related to the three teaching approaches and teaching strategies as identified in chapter 2. Figure 3.2 shows which statements relate to which teaching strategies. Details can be found in appendix 1.

Figure 3.2 – Honors teaching approaches, teaching strategies and ranking questionnaire items

	Ranking items in questionnaire (teacher assessment and self-assessment, honors and regular)
Creating community • Interaction, (peer) feedback, active learning • Encouragement, joy, inspiration • Availability, interest in students, commitment	46k 44e, 44f, 46e 44g, 44h, 46b, 46i
Enhancing academic Competence • Multi- and interdisciplinary thinking, multiple perspectives • Scholarly teaching, academic depth, involvement in research • Challenging learning tasks, difficulty, acceleration	44a, 44b 44i, 44j, 46c, 46d 46n, 46p
Offering freedom • Flexibility, allow for self-regulation, openness • Innovative teaching, experimentation, fun • Professionalism, novice relationship, challenge	44c, 44d, 46g, 46h, 46m, 46q 46f, 46o 46a, 46j, 46l

3.2.4 Attitudes and beliefs

As already discussed in chapter 2, teaching strategies do not exist in isolation but are related to teachers' underlying attitudes and beliefs: their conception of (honors) teaching and learning in higher education, their motivation to teach (honors) in higher education, and their perception of both honors and regular students. Part 3 of the questionnaire contains items that measure such attitudes and beliefs supplemented with five statements already introduced in section 3.2.3. The answers to the two open questions at the end of the questionnaire are not analyzed for this study.

For the description of the respondents' teaching conceptions twelve items suitable for higher education were selected from Denessen's 'Attitudes towards Education' 25 items questionnaire (Denessen 1999). These are items 48-59 in the questionnaire of this study, with a five-point Likert scale with its anchors defined as 1 = completely disagree, 5 = completely agree. Six items measure dispositions related to the teacher-content orientation, another six to the student-learning orientation (see chapter 2). In both cases, two items refer to ideas about educational goals, two to ideas about pedagogical relationships, and two to ideas about instructional emphasis, in line with what we discussed in chapter 2. To give an example, one of the twelve items reads: '*I find it important that students at the university can cooperate*' (student-learning orientation). The full list of items can be found in appendix 1.

Besides the twelve items drawn from Denessen's attitude survey, five items specific to the teachers' perception of honors teaching and learning in higher education were also included. These five items, also in the form of statements on a five-point Likert scale, refer to the respondents' general attitude and disposition with regard to honors education. They were mixed in with the 'teaching strategies' items (16-43); their numbers are 24, 25, 32, 37 and 43. These items are worded to gather some basic information about conceptions of honors: do teachers see honors mainly as a space where the very best students can excel academically, or rather as an innovation space where students can take risks and experiment? (Note that while the two positions are not mutually exclusive, the focus is quite different.) One example is the following statement: '*I think that taking risks should be at the center of honors education*' (item 24).

To explore the motivation of teachers for teaching in honors in higher education, elements of the 'Intrinsic Motivation Inventory' were adapted to fit the context of this study (Deci, Eghrari, Patrick & Leone 1994, Markland & Hardy 1997, Martens & Kirschner 2004, Ryan 1982), basically by adding 'honors' to the standard formulation of some of these items. This resulted in seven questionnaire items (60-66, with a five-point Modified Likert scale with its anchors defined as 1 = completely untrue, 5 = completely true.) that together describe the motivation and self-determination of the teacher-respondents. One of the items, for example, reads as follows: '*I have the feeling that I can decide for myself how I organize my honors education*' (item 60).

Teachers' perceptions of the qualities that are important in students who participate in honors and regular courses were assessed by presenting the teachers with two sets of the same multiple choice and ranking statements. Respondents were asked which characteristics (five out of a list of fifteen) they find most important for a student of an honors program (item 67) and which ones (five out of the same fifteen choices) they find most important for a student of a regular program (item 68). An extra sixteenth line was added ('*other, namely...*'). The list was derived from various publications addressing gifted and motivated learners and honors students (Cosgrove 2004; Freyman 2005; Gerrity et al. 1993; Heller 2007; Heller et al. 2005; Kaczvinsky 2007; Reis & Renzulli 2004; Rinn & Plucker 2004; Rinn 2008; Wolfensberger 2004). Two examples are the following: '*The student obtains good results in his/her courses*' (option b) and "*The student thinks in a creative way*" (option h).

3.2.5 Data collection

Both in the Netherlands and in the United States, the questionnaire was distributed among and filled in by honors teachers from institutions across the country. The American respondents were approached at the annual conference of the National Collegiate Honors Council (NCHC) in Philadelphia (November 15-19, 2006), and they filled in the questionnaire while at the conference. Dutch honors teachers completed the questionnaire online. First the data collection in the United States will be further discussed, after which the data collection in the Netherlands will be addressed.

The 844 member institutions of the NCHC are widely dispersed over the country and include all types, ranging from research universities to community colleges (see figure 3.3).

Most states in the U.S.A. were represented at the 2006 annual conference, while colleges and universities in the vicinity of the host city were overrepresented. A total of 1768 participants registered for the Philadelphia conference: 919 students and 849 professionals (teachers, deans, directors, administrators).

Figure 3.3 – NCHC membership 2006 (U.S. institutions)

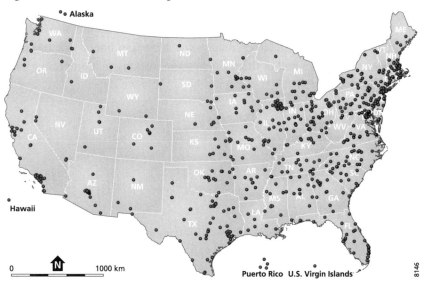

The NCHC gave permission to circulate our questionnaire – since it serves the purpose of academic research about honors teaching – among teacher-participants, on condition that the standard academic rules of privacy and confidentiality would be respected. Teachers entering the room for keynote sessions were handed a hard copy of the questionnaire, kindly requested to fill it in and to then drop it into a box at the NCHC table standing in the entrance hall. Not all teachers attending the conference were handed a questionnaire as they did not all attend the kneynote sessions. The response was considerable: 127 teachers returned a completed questionnaire (50% men, 50% women). As expected, the respondents had been recently involved in teaching honors students. The respondents were experienced teachers: 82% were over forty years old and 76% had more than ten years of experience in teaching regular courses. 40% of the teachers had more than ten years of experience in honors teaching. Almost half of the respondents worked both as an honors teacher and as coordinator of a program or as an honors director. Further background characteristics can be found in table 3.1.

All respondents could give their email address in case they would like to receive a summary of the outcomes of the questionnaire. Not all respondents did so, but those who did come from at least sixty different higher education institutions. These are distributed widely across the United States, with a bias towards the northeastern states (see figure 3.4 which also includes the interviewees' affiliations). Most of the respondents were faculty members in a humanities department, which reflects the American liberal arts tradition in honors. More than half of the teachers were working in a university-wide honors program.

Table 3.1 – Characteristics of U.S. respondents (n=127)

Question	Response	Abs	%
Age	20-30	1	0.8
	31-40	21	16.5
	41-50	38	29.9
	51-60	53	41.7
	over 60	14	11.1
Department	Humanities	61	48.0
	Science, Math & Technology	16	12.6
	Social Science	21	16.5
	Medicine	1	0.8
	Interdisciplinary	10	7.9
	Fine arts	2	1.6
	Other	12	9.4
	Missing	4	3.1
Type of honors	University honors program	74	58.3
	Departmental honors	4	3.1
	Honors college	28	22.0
	Other	21	16.5
Supported in teaching honors	Yes	123	96.9
	No	4	3.1
Teaching experience in honors	0-2 years	27	21.3
	3-10 years	46	36.2
	11 years and longer	51	40.2
	Missing	3	2.3
Teaching experience	0-2 years	3	2.4
	3-10 years	14	11.0
	11 years and longer	96	75.6
	Missing	14	11.0
Assessed honors work in last 2 years	Yes	109	85.8
	No	17	13.4
	Missing	1	0.8

Figure 3.4 – Participants' affiliations: Institutions of higher education (U.S.A.)

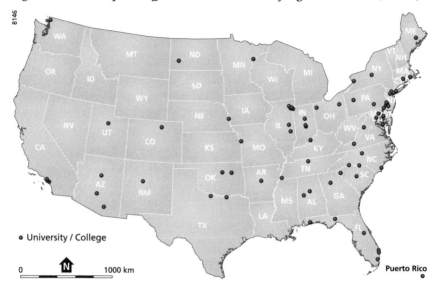

In the Netherlands, data collection took place in 2007. Honors education was on the rise at that time, although it was still a relatively new phenomenon at Dutch universities (see 1.2.2). In order to get a full picture of honors programs and honors colleges in the country (2006-2007), the author consulted previous stocktaking overviews of honors education at universities (Van Eijl et al. 2003; Van Eijl, Wientjes, Wolfensberger & Pilot 2005). As a next step, the Association of Universities in the Netherlands (VSNU) was asked to check and update these overviews. Out of the fourteen research universities in the Netherlands, eleven had honors programs or honors colleges (see figure 3.5). It should be noted that universities of applied sciences were not included in the survey; such institutions had not yet fully established honors programs at that time (Groothengel & Van Eijl 2008).

Figure 3.5 – Dutch research universities with honors programs (2006-2007)

Most honors programs were offered to undergraduates. Two of these eleven research universities had not only various departmental honors programs but also international undergraduate honors colleges with a liberal arts and sciences philosophy: Utrecht University (with University College Utrecht in the city of Utrecht and Roosevelt Academy in the city of Middelburg); and Maastricht University (with University College Maastricht). As many of the (young and small) programs might have relatively few teachers involved, it was decided to include in the survey all teachers in the Netherlands who were known to be active in honors education at research universities,

The director of every honors program known at that time and the director of education of each of the relevant faculties were asked to supply us with the email addresses of all their teachers involved in honors education. Co-operation was 100%. After some final checks and additions, the resulting list contained 768 names of teachers and their email addresses, distributed over eleven research universities (see table 3.2). Honors directors and directors of education were asked for permission to send a digital questionnaire to all the teachers involved in honors education. Again, everyone was cooperative.

Table 3.2 – Number of honors teachers at Dutch research universities, 2006-2007 (all teachers who received the questionnaire, N=768)

Institution	No.
Delft University of Technology	1
Eindhoven University of Technology	18
Erasmus University Rotterdam	19
Leiden University	59
Maastricht University	186
Of which: University College Maastricht	*(168)*
Radboud University Nijmegen	32
University of Amsterdam	51
University of Groningen	33
University of Twente	14
Utrecht University	339
Of which: University College Utrecht	*(200)*
Of which: Roosevelt Academy	*(36)*
Tilburg University	16

All 768 faculty members with (some) experience in honors teaching received an email with a request to complete the questionnaire (attached to the email). Non-responders were sent a reminder twice by email, again including the questionnaire. Total response was 41%: 313 teachers returned the completed questionnaire (68% men, 31% women – four missing values). As expected, most teachers had only recently become involved in teaching honors students and were therefore less experienced in honors than the American respondents. The Dutch respondents were also less experienced in regular teaching than the U.S. respondents. Almost a third of them worked both as an honors teacher and as coordinator of a program or as an honors director. There was a wide variety in the home departments of the Dutch respondents: Humanities as well as Science or Technology, with the largest group working in a

Social Science department. Further background characteristics can be found in table 3.3.

Table 3.3 – Characteristics of Dutch respondents (n=313)

Question	Response	Abs	%
Age	20-30	26	8.3
	31-40	80	25.6
	41-50	92	29.4
	51-60	89	28.4
	over 60	22	7.0
	Missing	4	1.3
Department	Humanities	59	18.8
	Science, Math & Technology	51	16.3
	Social Science	76	24.3
	Medicine	34	10.9
	Interdisciplinary	12	3.8
	Other	65	20.8
	Missing	16	5.1
Type of honors	University honors program	117	37.4
	Departmental honors	84	26.8
	Honors college	89	28.4
	Other	19	6.1
	Missing	4	1.3
Supported in teaching honors	Yes	211	67.4
	No	102	32.6
Teaching experience in honors	0-2 years	153	48.9
	3-10 years	134	42.8
	11 years and longer	9	2.9
	Missing	17	5.4
Teaching experience in regular education	0-2 years	21	6.7
	3-10 years	99	31.6
	11 years and longer	170	54.3
	Missing	23	7.3
Assessment	Yes	230	73.5
	No	35	11.2
	Missing	48	15.3

3.2.6 Analysis of the data

In order to avoid too much technical detail in the discussion of the results (chapters 4 to 6), all statistical techniques that were used in the analysis of the data will be summarized in this section.

Many questionnaire items have five-point Likert scales as answer categories. In line with Jamieson (2004), we presumed the intervals between the response categories to be equal and thus used interval-level measurement statistics for the Likert-scale questions.

Three dimensions of teaching approaches (community, academic competence and freedom) were taken into account in this study. For measuring the internal consistency of the statements allocated to each dimension, Cronbach's Alpha (1951) was used, which ranges in value from 0 to 1. For our purposes, a reliability of .70 or higher shows sufficient internal cohesion (Nunnally 1978, p. 245), although when measuring attitude a lower bound (0.5) is assumed to be acceptable (Tuckman 1972). Cronbach's Alpha was also used to measure the internal consistency of the scales allocated to teachers' motivation and self-determination and teachers' conception of teaching and learning (honors) in higher education.

In this study the standard deviation was used to measure the variability of the different scales (Gravetter & Walnau 2011). When variables were aggregated to another variable, the standard deviations were once again computed.

In order to analyze whether there is a difference between teaching strategies for honors and teaching strategies for regular courses, we used Cohen's Kappa (Cohen 1960). Data which contain a large proportion of zeros, such as the research data, give rise to a large number of chance similarities. The Kappa statistic is designed to correct for such chance similarities. Cohen's Kappa is an index of inter-rater reliability that is commonly used to measure the level of agreement between two sets of dichotomous ratings. So this Kappa indicator statistic gives a quantitative measure of the magnitude of agreement between respondents who are evaluating the same subject (Viera & Garrett 2005). For instance, in medical research Kappa measures if two doctors give the same diagnose for 100 patients. Here, this is turned around: Kappa measures if 100 teachers chose the same teaching strategy for two programs (honors and regular program). Kappa can lie anywhere in the range from -1.0 (consistent disagreement) to +1.0 (perfect agreement). A Kappa of 0 would equate to chance agreement. Kappa is high if most subjects are evaluated similarly by both respondents. In this case, we used Cohen's Kappa to analyze the opinions of each rater about teaching strategies for two different types of programs (honors and regular). Kappa is high if most respondents have an opinion about the teaching strategies that is consistent between an honors and regular program. So when Kappa is low – less than 0.4, as proposed by Sim & Wright (2005) – there is no similarity in their opinions about teaching strategies within honors and within regular programs. Thus, slight to no agreement among respondents indicate different teaching strategies for honors than for regular programs (proposed Kappa description by Byrt (1996)). When Kappa is higher, this is mentioned in the text as not convincing.

The teachers were also asked about the qualities students need in honors and regular education. To reveal whether the teachers really differentiated between honors and regular students, Cohen's Kappa was also used in this case.

A cross tabulation was made in order to examine to what extent teachers in the United States and teachers the Netherlands indicate the same teaching strategies for honors and regular education, at the statement level. With a chi square test we tested whether or not there are significant associations or differences. The same test was used to examine to what extent teachers in the U.S.A. and teachers in the Netherlands have the same perceptions of honors students and of regular students.

In order to find out whether there are significant differences between teachers' motivation between the United States and the Netherlands, the independent t-test was employed (De Vocht 2009).

To find out whether teachers' motivation correlates with the dependent variable 'creating community' (teaching approach), a multiple regression was made. The same analysis was used to explain 'enhancing academic competence' (teaching approach; dependent variable). All assumptions were fulfilled. This was not possible for 'offering freedom' (the third teaching approach) as the dependent variable.

The influence of class sizes on the approaches of creating community and enhancing academic competence was tested by an ANOVA. An ANOVA computes the variance of the variables and examines whether the population means are identical or not (Field 2009). In our analysis the independent variable was class size. This is an ordinal variable. As ANOVA is made for nominal independent variables this is also allowed for ordinal variables (Blalock 1979).

3.3 Interviews

Interviews play an important part in this study. Thirty experienced American honors teachers were interviewed, not only to confirm the outcomes of the literature and questionnaire surveys but also to understand their ideas about honors teachers and honors teaching. The interviews form an important enrichment of the questionnaire results in the level of detail, argumentation, examples and perspectives they offer. Section 3.3.1 describes the rationale and design of the interviews. Section 3.3.2 gives some details about the actual interviewing (data-gathering) process. In section 3.3.3, finally, the methods and procedures will be explained that were used for the processing and analysis of the interviews.

3.3.1 Design process

What do U.S. honors teachers say about the content and pedagogy of their honors teaching, when invited to do so in an open interview setting? Also, how do they think and feel about their role as honors teacher and about honors students? These questions were the entry point for the design of the interviews. It was not the intention to ask them specifically about teaching approaches and teaching strategies or about dispositions and attitudes, as presented in chapter 2, since this might limit the opportunities to get a broad and open impression about their 'lived experience' as an honors practitioner. The author considered it more interesting not to take too much of a steering role in the interviews but to check afterwards to what extent the interviews reflect, reinforce or put in perspective the findings of the questionnaire survey.

The interviews with American honors teachers were conducted by two researchers, both with sufficient expertise in honors research: the author of this study and a colleague from Utrecht University (Pierre Van Eijl). This joint task made it all the more important to agree upon a topic list for the open interviews. Basically it consisted of key words and questions that could be brought into the conversations (figure 3.6). The idea was to hold interviews of approximately forty-five minutes, with some fifteen minutes for orientation questions (mainly factual) and thirty minutes for a conversation about the honors teaching experiences, in a broad sense, of the interviewees.

Figure 3.6 – Topics of the interviews

Part 1 – Orientation (factual)	Years of experience
	Roles in honors (teaching, coordination)
	Area of specialization
	University, type of honors program
	Basic characteristics of honors program (mission statement, structure, elite group, rules, alumni success)
Part 2 – The personal practice of teaching honors (including opinions and beliefs)	Your teaching (what is specific to your honors teaching, in substance and methods; in what ways different from regular teaching)
	Your role as teacher (in helping to realize honors mission)
	Your motivation for honors (what do you like/dislike in it; ideas and feelings about honors students)

The first part of the topic list, the orientation part, may seem to be far more structured than the second part, particularly with regard to questions about the honors program in which the interviewee works as a teacher: these queries concern the mission statement, structure, activities valued by students, alumni success and the like. This is indeed the case; the difference is explained by the dual purpose of the interviews. On the one hand, they were intended to serve as input in this study about honors pedagogy, and part two of the topic list was particularly designed to this end. On the other hand, the interviews were supposed to provide input for an exploratory survey of U.S. honors practices, as part of a project funded by the Dutch Ministry of Education, Culture and Science. For this purpose, some more specific factual questions were included in part one of the topic list (for a report on this exploratory survey, see Van Eijl, Wolfensberger, Schreve-Brinkman & Pilot 2007). Overall, though, the topic list has the characteristics of a guideline for open interviews (Bryman 2004; Roulston, deMarrais & Lewis 2003).

Another initial decision was to not only conduct in-depth interviews with individual honors teachers, but also to have at least a few small focus group sessions along the same lines as the topic list. The author believed that, due to interaction within such focus groups, group conversations might reveal and clarify information that would not have emerged in individual interviews (see the arguments put forward by Breen 2006; Krueger 1994).

The interview design was tested in a pilot study with seven faculty members of the Department of Geography and Planning, Utrecht University, the Netherlands. The purpose was to explore whether the topic guide would stimulate the teachers to share their thoughts and experiences in honors teaching. The wording of some questions was adapted slightly in response to their reactions. Finally, the draft interview topic list was discussed with two experts, one from the Netherlands and one from the United States, and no further changes were proposed.

3.3.2 Data collection

Qualitative research includes meaningful sampling or 'purposive sampling', since all participants should have substantial experience in honors education (Bryman 2004). The first step was to approach all 38 site visitors listed on the NCHC website, as site visitors have guaranteed expertise and experience in honors teaching. Our aim was to conduct interviews with ten of them. The site visitors suggested additional interviewees: teachers with a track record in honors teaching from a wide range of institutions. The actual interviews took place during a six-week period prior to the 2006 annual conference of the NCHC in Philadelphia and at the conference itself. Participants were informed that the session would be audio recorded.

Thirty American honors teachers were interviewed. This number was considered sufficient, given the fact that the researcher wanted to understand the common perceptions and experiences of a rather homogeneous group of individuals (Guest, Bunce & Johnson 2006). The expectation of (a high degree of) homogeneity is based on the fact that experts – in this case experienced honors teachers – tend to agree more with respect to their expert domain than novices (Romney, Weller & Batchelder 1986). According to Guest et al. (2006), when the group of participants that is interviewed is relatively homogeneous, in the open coding process of qualitative analysis, the point where no new themes appear – the data saturation point – is reached after coding twelve interviews, as by then 90% of the codes have been assigned. This is an additional reason to assume that thirty is a sufficient number of interviewees (eighteen in individual interviews, four in the two focus groups with two teachers, eight in the two focus groups with four teachers).

Figure 3.7 – Participants in the interviews

Nr	Name	Department	State
1	Alexander	History	Pennsylvania
2	Andrea	Honors staff	Pennsylvania
3	Ann	Psychology	North Carolina
4	Aroha	American Studies	Pennsylvania
5	Betty	English	New York
6	Henry	English	South Carolina
7	Hermione	English	Florida
8	Janine	English	New Mexico
9	John	Mathematics	Florida
10	Jorim	Political Science	South Carolina
11	Jude	Honors staff	Rhode Island
12	Kate	Honors staff	Pennsylvania
13	Lillian	Honors staff	Pennsylvania
14	Marin	Honors staff	Pennsylvania
15	Martin	Economics	Florida
16	Moses	Political Science	Oklahoma
17	Nancy	Honors staff	Pennsylvania
18	Noa	Honors staff	Illinois
19	Orlanda	Honors staff	Pennsylvania
20	Patrick	Music	North Carolina
21	Peter	History	Washington
22	Pierre	Communication	Pennsylvania
23	Robert	Political Science	Oklahoma
24	Rosa	-	Delaware
25	Rosalie	English	New York
26	Rudolf	English and American studies	Connecticut
27	Samuel	Psychology	New York
28	Silver	English	South Carolina
29	Tim	History	Washington
30	Walter	Religion	Pennsylvania

All thirty interviewees had several years of teaching experience in honors and regular teaching and were committed to honors programs, as shown by their attendance at the conference and/or their further involvement, for example as a site visitor, in the NCHC. Most of them worked not only as teacher but also as director of an honors program or as dean of an honors college. Figure 3.7 gives an overview of the thirty interviewees. This display requires some explanation. The names are fictitious. All transcribed interviews have a number and the people who were interviewed have been given these fictitious names, in alphabetical order (Alexander for interview 1, Walter for interview 30 – please note that the contributions of one individual in focus group discussions have been reorganized into one numbered interview transcript). The advantage of giving these names is that we can refer to them after quoting from the interviews in the following chapters, instead of having to refer, unpleasantly, to a 'number'. The interviewees represent sixteen different higher education institutions in the United States located in twelve states (see also figure 3.4).

3.3.3 Analysis of the data

The recorded interviews and focus group discussions were transcribed verbatim, and subsets were constructed for the comments made by individuals during the focus group interviews. This resulted in thirty bodies of transcribed text that were subsequently subjected to content analysis. Analyses of the textual data were accomplished with the use of the qualitative analysis software package ATLAS.ti, version 06 (ATLAS.ti Scientific Software Development GmbH). The transcribed interviews were entered into the Atlas program. All data that could have led to the identification of the participants were removed from the transcripts.

First the transcripts were categorized with four main codes which are relevant to the present study, namely: teaching approaches; dispositions towards and beliefs about honors education; motivation for honors teaching; ideas about and attitudes towards honors students. In line with the framework developed in chapter 2, all text under the code 'teaching approaches' was further categorized, as far as possible, under three sub-codes: creating community, engendering academic competence, and offering freedom. After that a new iterative process started for the text under all (sub-)codes in order to find the main themes that the teachers addressed in the interviews. The analysis as a whole relied on an iterative analytic process in which themes were refined as the analysis progressed and then revised based on conversations between the researchers and consecutive close readings of the transcripts (as in Light

& Calkins 2008, p. 31). During the analysis, a codebook was developed by two independent researchers (the author and colleague Wolter Paans, Hanze University of Applied Sciences, Groningen) using a standard iterative process (MacQueen, McLellan, Kay & Milstein 1998) in which each code definition has four parts: a brief and a full definition, a 'when-to-use' section and a 'when not to use' section, and examples, consisting of quotations pulled from the data.

As indicated above, the data analysis process began with coding. The two researchers compared and discussed their categorizations. In case of a lack of agreement, the disputed fragment was examined again in light of the whole interview to interpret it in context. This was followed by discussion until inter-coder agreement was reached for all allocations. In cases of remaining doubt, a third researcher was involved. Those interview fragments that could not be related to any of the codes or to a possible new code were labeled as 'no code' and discarded (removed from further analysis).

After the successful allocation of interview text to the four main codes, a similar and second step was the allocation of text classified under the code 'teaching approaches' to three sub-codes: community, academic competence, and freedom. It became clear that much of what the American teachers had said about teaching strategies could indeed be categorised under these three sub-codes. The process of attaining inter-coder agreement followed the same procedures as those for the first step. Unclassifiable text fragments were brought under a non-coded fourth group.

The next step was to find out what the main themes and issues are that the American honors teachers speak about under each of the rather broad initial codes: beliefs about honors; motivation for honors; notions about honors students; the creation of community as teaching approach; enhancing academic competence as teaching approach; and offering freedom as teaching approach. To this end the researchers chose an open coding approach analogous to procedures of the grounded theory approach (Charmaz 2006; Strauss & Corbin 1990). By creating themes, a higher level of data conceptualization may be reached. The data were broken down into discrete parts, examined, compared for similarities and differences, and discussed. In this manner, for every code, the two researchers – independently from each other – analyzed the text in order to reveal dominant themes, topics or issues. Themes were labeled whenever possible by using the words expressed by participants (in vivo coding, see Bryman 2004, p. 547). For every category, the themes discovered by the two researchers were compared, discussed, and sometimes presented to a third researcher in order to attain inter-coder consensus, very much in the same way as discussed for previous steps.

The resulting themes – for example the themes and aspects that teachers mainly brought into the conversation with regard to their motivation or about creating community as a teaching approach – are in fact an important outcome of the analysis of the interviews and will therefore be discussed in chapters 4 and 5.

3.4   Methodological caveats and limitations

This study has some methodological limitations. The research design solely takes into account teachers' own perceptions of their teaching. Observations of their actual teaching were not included. Previous studies have indicated the complex relationship between cognition (what teachers say they think, want or do) and their actual behavior (Mathijsen 2006). One example of potential inconsistency is the 'value-conflict' that may arise in the classroom when a teacher wants to adhere to her or his subject but equally wants to allow room for a student's interest, even if this does not fully fit the teacher's plans. The author is confident, though, that the results are a very close proxy for what the honors teachers actually think, want and do. Many of the questions in the questionnaire are factual and non-confrontational. More importantly, the honors teachers show a high level of agreement and consistency in their answers and in the conversations.

Secondly, there may be some bias because of the selection of respondents. The way in which the questionnaire was distributed differs between the U.S.A. and the Netherlands. In view of the method of data collection in the U.S.A., there may have been a stronger self-selection among the respondents to the American questionnaire. Although there are relatively many teachers with experience in (honors) teaching (table 3.1), the teachers' characteristics do show dispersal.

In this study the Dutch teachers' comprehension of honors teaching is to be explored and only a baseline comparison with the American teachers' comprehension is to be made; as it turns out, surprisingly few differences are notable. The U.S. respondents all attended the NCHC conference, which means that they have a particular interest in and motivation for honors teaching. This might even mean that they are to some extent predisposed to perceive differences between honors and regular standards of learning and teaching. The Dutch respondents were in a sense honors pioneers in their country and might therefore have biased opinions, although this is difficult to substantiate. Furthermore, teachers were explicitly asked to make a comparison between honors and regular study. This juxtaposition may induce somewhat exaggerated differences between the two in the answers, to an extent that is not really experienced by the respondents in their daily practice. The author believes, though, that this limitation is largely overcome by the mixed methodology: the interviews add a great deal to the questionnaire survey.

4 American honors teachers: thoughts about honors education

4.1 Introduction

It is the purpose of this chapter to describe, analyze and contextualize what American honors teachers think about their honors teaching, their role as honors teachers, and their honors students on the basis of survey data as well as interviews. Teachers' ideas about honors form the core of the chapter, but the first section (4.2) expands on their conceptions of teaching and learning in general: are teachers relatively more teacher-content oriented in their approach, or rather more student-learning centered? Section 4.3 highlights the teachers' ideas on honors education. This is followed by sections about their motivation for teaching honors (4.4) and about their perceptions of honors students (4.5). Throughout the chapter, survey outcomes will be combined with interview data. This chapter sets the scene for what will be the focus of the next one: the teaching approaches and teaching strategies of the American honors teachers.

4.2 Conceptions of teaching

The notion of basic orientations towards teaching and learning was introduced in chapter 2, particularly the distinction between a teacher-content orientation and a student-learning orientation. It was explained that Denessen conceptualized three dimensions of such orientations, namely (ideas about) educational goals, pedagogical relation, and instructional emphasis. A balanced set of twelve statements from Denessen's scale for measuring teachers' orientation was selected for inclusion in our questionnaire (two statements per dimension for each of the two orientations). The statements interrelated at face value. The results show the orientations towards which American honors teachers are most inclined. It should be noted that the orientations are not mutually exclusive.

Table 4.1 displays the results (mean scores and standard deviations) at the level of each item individually for each of the dimensions and for both orientations. It is noticeable that the conceptions of the 127 honors teachers tend more towards the student-learning orientation than to the teacher-content orientation (table 4.1). Another observation is that for all items the average scores are higher than 3.0 on a five-point scale, except for one statement ('... *I find competition among students important*' – see table 4.1). This means that the teachers combine ideas that relate to both orientations, although for all statements for the student-learning orientation the mean scores are higher than 3.5. It is interesting that internal consistency is stronger for the teacher-content items (Cronbach's Alpha 0.64) than for the student-learning oriented items (Alpha 0.59). This is in line with other research (Denessen 1999; Light & Calkins 2008). It is explained in other studies by the more diverse vision of the student-centered orientation and the more rigid approach of the teacher-centered orientation, with its strong focus on the 'traditional fundamentals of education'.

The tendency of the teachers towards the student-learning orientation is most evident for the dimension of 'instructional emphasis'. For this dimension, the statements for the teacher-content orientation focus on grading and competition, whereas those for the student-learning orientation focus on co-operation and mutual learning (see table 4.1).

The author takes these findings about teaching and learning orientations at face value, while realizing that they only provide rather basic evidence for the fact that honors teachers are relatively more inclined towards the student-learning orientation. The exercise made clear that the distinction is not black and white. The respondents have some high mean scores for items that – according to Denessen's conceptualization – also reflect 'traditional' values of the teacher-content orientation. After having discussed teachers' conceptions of teaching, we now turn to their ideas about honors education.

Table 4.1 – Teaching orientation scores, by pairs of related statements, U.S. teachers (n=127)

	Statement	Mean Score	SD
	TEACHER-CONTENT ORIENTATION		
Educational goal	If students want to achieve something later in their life, they have to learn a lot at the university.	3.5	1.0
	A good education is the key to success in society.	4.1	0.7
Pedagogical relation	Order and discipline are important at the university.	3.2	1.0
	I consider it important that students behave well at university.	3.5	1.0
Instructional emphasis	Grading is a good boost for the studying of students.	3.3	0.8
	For optimal learning results at the university, I find competition among students important.	2.7	1.0
	STUDENT-LEARNING ORIENTATION		
Educational goal	It is the job of the university to educate students to become critical citizens.	4.4	0.7
	It is the job of the university to pass on values and standards.	3.6	1.0
Pedagogical relation	Involvement of the students in the university is important.	4.1	0.8
	It is important that the university takes the wishes and interests of the students into account.	3.8	0.8
Instructional emphasis	Students can learn a lot from each other too.	4.6	0.5
	I find it important that students at the university can cooperate.	4.0	0.7

4.3 Honors education

"I always try to remind students that being elite does not necessarily mean the same thing as being elitist, and we focus on how important it is that they put their talents to good use, that they live their lives ethically and humanely, always mindful that honors is also about honor, not just about achievement and rewards" (Henry).

During the interviews, the teachers were not directly asked what – to them – the essential characteristics of honors education would be. But during the conversations about half of them did make statements that reflect what they see as the core of honors. 37 such fragments were found in the interviews. Three recurrent themes among these interview fragments were brought up rather frequently plus two minor themes that were each mentioned twice. We labeled the themes as:

- outstanding performance (17 fragments);
- distinct group (8 fragments);
- honors as recruitment instrument (5 fragments);
- other themes: innovation, satisfaction (4, respectively 3 fragments).

The various themes that were identified when analyzing the interviews will be discussed individually. The author will also refer briefly to questionnaire statements in the course of this section. The questionnaire contained five statements that refer explicitly to a general characterization of honors education (see chapter 3). The aggregated answers to these five Likert-scale items (five-point scale) are depicted in table 4.2.

Table 4.2 – General characterizations of honors education – questionnaire items, U.S. teachers (n=127)

Item	Statement	Mean	SD
24	I think that taking risks should be at the center of honors education.	3.9	0.98
25	I think that honors education should be focused on evoking excellence.	4.2	0.85
32	Honors education is more focused on the development of talent than my regular education.	3.1	1.05
37	I consider it important that an honors student belongs to the top 10% of the student population with regard to grade average.	3.1	1.15
43	I use honors as an 'educational innovation room'; I try out different education methods and tests.	4.1	0.78

4.3.1 Outstanding performance

What characterizes honors education most, according to the teachers, is outstanding performance. The teachers are aspiring to elicit exceptional work. *"The ability to settle for nothing less than excellence, that is to be expected"* (Pierre). The high mean score (4.2 on a five-point scale) of the reactions to the next questionnaire statement underlines this: '*I think that honors education should be focused on evoking excellence*' (table 4.2). The American honors teachers believe that honors programs are a symbol of the institution's attitude towards excellence. Among the teachers we encountered a feeling that their institutions had what Kuh, Kinzie, Schuh & Whitt (2005) describe as *'a cool passion'* for excellence. That is, *"an undergirding, institution-wide commitment to student learning and making the necessary changes in institutional policies and pedagogical practices to help students realize their potential"* (p. 77). Kuh et al. call this *'a cool passion'* because it maintains a steady fire that is critical and creative while withstanding icy logic or frigid resistance. One of the teachers phrased it as follows: *"I can give you a characteristic. When I see students that love what they are doing and I see teachers that love what they are doing, then I can tell that they have a good administration. It's very simplistic, but still"* (Nancy).

Excellence may be a key word, but this is certainly not the case for 'talent development'. One interviewee said, when asked if there were examples for the development of talents, that *"Talent development is not a term with which I am familiar"* (Robert). Another teacher said that *"I haven't seen the words 'talent development' in any program review documents. Still, development of talents seems like an obvious, implicit goal of honors education"* (Henry). In spite of the pre-testing of the research instruments, the notion of 'talent development' slipped through in the interview questions and questionnaire. American honors teachers apparently think of talent as innate, as something to be used but not to be 'developed'. This may explain the lukewarm (mean score 3.1) and dispersed (SD 1.05) reactions to the questionnaire statement that uses the notion of 'talent development' (table 4.2).

In their remarks about outstanding performance, the teachers stress the process of learning (effort, engagement, initiative) more than its outcomes (such as high grades). This focus on outstanding quality in the learning process is reflected in many of the interviews. *"I would say that the main goal is to figure out how to get the individual more engaged in their individual learning process. To make them more dedicated to learn more in this one area; to go for finesse and not accept the mediocre. That they'll demand more from themselves until justice has been done to the topic"* (Pierre). The same teacher explains further that honors students should stand out in effort and in depth of academic work: *"I expect a higher level of work, more finesse and style. Sitting there giving me a bunch of URLs for research is not research, it's lazy. I expect more. You'd better be citing journals in my honors classes and they'd better be current. My role is to try out how to make them excel even more and to make them excel in something different"* (Pierre). Others expect honors students to stand out in their originality and independent thinking: *"I mostly give the same assignments, but what I get back from honors students does more for me. I never expect them to parrot my views. I encourage them to have their own views as long as they have good reasons for them"* (Alexander). Honors students are supposed to do something 'special' compared to students in regular courses. What it is that makes their learning process special or different is not always expressed in qualifications such as 'outstanding' or 'excellence'. This teacher expresses it in plain language: *"They [the students – MW] should be relatively more self-directed and independent in their academic work. Further they should be able to integrate methods and concepts from different disciplines in dealing with complex questions"* (John).

Several of the teachers praise effort. They believe in offering opportunities that stretch students' abilities. But some teachers deplore the students' competitiveness and fixation on grades. *"They can be too competitive when it comes to grades, which results in the jockeying for the A, which can be extremely frustrating"* (Pierre). High grades, according to the teachers, are not the essence of honors education. One of the questionnaire statements was about grades: *'I consider it important that an honors student belongs to the top 10% of the student population with regards to grade average'* (see table 4.2). The mean score was not high (3.1 on a five-point scale) and the standard deviation (1.15) reflects wide diversity in the reactions. It might be self-evident to the teachers that honors students generally get high grades; they certainly dislike extremely grade-driven honors students. There is strong agreement that honors is not solely about an outstanding GPA: *"An undergraduate honors program adds substantive value to a student's degree that goes beyond merely what is shown on a transcript or diploma"* (Henry). Or, as already quoted at the opening of this section, *"honors is also about honor, not just about achievement and rewards"* (Henry). Nevertheless, various teachers confirm that outstanding outcomes in their honors program do make a difference in the further career of honors alumni: *"Much of the evidence is anecdotal, but I believe that graduates of honors programs probably pursue graduate and professional training in greater percentages than non-honors students, and they probably have higher GPAs and are more successful in these endeavors. I would also suspect that they move up the ladder a bit more quickly once they have settled into careers"* (Martin). One of the others is of the opinion that this is the general impression of

American honors teachers: "*[I think ...] that any honors program can produce impressive evidence of alumni success in graduate and professional schools, jobs, community*" (Henry).

4.3.2 Distinct group

Streaming is common practice in American honors education: honors students sit together in special honors classes, which are only accessible to participants in the honors program. Because of this – though also because of other practices such as special honors student dorms – the students form a distinct group, sometimes referred to as an 'elite'. Elite is a contested concept, also among the honors teachers. Honors students may be "*a kind of elite*" (Orlanda), but the teachers shy away from elitism: "*Egalitarianism is a highly valued commodity*" (Samuel).

The fact that honors students sit and work together as a rather homogeneous group with strong motivation and academic potential is seen as one of the core characteristics of honors education. Streaming helps create high expectations: "*I believe that most of the time, knowing that they are in these special circumstances raises the expectations of the students in a constructive way*" (John). The special circumstances include small classes, often of twenty to twenty-five students. As one of the teachers (Alexander) said, teaching in small honors classes benefits students, not least because honors students like to get involved in discussions. The 'elite-ness' of being a separate and distinct group is generally considered as highly stimulating: "*I hope that being 'elite' influences students positively to be serious, ethical, creative, deeply engaged in developing their talents*" (Henry). Interestingly, this teacher uses the words 'developing talents'; this is the only case in all of the interviews where the term is used spontaneously. The distinct honors group with high expectations is also a setting where teachers are triggered to do their best: "*The teacher must be willing to have the students 'shine' and sometimes show novel ways of thinking*" (John).

The theme of distinctness, as a trait of honors education, is closely linked to the teaching approach of creating a sense of community and connectedness. In chapter 5, the interviews will be analyzed from this perspective.

4.3.3 Recruitment

Various teachers also pointed out that honors programs may be used as a marketing tool; they are certainly seen as an effective asset in the recruitment of good students and good teachers. "*I believe* [...] *it* [an honors program – MW] *becomes an important mechanism for recruiting students of a university*" (Nancy). One of the teachers was very clear about why this is the case: "*I think that in our current higher education climate of fierce competition for talented students, any school without an honors program is seriously disadvantaged. Honors programs, especially in larger universities, offer students the high-quality, close community experience of a small, academically elite college within the larger context of a big institution*" (Henry). He continued by explaining that this is equally true for attracting motivated faculty: "*What dynamic, motivated, eager teacher would not want to accept a position at an institution with an honors program that demonstrates the school's commitment to excellence in teaching and learning?*" (Henry). A similar perspective came across in another interview: "*If the program enjoys institutional support and is highly regarded both on and off campus, it will often attract the best and brightest faculty who wish to engage these types of students*" (Martin). The links between institutional ambition (striving for excellence), honors programs and recruitment (of good students and good teachers) are clearly perceived as important. This strategic institutional function of honors is among the first things mentioned by some of the teachers when talking about their honors program. One of the interviewees gave her own university as an example: "*For the university honors is the driving force for getting the best students. If you just look at the honors program, we would be ranked amongst the best selective colleges in the country. A lot of students pick the University of X because of the honors program. So attracting the best students is the added value, which also results in faculty members being happier and in enhancing the classroom experience for all students*" (Rosa).

4.3.4 Other themes: innovation, satisfaction

"*The honors program has served as a kind of incubator for all kinds of good teaching initiatives, it just happened that way, problem-based learning is just one example. There are lots of examples where projects launched in the honors program went university wide [...] I think it is a combination of dedicated faculty interacting with interesting, motivated and somewhat demanding students. This creates a very dynamic relationship, which gives these interesting educational results"* (Rosa).

Although it was not an explicit topic in the interview agenda, many teachers would agree that honors education is about innovative teaching. One of the questionnaire items referred to this issue: *'I use honors programs also as an 'educational innovation room'* (see table 4.2). The response was highly affirmative (mean score 4.1). During the interviews, one of the teachers put it very simply: *"Honors is a stimulus for teaching innovation"* (Henry).

Innovation and experimentation involve risk. The teachers used the word 'risk' or 'risky' spontaneously eighteen times while they were talking about their honors experience. One of the teachers observed that *"Pushing harder is an example of taking risk"* (Pierre). In the questionnaire, the respondents agreed rather strongly with the statement *'I think that taking risks should be at the center of honors'* (mean score 3.9, see table 4.2). The conversations with teachers made it clear, however, that we should not draw any conclusions from this score. Some teachers were unsure whether 'risk' in this survey item referred to risk for teachers, for students, or for both.

Another association with honors that came up several times during the interviews is the notion of satisfaction. *"The opportunity to work with people who are so talented is extremely rewarding"* (Rosa). Or: *"(...) the payoffs would be more personal satisfaction and that there is more satisfying of inner curiosity"* (Patrick). In this context, it is interesting to note that none of the interviewed teachers brought up external motivation factors such as extra salary or more prestige (for the teacher). But they do spontaneously mention the pleasure and satisfaction of working with honors students as their reward. The same holds when they talk about honors students, as we saw earlier: they stress the students' intrinsic motivation; and they are more negative about external motivation, such as striving for high grades or prestige, if such factors would dominate among a student's reasons to participate in honors. The reward of satisfaction brings us to a discussion of what motivates teachers to participate in honors, which is the topic of the next section.

4.4   Motivation

"A lot of people call me the Pied Piper of Hamelin, where everybody sort of flocks around me. I think it is because I respect all of their opinions. If somebody comes up with a really stupid thing, I won't tell him it's stupid, I'll ask him to defend it better. Also, when I lecture about history I always bring in a couple of stories. Those kinds of things people remember. I think I'm enthusiastic about history and that shows" (Alexander).

The 127 American honors teachers who filled in the questionnaire get remarkably high scores on their motivation for honors teaching. As explained in chapter 3, the author used the seven-item version of the 'Intrinsic Motivation Inventory' (Martens & Kirschner 2004), slightly modified by adding the word 'honors' to four of the seven items. The mean score for all seven items is higher than 4.0 on a five-point scale and ranges between 4.1 and 4.4. Self-determination and motivation are closely related (see chapter 2) and the seven items refer to both aspects (see table 4.3). Statistical analysis showed that the cluster of seven items holds as a reliable scale for teachers' motivation and self-determination. (Cronbach's Alpha 0.75). The general picture is that teachers like their honors classes very much, feel free to organize their honors classes, get new ideas thanks to their involvement in honors, and cover subject matter in these classes that is in line with their personal interest. On top of that, they see themselves as good teachers with the desire to be among the best and to engage in new challenges.

Table 4.3 – U.S. teachers' intrinsic motivation for honors teaching (n=127)

Statement	Mean	SD
I have the feeling that I can decide for myself how I organize my honors education.	4.1	0.9
I am extremely motivated to teach in honors.	4.3	0.9
My honors education makes me think of matters I had never thought of before.	4.2	0.9
My honors course fits, with respect to content, my personal interests.	4.1	0.9
I think that, in comparison with other teachers, I teach well.	4.1	0.7
I want to be one of the best of my work associates.	4.4	0.7
I find it important to be challenged to get the most out of myself.	4.4	0.7
Score of motivation scale	*4.2*	*0.53*

The atmosphere during the interviews reflected this impression – that the teachers have a strong intrinsic motivation for their honors teaching. The interviews took place in a positive atmosphere. The teachers were remarkably positive about their jobs, about honors, about their students and indeed about themselves as teachers. Teachers' motivation and self-determination for honors teaching was not actually the subject of the interviews. But in the open interview setting, which broadly followed the topic list, teachers said what they liked or disliked about honors teaching and what they thought about themselves as honors teachers.

Analysis of the interview transcripts resulted in 24 text fragments that refer to the interviewees' motivation for teaching honors. It was not easy to discern clear themes within this collection of fragments, due to overlap between many of the arguments that were put forward. Nevertheless, through the iterative process as explained in chapter 3, the researchers decided on the following themes:

- The pleasure of working with honors students and helping them to fulfill their potential (7 fragments).
- Enthusiasm about being able to share much of their academic field – in depth – with the students (9 fragments).
- The challenge that comes with honors teaching (8 fragments).

The American honors teachers who were interviewed perceive honors as fun. When the teachers talked about their motivation for honors teaching, they said that their encounters with honors students were crucial. "*I get a lot of satisfaction out of working with students who are very motivated and want to get the best out of their education*" (Rosa). Interaction with the honors students is clearly an important motivational factor for honors teachers. "*Those seeking rewards in teaching motivated students will be attracted by honors*" (Jude). Throughout the reactions, we discern a reciprocal relationship between faculty motivation and student motivation. The feeling of being able to teach and support young, motivated and talented people appeals to the teachers. "*I feel that the college years are so important to a young person in terms of growth and development. That's the time they really are becoming who they will be. The opportunity to work with people who are so talented, personally I think it's extremely rewarding*" (Rosa). Some teachers go so far as to express their gratitude and pride about being able to support the development of honors students. One of them told us *"I think a lot of the honors students are excellent and I don't know how many of them were already excellent or whether I have been bringing it more out of them. I have had some students that, sometimes after they graduated and moved on, I get emails from. They talk about how a class moved them or how they decided to do something differently with their lives, because of me. I like to be an inspiration and give honors students the feeling that what they can learn now is something that they can continue to learn, a sort of lifelong learning"* (Alexander).

For some teachers, the (motivating) pleasure of helping students in their development is mixed with content-driven motivations. It is the synergy of doing more for the students and doing more with the academic field in which the teacher has specialized. Because of such mixed motives, one of the teachers told us that he finds honors teaching particularly stimulating with more senior students: *"It depends on the topic. If it's an upper level course, I would definitely prefer honors, because I know that I could get a lot of great products out of the students. We are talking about products that will be published on a national level, for example. For beginner courses, it really depends on the subject. There's something inherently good about introducing a student to college and making sure that they start off on the right foot. I like that aspect of teaching. So to some extent I could argue that I like teaching non-honors entry-level courses. But when it comes to an advanced class I definitely prefer honors classes"* (Pierre).

When students express their enthusiasm for the academic field of their honors teacher, the teacher may also be more inclined to really show his enthusiasm for that field of study, sometimes in novel ways. Alexander, for example, clearly demonstrated this: *"I give the students the idea that all their ideas and opinions are worthy and I try to encourage people to talk [...] I am not so much teaching about history, I teach them to be enthusiastic about history. If I can give them enough stuff, that makes them want to find out more, they will go on to teach it themselves, get the books and investigate further. What I do sometimes, I bring in my guitar with me in class to show them how music evolved my history. When I brought in my guitar [the first time], I was very nervous for them to think what I as an intellectual was doing with a guitar, but it worked well [...] I give the students the idea that all their ideas and opinions are worthy and I try to encourage people to talk. I try not to take myself so seriously, some professors are very serious, I try to be more ordinary, not like some oracle sitting up there telling the truth"* (Alexander).

The overall impression from the interviews is that the positive motivation of the teachers makes them act in a relaxed and authentic style in class. They combine this with an engagement that not only sets the standard for the students but also encourages them towards deep learning and excellence. Motivation (both of teachers and students) helps to create an informal, relaxed yet demanding class atmosphere, and the other way around. Teachers express this mechanism in many ways: "*I am more formalized in my regular courses*" (Pierre); or "*I always left the classes feeling a little bit high.*" (…) "*I always cannot wait for Monday morning; I can't wait to get back into class after the weekend. I am pretty relaxed with my students and they sense that and they feel that they can say things*" (Alexander).

Teachers experience various challenges within their honors classes. They find these challenges motivating, since challenges break routines, require hard work and sometimes involve risk. The challenge of honors education is therefore considered exciting, at least by a number of interviewees. Pierre mentioned some of the inherent risks in honors teaching which make the experience extra interesting: "*I think it's a risk of taking our students further than they think they can be taken. Because they think that there will be potential backwash, it's demanding too much of them. It's risky for students to dislike you for pushing them further than they thought they could be pushed. [...] If my evaluations are not good, I could be removed from teaching in honors or my renewal could be questioned. My allocations of that class could be questioned. [...] In my honors classes you will have to work very hard to get the same grade as in a non-honors class. That's also the risk. Do you risk potentially hurting yourself by demanding a lot of those students? It is a hard balance to find. In honors classes you will find yourself explaining the grades a lot more. I usually give a six-page feedback on the projects. A project is about ten pages*" (Pierre).

During many of the interviews, teachers indicated that they had to work very hard in their honors classes in order to get the same '*student satisfaction scores*' on standard class evaluations as from their non-honors classes. Student satisfaction evaluation results are important for faculty: for instance, to get tenure, to be promoted or to be allowed to stay in the honors program. For such reasons some teachers see a risk in demanding a lot from honors students (Moses), but this challenge tends to boost their motivation rather than to diminish it. This section concludes with a long interview fragment (figure 4.1) that clearly illustrates the types of challenges and risks that may be part of teaching honors. The fragment also makes it very clear why many honors teachers perceive such risks as an extra asset and a motivating factor rather than as a problem.

Figure 4.1 – Example of challenges within an honors course

"I think research has to be broadly understood. It is not just about research. (…) This course, rituals in gender, that I taught, is a good example. I really wanted to think about feminist art, say art since 1945. Knowing that nobody knows about this stuff – in the curriculum of T. we don't have this. But I'm also very interested in rituals especially with respect to classroom treatment, about how a classroom is a very ritual space. I wanted to talk about that and about how gender equated to it. So I taught this course three times and every time it was really different. The third time was especially amazing, because one of my friends, who is running the T. art gallery, asked me if we wanted to do a show of art. I couldn't ask my class first, because she had to book it already, so I said yes. Nobody in my class is an artist, because it's a women's studies class. So we ended up having a show there and it was an incredible experience. Everybody turned their pieces in on time. Someone of the class offered to be in charge of the exhibit on one condition: that I would not interfere. The show was just fantastic, the way she arranged our work it looked like we were serious artists. The night before, when I was finishing my piece I thought about backing out, since I'm the professor. However then I thought, "No, I can't get to class without it". That's what I mean by providing situations where I have no choice but to take risks myself. I told them that they were not going to be graded on the piece, only on the passion and commitment in doing their job. I said: "I have a piece too and I don't want you to give me a bad grade on my piece, because I'm not an artist either." So we need to actually make something, do something, show something for this and really put ourselves out. I'm always trying to get people to do that and that's how I stimulate myself to also go to the edge" (Aroha).

4.5 Students

[What are for you the characteristics that make it an honors education?] *"I think a considerable part of the burden is on the student and on the students as a group. We, as instructors and administrators, assume that these people can and will work hard enough to understand things by themselves at a level at which other people just won't. As a consequence it's not that they work harder, they work differently"* (Rudolf).

Teacher' perceptions and expectations of students can shape their honors pedagogies, leading to different educational practices, as already suggested in chapter 2 (Rosenthal & Jacobsen 1992; Weinstein 2002). Both the questionnaire data and the interviews reveal which perceptions and expectations the American honors teachers have of their honors students. We shall first discuss the survey outcomes and then turn to the results of the interviews.

Two items in the questionnaire specifically address teachers' opinions of (honors) students: items 67 and 68 (see appendix 1). Both items are of the multiple-choice/ranking type. The teachers were asked to select the five (out of fifteen) characteristics they find most important for a student in an honors program (item 67) and, similarly, the five (out of the same fifteen characteristics) they find important for students in a regular higher education program (item 68). The results are shown in table 4.4. The numbers in the table indicate by what percentage of the 127 respondents a particular statement was placed in their top-five. The Kappa statistics show that most of the outcomes (the two rankings compared: for honors students and for regular students) have slight to weak similarities. This means that the teachers made conscious choices that exhibit a clear difference in opinion about the qualities that are important for honors students compared to those considered important for students in a regular program.

The top-three in both rankings appear in bold in both columns. These top-three suggest that, according to the teachers who participated in the survey, the key words for honors students are initiative, curiosity and creativity. For students in regular programs, the key qualities are motivation, curiosity, and effort. Some of these differences are modest: the teachers believe that honors students as well should be motivated and invest effort in their studies (in fact, these two qualities rank fourth and fifth in the honors top-five). For creativity, a quality the teachers value in honors students, the ranking difference is considerable (63.0% and 25.2% respectively). To a lesser extent, this is also the case for 'showing initiative and carrying it out' (70.9% and 49.6% respectively). Two other qualities that are prioritized very differently for the two student groups are preparedness to take risk and being on schedule with coursework (valued much more for students in regular programs).

Table 4.4 – Qualities considered most important for honors students and regular students, U.S. teachers (n=127)

Student quality	% in honors top-5	% in regular top-5	Kappa
Shows initiative and also carries it out	**70.9**	49.6	0.137
Is curious	**68.5**	**66.1**	0.267
Thinks in a creative way	**63.0**	25.2	0.275
Is motivated in his/her courses	56.7	**73.2**	0.244
Is prepared to invest considerable time in his/her courses	51.2	**63.8**	0.207
Is prepared to take risks in his/her academic career	47.2	16.5	0.231
Is involved in the academic community	34.6	21.3	0.292
Stimulates other students within the education program	31.5	12.6	0.085
Has a passion for research	16.5	3.9	0.014
Obtains good results in his/her courses	8.7	26.0	0.216
Values my knowledge about a given subject	8.7	22.0	0.326
Is not behind with his or her studies	4.7	44.1	0.118
Is easy to get along with	1.6	5.5	0.203
Behaves well in class	0.8	15.7	-0.015
Can keep an appointment	0.8	11.0	0.120

The differences in assigned qualities are largest for creativity and readiness to take risk (considered much more important for honors students) and for remaining on schedule (not getting behind) with coursework (considered much more important for regular students). It is important to keep in mind that the respondents had to compile a list of their top five choices out of the fifteen qualities. This does show what they consider most important, but it does not mean that other qualities, outside the top-five, are considered unimportant.

The interviews did not include many questions (topics) about students and student qualities (see 3.3.1). In fact, the only points of attention were types of activities valued most by honors students, and honors students' self-perceptions as a distinct or 'elite' group. However, while talking about diverse aspects of honors, the interviewees spontaneously offered stories about their honors students. In general they were positive about their honors students; none of them expressed worries or a fear of setbacks, with the exception of students who are over-competitive and/or over-committed.

Twenty of the interviewed teachers made observations about (their) honors students during the interviews. The researchers identified 77 relevant text fragments. Using the procedures set forth in chapter 3, the researchers identified four themes that these passages have in common; together, the themes occur in 60 of the 77 text fragments. The other 17 text fragments were singular statements, sometimes very brief, and in all cases hard to classify. These are the four common themes:

- Honors students are engaged, dedicated to learning and willing to go further (24 fragments).
- Honors students are academically and personally more advanced than their peers and work harder and differently (17 fragments).
- Honors students are strong communicators and eager to discuss the subjects they are interested in (12 fragments).
- Honors students may be over-competitive or over-committed (7 fragments).

Teachers experience honors students as engaged and dedicated. "*They are willing to go above and beyond what is required for the assignment. I think in the honors program there is to some larger extent the desire to learn, to challenge a teacher and to challenge the self. That is probably the biggest difference between a regular student and an honors student*" (Pierre).

Various teachers stressed that honors students are not only dedicated to their study, but that their inquiry goes beyond the boundaries of their courses. "*Honors students show evidence of intellectual engagement beyond merely making good grades; (…) evidence of a willingness to grow and learn beyond the formal classroom setting*" (Jorim).

Because of their strong engagement and commitment, many honors students are eager to become involved in research and in teaching. One teacher commented that "*More honors students tend to get more engaged with helping with their teacher's work. Some of my honors students are literally helping me with my research right now. We also have some programs in which students can become teachers and they assist us with the teaching of our courses. Some other major differences are that they are more engaged, they talk more, and they are willing to go further*" (Pierre). Another teacher stressed the strong engagement of students in classes: "*I was asked to teach this class in 2001 and a lot of other teachers said to me that the honors students had a very high opinion about themselves and that they were hard to deal with. I didn't think that at all. I loved it from the first moment. The students are so engaged and they're answering questions, have critical comments and it was just inspiring"* (Alexander).

Honors students are also perceived to be academically and personally more advanced than their peers. According to the teachers this means that they are quicker and work not only harder but also in a different way. The academic potential of honors students was noted by many of the teachers in comments such as *"It's easier to teach honors students, because they have more academic skills"* (Walter). One of the teachers told us that honors students are more advanced and thus more professional in doing their reading and preparing for classes; this means that the teacher enters honors classes with a different feeling than regular classes: *"I think that there's a level of trust in the honors experience that I don't typically find in regular classes, where I am sometimes struggling to make sure that people are doing the reading and are prepared for the test. I go into an honors experience with a level of trust, which means I can expect more and deeper things out of them and that I don't have to be worried about the content. Not that I'm not disappointed sometimes"* (Silver). The same teacher gave an example to illustrate that many honors students, in his opinion, have strong and mature personal skills such as perseverance, courage or willpower: *"I'll use an example. I had a student two years ago, who in terms of her statistics, was in the middle of the pack, just about an average honors student. I had her in a first-term honors course and she set the curve. That's very unusual in an honors course, there's usually a cluster of people. The thing that distinguished her simply was courage. She had the willingness and the ability to ask the hard question. Those are not measurable things"* (Silver). In many interviews, teachers observed that their honors students often have multiple talents, such as for music or for sports. Honors students do *"astonishing things, in various walks of life"* (Betty).

Honors students are strong communicators, a quality highly appreciated by the teachers. *"Usually the students are very vocal; they interact in very strong ways with each other. They get to show, also to each other, their excellence in verbal exchange. Normally, due to large classes, only written excellence is tested"* (Walter). During the interviews, many of the teachers made brief remarks suggesting that they see honors students as good debaters, good speakers, good writers and also good listeners.

As a counterpoint to the very positive perceptions described above, teachers are more negative about the tendency for honors students to be over-competitive (particularly when this leads to a fixation on grades) and sometimes over-committed. With regard to competitiveness, teachers do see that this attitude can also contribute to outstanding performance, like winning prestigious awards or scholarships. The other side of the coin is that very competitive and grade-driven honors students may lose the pleasure of intellectual exploration for its own sake and of the 'honors experience' as largely a joint adventure. "*One of the things honors students are most terrified of is being assessed and getting less than an A. One of the things I find very important to do is help to break away from two things: being perfectionists and being competitive*" (Rosalie). One of the interviewed teachers made the observation that it is maybe naïve to assume that grades should not be that important to an honors student: "*I think it's a little bit idealistic from a professor's point of view. We want them to come up with ideas and generate things and apply it outside the classroom. That happens sometimes in our experience. What also happens is that students in the honors program want to know how they are going to be graded. So it is true that they are more open in terms of thinking about things, but when it comes to their grade, they become very crazy*" (Ann).

Ambitious honors students may also over-commit themselves, academically and socially at the same time, which may result in stress, lack of focus, and underperformance. Some of the teachers have pointed out this danger: "*I think there are some students that want to do too much, because they are very confident, they like a lot of things and they take it all on*" (Lillian). "*In my experience, honors students have many talents, but live in a world that pushes them to pursue only one avenue of personal achievement. This pressure to be unitary creates genuine confusion, and often self-doubt*" (Betty).

The share of relevant interview fragments presented in this section was small but indicative. Teachers clearly see honors students as engaged and dedicated, academically able individuals, often with remarkable personal skills, as good communicators and as students who may develop the negative tendency of becoming too competitive or over-committed. These qualities were extracted from interviews during which few direct questions about honors students were raised. The comments of the interviewees came up spontaneously during the conversation. The structured questions about honors students in the questionnaire, filled in by 127 teachers, resulted in an image of the honors student as motivated, curious and creative.

4.6 Conclusions

This chapter gives an impression of some of the dispositions, opinions and attitudes of American honors teachers: about their basic orientation towards teaching and learning, about how they characterize honors education in general terms, about their motivation to teach honors students and about honors students. Some of the findings were derived from the questionnaire survey. The interviews provided considerable additional detail and insight.

The teachers show more characteristics of a student-learning orientation than of a teacher-content orientation. The teachers believe that honors education is a setting for outstanding performances. The distinct group of students with strong motivation and academic potential, sitting and studying together is seen as important for honors. The teachers believe that honors is a setting that allows for educational innovation, offers considerable inherent satisfaction to the teacher, and that may be instrumental for recruitment purposes.

The honors teachers show very high intrinsic motivation, which they ascribe – at least partially – to the pleasure and fun that comes from teaching and coaching able and motivated students, to the possibility to go deeper into their academic subject with honors students, and to the challenges that come with teaching honors students. They see honors students as motivated, curious and creative; they praise honors students' dedication and engagement, their academic and personal skills, and their communicative abilities. But the teachers are somewhat concerned about the tendency of honors students to become too competitive or over-committed.

The information provided in this chapter forms a backdrop to the discussion in chapter 5 on the teaching approaches and teaching strategies of American honors teachers.

5 American honors teachers: approaches in honors education

5.1 Introduction

Both in the survey and during the interviews, the American honors teachers have given a wealth of information. They have told what they see as important teaching strategies in honors classes and identified the differences they perceive between honors teaching and teaching regular university classes. We shall first look at those questionnaire items asking the respondents which aspects of teacher behavior they consider most important in honors classes and in regular classes (items 44-47, see appendix 1). The results are discussed in section 5.2. After that, we turn to the three teaching approaches that were presented in chapter 2 as pivotal to honors education: creating community, enhancing academic competence, and offering freedom. Section 5.3 examines the survey results in light of these three dimensions: to what extent do the survey data support the assumption that teachers consider these approaches more significant to honors teaching than to the teaching of their regular classes? Section 5.4 presents the interviews conducted with American honors teachers. The discussion is again focused on what they say about these approaches in honors teaching.

5.2 Honors classes and regular classes: priorities in teacher behavior

"I'm looking for teachers with broad minds, who are creative, who want students to have input in the courses, who can engage students. I look for teachers that can inspire their students so that they go much further than what anybody in

their right mind should do in coursework. So I'm looking for teachers who have interdisciplinary interests, who have interests outside the classroom, who are willing to invest personal time with students, willing to take them on field trips and are willing to take them into risky situations intellectually" (Aroha).

In items 44 and 45, the respondents were asked '*... to indicate which three characteristics you find especially important for a teacher of an honors program, and which three characteristics you find especially important for a teacher of a regular program'*. In both cases, they were given the same ten options to choose from (see appendix 1). The teachers were not asked to reflect upon themselves as honors teachers but to make a choice that might refer to any honors teacher. The results are presented in table 5.1.

The Kappa values suggest that the teachers did indeed make two independent rankings (for honors programs and for regular programs), as was the intention. The Kappa values also suggest that they gave sufficient thought to the distinction between the two settings and that they did not assign the same priorities to both contexts. The only option for which Cohen's Kappa is not convincing is 'enjoys teaching'.

Table 5.1 shows how often each strategy occurred in both top-three lists. The three most frequently chosen options in both rankings are printed in bold. The most important teaching strategy for honors is thus inviting students to participate actively (chosen by 82% of the respondents). Next come the options 'makes connections with other areas of study' (51%) and 'makes the course exciting and has confidence' (33%). The priority given to these three aspects of teacher behavior, respectively, resonates with the importance attached to community (active participation) and academic competence (respectively multiple perspectives and the notion of confidence). That relation will become clear in the next sections. The ranking of strategies for teaching in regular programs was quite different. Teachers were supposed to offer well-organized subject matter (58%), formulate clear and shared goals for their classes (46%), and enjoy teaching (38%). Structure is emphasized; the respondents might have put 'pleasure' in third place because they assumed that in regular programs the students need an enthusiastic teacher to keep them motivated, more so than in honors programs. But this is mere speculation. The most frequently chosen strategies for teaching in honors and non-honors are very different, but beyond the top-three, the rankings show some resemblance. Inviting students to participate actively in classes and making a course exciting (and having confidence) also rank high among aspects of teacher behavior that are important in regular classes (both 35%).

Table 5.1 – Top-three teaching strategies for honors programs and for regular programs, U.S. teachers (n=127)

Strategies	Honors top-three (%)	Regular top-three (%)	Kappa
Invites students to actively participate	**81.9**	34.6	0.052
Makes connections with other areas of study	**51.2**	18.9	0.177
Makes the course exciting and has confidence	**33.1**	34.6	0.192
Is interested in students as individuals	32.3	12.6	0.207
Appreciates questions and remarks	26.0	18.9	0.169
Enjoys teaching	24.4	**37.8**	0.550
Is available to his/her students and is easily accessible	23.6	22.0	0.107
Places different points of view opposite each other	19.7	10.2	0.148
Formulates clear and shared goals for the class	8.7	**45.7**	0.101
Offers well-organized subject matter	6.3	**57.5**	0.039

It is notable that the frequency of choosing an individual option differs between honors teaching and non-honors teaching. Two options – inviting students to participate actively and making interdisciplinary links – were chosen far more frequently for honors teaching than for regular teaching. The two items referring to structure – offering well-organized subject matter and formulating clear goals – were assigned one of the highest priorities for teaching regular classes but one of the lowest for honors teaching

While designing the questionnaire, the author realized that honors teachers might answer such questions differently if asked to apply them to their own teaching practice, not to honors teaching in general. Thus, two additional multiple-choice/ranking items were included in the questionnaire. These were cast in the first-person singular: '*Please indicate which five qualities of yourself make you especially appropriate to teach in an honors program and which five qualities make you especially appropriate to teach in a regular program*' (items 46-47, see appendix 1). To answer, the respondents could choose from a list of seventeen options. These were formulated differently than the ones shown in table 5.1 to discourage repetitive behavior while filling in the questionnaire. But all the options were derived from the same dimensions of

94

teaching approaches (community, academic competence, freedom; see also section 3.2.3). The results are given in table 5.2, with the five most frequently chosen options in both cases shown in boldface.

Table 5.2 – Respondents' personal top-five teaching strategies: honors teaching and regular teaching, U.S. teachers (n=127)

Strategies	Honors top-five (%)	Regular top-five (%)	Kappa
I challenge students	**78.7**	**53.5**	0.212
I am prepared to deviate from traditional education methods	**63.8**	21.3	0.184
I give students room for their own choices	**56.7**	17.3	0.189
I grant students much responsibility	**48.8**	11.8	0.150
I inspire students	**47.2**	27.6	0.467
I give the students new ideas	39.4	23.6	0.149
I give useful feedback	29.1	**55.1**	0.320
I am demanding	24.4	25.2	0.472
I know a subject well	23.6	**42.5**	0.282
I am friendly	18.1	29.9	0.471
I am clear about my expectations of students	15.0	**58.3**	0.111
I explain well	9.4	**51.2**	0.088
I understand quickly what a student asks or remarks	6.3	18.1	0.110
I correct work quickly	4.7	13.4	0.486
I discuss course subject matter at a fast pace	1.6	2.4	0.388
I am good at keeping discipline	1.6	3.9	0.562
I make sure that students keep appointments and deadlines	0.8	3.1	0.392

As before, the results show that teachers make a clear distinction between honors teaching and non-honors teaching. Cohen's Kappa is low for twelve out of the seventeen options, which indicates that the respondents have made two sufficiently independent rankings. Options with a more dubious Kappa do not stand out in either of the two rankings. Referring to their own behavior, the teachers chose the following options most frequently for honors teaching: they challenge students, are prepared to deviate from traditional educational methods, give students room to make their own choices and grant them responsibility, and inspire them. For their regular courses, the American teachers valued the following qualities most in themselves: they are clear about their expectations, give useful feedback, challenge their students, explain well, and know their subject well. Again we see a strong focus on structure in what teachers consider important for their regular classes. They do see the importance of challenging students academically in both their honors and regular classes, but this option was chosen far more frequently within the honors top-five.

Every ranking item (also called option) in questions 44-45 and 46-47 was derived from the three dimensions (community, academic competence, freedom; see also sections above and 3.2.3 in the methods chapter). The ranking items for honors teaching were identical to those for regular teaching. This makes it possible to draw comparisons between honors and regular education with respect to the relative importance of community, freedom and academic competence, as is done in table 5.3. For table 5.3, the options (as shown in table 5.1 and 5.2) have been aggregated and related to the three dimensions of teaching approaches set forth in figure 3.2, with the caveat that structure has been introduced as a fourth dimension of the teaching approaches. As set forth in figure 3.2, eight ranking items (numbers 44e, 44f, 44g, 44h, 46b, 46e, 46i and 46k in the questionnaire – see appendix 1) are related to 'community' as a teaching approach; for example, 'Invites students to actively participate'. Likewise, eight items are related to academic competence. It was decided for this exercise to divide the eleven ranking items regarding freedom into two categories: six items are related to offering freedom and five to offering structure (see also section 2.2.3). One example of those five (numbers 44c, 44d, 46g, 46m and 46q in the questionnaire – see appendix 1) is 'Offers well-organized subject matter'. The table shows how often strategies related to each of the four dimensions were mentioned for honors and regular education.

In honors education, as table 5.3 indicates, the strategies related to freedom are seen as most important, followed by those related to community and academic competence. All of the mentioned teaching approaches are also important in regular education, though some striking differences emerge. Teaching strategies related to freedom were least frequently chosen for regular programs. Strategies related to offering structure are seen as important for regular teaching but rarely for honors classes.

Table 5.3 – Importance of community, competence and freedom/structure for honors and regular education, U.S. teachers (n=127)

Approaches	Number of items chosen			
	within honors programs		within regular programs	
	abs.	%	abs.	%
Community	336	34.0	278	29.1
Competence	213	21.6	268	28.1
Freedom	396	40.2	194	20.3
Structure	41	4.2	214	22.5
Total	986	100.0	954	100.0

In summary, while it is important to challenge all students, the ways to do so differ for honors and regular students. The items discussed in this section were designed in such a way that the results would indicate what teachers consider the most important aspects of teacher behavior in honors or regular classes. The results do not imply that the options infrequently appearing are considered irrelevant or unimportant. What the data do show is that teachers have very different perceptions of teaching honors classes compared to regular classes. In terms of the required teacher qualities, teacher behavior and classroom strategies, they stress structure-related aspects for regular teaching. For honors teaching, they give priority to strategies conducive to creating community, enhancing academic competence and offering freedom. This interpretation will be substantiated in the next two sections.

5.3 Teaching approaches – survey results

Part 2 of the questionnaire also contained 24 items about teaching strategies (among the items numbered 16-43, see appendix 1). In chapter 3 these were called comparative items, since they require the respondent to compare teaching in honors and non-honors education. All 24 items concern one or another of the three teaching approaches identified in chapter 2: ten are related to creating community, eight to enhancing academic competence and six to offering freedom (see figure 3.1).

For example, '*I assign more challenging assignments to honors students than to regular students*' (item 29) is clearly related to the teaching approach of enhancing academic competence. The results will be discussed in more detail for each of the three approaches.

5.3.1 Creating community

Community as a dimension of honors teaching was measured using ten statements in the first-person singular. These were rated by the teachers on a five-point scale, with its anchors defined as 1 = completely disagree, 5 = completely agree (see figure 3.1 and appendix 1). With five of these ten statements about teaching practices within honors and regular programs a community scale was created (Cronbach's Alpha= 0.74). This is an indicator of the teacher's opinion on the relative importance of community in honors classes and regular classes (see table 5.4). The responses were averaged to form composite scores (M= 3.5; SD= 0.75). Five statements were not included in this community scale, also due to flaws in the way these items were phrased. One item did not differentiate between honors and non-honors ('*My relation with honors students is equal to my relation with regular students*'); two items did not fit for the scale because the comparison was spread over two separate statements ('*I know all my honors students by name*' and '*I know all my regular students by name*'); and two other items did not correlate enough, also the order of the subjects of comparison was reversed.

Table 5.4 – Creating community as a teaching approach, U.S. teachers, 5 statements (n=127)

	Statement	Mean	SD
I	I stimulate honors students more than regular students to think about personal wishes and goals.	3.1	1.22
II	I think honors students are more active in the academic community than regular students are.	4.0	0.94
III	I think that honors students will be our leaders of the future rather than regular students.	3.5	1.00
IV	My approach to honors education has more active teaching and learning methods than my approaches in regular class.	3.6	1.26
V	The personal interest of a student plays a bigger role in my honors education than it does in my regular education.	3.2	1.23
	Score of community scale	*3.5*	*0.75*

As it turns out, creating an objective measure of 'creating community' is no easy task. Indeed, some of the individual statements that were used may be questionable. The five statements correlate with one another and form a valuable basis in terms of content. The mean score for two of the statements, I and V, is not convincingly high (on a five-point scale). In three cases, statements I, IV and V, the standard deviation reflects considerable diversity among the answers. Statements II and III have an indirect relationship to teaching strategies: it is assumed that teachers have to be involved with their honors students and know them rather well (community strategies) in order to be able to judge their level of engagement in the academic community (II) and leadership potential (III). Statement V might also be considered relevant to 'offering freedom' as a teaching approach. Nonetheless, it was taken as an indicator of 'creating community' since it assumes that teachers are informed about the personal interests of their students, which is a community trait.

The general picture is that teachers encourage interactivity and active learning in honors classes. They give attention to the personal interests and needs of honors students. And teachers indicate, although indirectly, that they know their honors students well. This seems to fit in with the finding that 55% of the honors teachers say they know the names of all their honors students (completely agree) versus 41% who say they know all the names of their regular students (completely agree).

Class size may have a major impact on the scores teachers give to community related survey items. Size influences the opportunity for interaction between teacher and students. Also, the sentiment that smaller is better could influence the outcomes, although a decade of research on the relationship between class size and student achievement failed to produce conclusive results (Okpala, Smith & Jones 2000). An Anova analysis was conducted in order to check for such bias in the results. It turns out that there are no significant differences in scores on the community scale between teachers who have reported relatively large average class sizes (for honors and non-honors) and teachers who have reported relatively small classes.

The relationship between the community scale and teachers' intrinsic motivation was analyzed through a correlation analysis. Variation in teachers' motivation explains 6% of the differences in creating community. Details of the analysis are presented in appendix 2a.

5.3.2 Enhancing academic competence

Eight statements in the questionnaire are related to enhancing academic competence as a teaching approach for honors education. All eight items were included in the academic competence scale, which was shown to be sufficiently internally consistent (Cronbach's Alpha 0.76, see table 5.3). The overall mean Likert score for all eight items is 3.3 (see table 5.5), showing a slight inclination of the teachers to apply the strategies for enhancing academic competence to a greater extent in honors classes compared to regular classes. The individual statements give more insight into the teaching strategies for the enhancement of academic competence (table 5.5).

The American honors teachers differentiate the most between honors and regular for the following three statements (Likert scores 3.5 or higher):

- They give honors students more challenging assignments (I).
- They want honors students to be more involved in research (VII).
- They assess honors students in a different way (III).

At the other end, we find the least convincing differentiation in teaching strategies between honors and non-honors for items V and VI: teaching more fundamental content knowledge and application of knowledge to real situations. The lack of effectiveness of these items may well be explained by their phrasing. Indeed, 'fundamental content knowledge' (V) may be perceived as 'basic knowledge', which is obviously equally important in regular courses; the same may be the case for applying knowledge in real situations (VI). Standard deviations are generally high, meaning that there was a rather wide distribution of the individual scores.

Again, teachers' class sizes may influence their scores on academic competence items. Anova analysis showed no significant differences in academic competence scores between teachers with relatively large classes and those with relatively small classes. The relationship between the scales of academic competence and teachers' intrinsic motivation was analyzed through a correlation analysis. Variation in teachers' motivation explains 21 % of the differences in enhancing academic competence. Details of the analysis are presented in appendix 2a.

Table 5.5 – Enhancing academic competence as a teaching approach, U.S. teachers, 8 statements (n=127)

	Statement	Mean	SD
I	I assign more challenging assignments to honors students than to regular students.	4.1	1.03
II	I assign more time-consuming assignments to honors students than to regular students.	3.3	1.19
III	I assess students in the honors program differently than I assess students in the regular program.	3.5	1.23
IV	My methods to evaluate honors education are different from my methods to evaluate regular education.	3.3	1.17
V	I teach my honors students more fundamental content knowledge than my regular students.	2.7	1.18
VI	I teach my honors students more often than my regular students how they can apply their knowledge in real situations.	2.8	1.12
VII	I find it more important that honors students, rather than regular students, are intensively involved in research early in their education.	3.7	1.08
VIII	I teach my honors students more about different points of view than I teach my regular students.	3.3	1.29
	Score of academic competence scale	*3.3*	*0.71*

5.3.3 Offering freedom

Six of the 24 questionnaire items that are discussed in this section refer to the teaching approach of offering freedom. These six statements do not have the internal consistency needed to consider them as a 'freedom scale'. To create such a scale, apparently more and differently formulated statements would be required. Four items did not include a straightforward comparison between honors programs and regular programs. And one other statement reversed the order of the subjects of comparison ('*I have more fun with my regular students than with my honors students*'). The statements will therefore be examined separately (table 5.6).

Table 5.6 – Items related to the teaching approach of offering freedom, U.S. teachers (n=127)

Item		Mean	SD
I	I find it hard to teach students smarter than me.	1.8	0.96
II	I give honors students more freedom (with respect to choosing topics and time-management) than regular students.	3.9	1.12
III	I give feedback to my honors students as if they are junior colleagues.	3.1	1.15
IV	I have more fun with my regular students than with my honors students.	1.9	0.91
V	I refer students to experts when their questions or interests are beyond my area of expertise.	4.4	0.73
VI	I use honors also as an 'educational innovation room'; I try out different education methods and tests.	4.1	0.78

Table 5.6 shows that the teachers mostly apply the following strategies in their honors classes:

- They allow their honors students more freedom in choosing study topics and in their time management (II).
- They encourage students to find expertise elsewhere, outside the classroom (IV).
- They use honors classes as a space for innovation and experimentation (IV).

Statement II may have been too indirect and not properly understood by the respondents, which may explain the less pronounced outcomes. The idea was that 'feedback (...) as if they are junior colleagues' implies giving only constructive suggestions and leaving it to the other how to use these suggestions (as a proxy for offering freedom). Statement I assumes that offering freedom comes with trust and with a real sense of equality. Teachers who perceive very smart students as a threat are probably not inclined to offer them a lot of freedom. Statement IV, which like I is also reversed, assumes that inherent pleasure in honors teaching makes it more likely for a teacher to allow the students more freedom of choice.

Summarizing all of the above, the empirical analysis suggests that teachers employ different teaching strategies for honors courses than for regular classes. With honors, they place more emphasis on community and freedom. Academic challenge is created by a stronger focus on interdisciplinary perspectives and research. Finally, teachers consider rigorously structured teaching as unsuitable for honors classes but more suitable for regular classes.

5.4   Teaching approaches – teachers' stories

How teachers perceive their teaching strategies within honors education will be described in more detail here. This section reports on findings from the interviews conducted with thirty American site-visitors and teachers. Two researchers examined the verbatim text, as explained in chapter 3. First they categorized all fragments that have a bearing on honors teaching strategies; the next step was to explore how teachers approach their honors teaching with regard to creating community, enhancing academic competence and offering freedom, as defined in chapter 2. No direct first-person questions were asked about those teaching approaches. The focus of the interviews was on honors education itself; only occasionally were the respondents asked to draw a comparison between honors and regular education.

Teachers spoke readily about their teaching experiences and gave all kinds of examples. In total 160 fragments about teaching strategies were classified according to the three teaching approaches: 57 of those were coded 'creating community' (section 5.4.1); 68 as 'enhancing academic community' (section 5.4.2); and 35 as 'freedom' (section 5.4.3). It became very clear during the classification task that the conceptual and theoretical foundation laid out in chapter 2 served well for the identification of teaching approaches in honors, as expressed in the interviews. Only a limited amount of fragments could not be coded and those fragments had not coherence. Creating community, enhancing academic competence and offering freedom are the three teaching approaches that stand out as essential in honors teaching. The next step was to label common themes in the text fragments as community, academic competence or freedom. This was not always easy, since many remarks of the interviewed teachers related to more than one teaching strategy.

In most fragments, the teachers are telling about their own experiences. However, teachers who also worked as, for instance, honors directors or site-visitors had additional experiences, which will be reflected in the text selections presented in the next three sections.

Figure 5.1 – The honors teacher – a mosaic of qualities and teaching strategies

An honors teacher:

Provides an environment conducive to free inquiry, has high academic standards, works well with students, and is open to new things (Noa)

Has to get the students to challenge themselves (Martin)

Has to cultivate in students an attitude of inquiry and discovery, such that students develop an ability for self-teaching (Jorim) and are willing to take risk (Aroha)

Challenges students, challenges their assumptions, provides provocative readings; constantly thinks of ways to try to keep classes exciting and imaginative (Rosa)

Has a passion for the subject matter and for sharing it with students (Hermione)

Gives guidance, but not too much (Peter)

Is an interdisciplinary thinker who encourages students to think across boundaries and to make connections among subject areas and between academic learning and personal lives (Henry)

Frames issues, leads discussions, and keeps quiet (Betty)

Shows novel ways of thinking (John)

Uses plenty of active learning strategies, engaging students in learning not only content material but also how to learn and why, and about themselves as learners (Henry)

Draws directly on a student's experience and interest and empowers students to contribute actively (Peter); Is spontaneous and has liveliness (Rosalie); has flexibility (Silver) and is a risk-taker liking challenges (Tim)

Has respect for student opinions (Hermione) and commitment to students' learning (Robert)

Has a willingness to be a co-student (Hermione) and takes a personal interest in students' success (Martin)

During the interviews we asked the teachers to describe qualities of honors teachers that, in their experience, are effective in evoking excellence among their students. This question echoes some of the questionnaire items described above, for instance items 44 and 46 (see appendix 1). Some of the short replies given by the interviewees to this question are compiled in figure 5.1. This figure is a mosaic of teachers' qualities and teaching strategies that most respondents would see as important in honors teaching. Although many of these statements refer to creating community, to enhancing academic community or to offering freedom, they will not be used in the following sections as illustrations.

5.4.1 Creating community

"Another factor is that the students develop a sense of community, that they belong to something. Because of that they tend to reinforce each other, they form study groups, develop good study habits" (Moses).

Although the interviewers did not explicitly ask about creating community as a teaching approach, 24 of the teachers talked spontaneously about creating community. Altogether, 74 fragments were subsumed under this heading. Of these text fragments, 57 related to actual teaching strategies; the other seventeen referred to institutional conditions for creating an honors community. This last group will be discussed first; then we shall turn to the actual teaching strategies.

"Every university college has a culture and every honors program has a culture. The main job of a director of an honors program is to do something to improve this culture" (Tim). More than half of the teachers stressed the importance of the preconditions for creating community. They see such preconditions partly in the structure and consistency of the honors curriculum and partly in the infrastructure offered by the institution, like housing for honors. Through examples, the teachers make it clear what they mean by an honors culture and by an institutional culture that supports the honors community. They mention the importance of an honors office and of specific facilities. *"Our honors freshmen have to live together. That helps us to develop that community"* (Rosa). *"We have a lounge. It's a big lounge, very casual. Students can come by and hang out. We allow them to stay here after work. It's also the fact that they are trusted to hang out here, when we are not here"* (Orlanda). Several teachers give examples of how the social and co-curricular activities may

induce the students to collaborate and make them familiar with the honors culture. "*We have open house. We have dinners; we have various campus activities that bring students to the campus*" (Rosalie).

The preparation for professional life and graduate school is also part of the honors education. One of the teachers mentions the active support infrastructure that many honors programs offer: "*It's also the trend for honors programs to take on the role of helping students to prepare for these major national awards (…). They help them to prepare the essays and prepare for the oral questioning, so the role of the honors programs is getting broader for the university*" (Nancy). Rosa also stresses the special facilities that help to create a feeling of being a distinct group: "*We work hard to give them a small college experience within all the assets of a large research institution. They get individual attention and specialized advising. They are encouraged to study abroad, to seek an interesting internship, to double their major or add a minor. We work intensely with students to get them competitive for national scholarships*" (Rosa). This goes hand in hand with an emphasis on and pride in output like prizes, grants, acceptance rates at prestigious graduate schools; all those achievements nourish the community feeling. "*We have that* [alumni survey – MW] *and we also have tracking on how well they do in honors courses. We can check for the last fifteen years. Usually 95 percent of the honors students have an average grade of A or B. So participation in honors is not destroying their grades. Also, when you look at our students who have won major national and international scholarships, most of those students have been honors*" (Moses). The teachers give examples from a context where a kind of 'parenting-guidance' is considered normal, even in undergraduate university education. We should keep in mind that in the United States young people are only considered adults from age 21 onwards. It is also partially for that reason that it is considered quite normal for university teachers to take part in many aspects of (honors) social and cultural campus life outside the classroom.

Three main themes emerged during the content analysis of the interviews. These are the themes most commonly expressed by the teachers with regard to the creation of an honors community. The three themes that capture the teaching strategies related to the teaching approach of creating community are as follows:

- Create an atmosphere – by showing genuine interest in the students and giving them supportive feedback – in which students learn from each other and develop a strong social network (24 fragments).
- Offer students ample opportunity to take initiative, so that they can develop their leadership skills (15 fragments).
- Give support and advice to students that would help them improve their personal and intellectual development, including learning skills (18 fragments).

Theme one: Create a supportive atmosphere

The first theme is about teaching strategies that help to create a community characterized by peer learning, camaraderie and a strong social network. Such a community is not restricted to the classroom. During honors classes, however, teachers may employ strategies that help to build a strong honors community, for instance by means of their style of communication and feedback. The right atmosphere is crucial: "*There's usually a good deal of humor. There's a relaxed and intense atmosphere and a good deal of chance for students to test their verbal skills with each other. When you look beyond the university, the first way people are going to know if you are intelligent or not, is your verbal ability*" (Walter). Part of the key to success in creating this atmosphere is having an eye for one another. As one honors teacher said, "*It is important, I think, to find out what these students have done, what they enjoy and then what they project into the future. They all have good grades, but you can have a student for example that is a ballet dancer. Then you see that this student has some depth*" (Tim). "*I try to create an atmosphere in which whatever they like to do, is also given time in the school settings. That makes them feel that they want to stay there and study there, rather than go someplace else*" (Rosalie).

Teachers intertwine interpersonal interest and academic competence to create this atmosphere: "*When I'm teaching a class, I stress the competence, but outside of the class I stress the relationships. I personally believe that teachers should be getting involved with students outside of the classroom and they should be involved in programs on campus*" (Patrick). "*I loved it when students were standing around talking after class about something we dealt with in class*" (Alexander). Teachers think that the activities most valued by students are *"those that connect them to others in their honors community and have tangible value regarding their academic interests"* (Jude).

Interpersonal interest is mentioned as one of the key factors to create an atmosphere through which community is sensed. The teachers indicate that it is important to have the capacity to initiate interaction not only between teacher and students but also among the students. *"There are honors programs with numbers of students ranging from ten to thousands and even when there is thousands, they are able to create this community. It's an atmosphere that is created by relationships and a space"* (Rosalie). *"It allows the honors students to develop all sorts of camaraderie among themselves. What I have been able to see is that honors students have other honors students as friends and tend to have classes together. It is interesting to see that comradeship develops in a more diverse way, where it usually develops around race and ethnicity"* (Walter).

The honors community is co-created by these bonds between students, and a strong social network benefits the learning experience. Moreover, those bonds also benefit honors alumni: *"Our alumni received immense benefit from the network of friends and connections they received in honors, and I think that's generally true of honors alumni"* (Hermione).

Besides interpersonal interest, the honors teachers use communication and feedback to create community. When teachers talk about this, they tend to make connections to how they enhance academic competence among students. For instance, in one of the focus groups, teachers stressed the importance of verbal communication and feedback: *"They have to present [their thesis – MW] in public"* (Tim). *"Yes, and I have a lot of the students come to this series of colloquia. They do it once in the research stage and once in the writing stage and their mentor usually joins them. They talk about their project in a circle of around thirty students. So everyone has to give feedback on the progress of the project. Yes, those feedback sessions are also a way to create community"* (Rosalie).

Theme two: offer opportunity for initiative

Offering opportunities to students to take initiative and develop leadership skills is the second main theme in regard to the teaching approach of creating community. Teachers stress the importance of offering those leadership activities. As Henry puts it: *"Leadership activities clearly help develop confidence,* commitment, and competence as students learn not only practical skills of motivating, organizing, and communicating with others but also personal traits such as courage, risk taking, resilience" (Henry). Such newly acquired leadership skills subsequently help students to play a stronger role in creating the honors atmosphere. Teachers give various examples of how to offer opportunities for initiative and leadership: sometimes in class through a project closely related to content; sometimes by specific activities, like a writing-fellow program. "*Ones* [MW: co-curriculum activities] *that involve serious and responsible commitments to important issues in the community are valued*" (Hermione). The examples the teachers gave of how to offer opportunity for student initiative and for the development of leadership skills are very diverse. Three examples will be cited here. "*I have found that certain kinds of artistic production like theater or group service projects or commonly shared field trips have generated enthusiasm (…) Some otherwise quiet students learn to express their underdeveloped talents when given this kind of opportunity. The theatrical production had students commit a major block of time and used several different skills in addition to acting. The others called on leadership, organizational, and production skills*" (John).

Some programs create positions for more mature honors students that may help them to develop leadership skills. "*In the residence halls we have peer mentors. Those are honors students and they can do that from their sophomore year. We have a writing-fellows program, where undergraduate honors students take an advanced composition course and then they work with freshmen to help them with their writing. We have orientation assistants who help the incoming freshmen each summer and those are always honors students. Then they have a lot of leadership opportunities all over campus. They are typically in leadership positions all over campus*" (Rosa). Giving honors students a sense of ownership of their community is also essential. "*Letting the students take a lead in a lot of what happens helps to build the community, because it's their own trying to encourage their own to participate and come up with different ideas. We use students in almost every activity we do. We really use our own students to sell the program in the university, for example when families come in to visit. It gives the students a sense of ownership as far as what's happening in the program and how the program is evolving helps building this feeling of community*" (Marin).

Theme three: support and advice

The third theme underlines the particular importance of relatedness between the teacher and the honors student. Teachers say that honors students seek support, advice or guidance and that they will easily accept those responses when they experience relatedness with the teacher. On the one side, teachers want to give support and advice, but they realize that they can only give advice when they know what is going on in the students' lives and that their guidance will only be accepted when there is a relationship. So this third theme has a clear element of reciprocity. *"The relationship is necessary for the support. These kids have to work hard and for that they need the support"* (Rosalie).

One of the interviewed teachers, Ann, gave the following example: *"What I encourage the students to do is to think of a major that fits their personality. So I talk with them about what they want to do. I tell them to find out what they want to do, but not to do what their parents want them to do, because eventually they will end up as a senior and decide that they don't want to be for example an accountant or a nurse. So if you have a very competent student and you can get them to open up, the best thing that you can do for the student is to get them to choose their life based on their feelings instead of expectations. I'm a role model in this case. I changed my major in my senior year. I waited until my senior year, because I thought my parents wanted me to be a doctor"* (Ann).

Teachers also speak about one-to-one relationships that can arise, thanks to, for instance, a capstone or a research project. Those relationships are highly valued; the teachers call them an essential part of the honors community and teaching. However, these bonds are not necessarily discipline-bound or research-oriented. As Rosalie puts it, *"You have the relationship with the person, not with the major. (…) This one-on-one relationship between faculty and honors students really can become important and might result in lifelong bonds. It's a relationship, I had breakfast with one this morning"* (Rosalie).

To illustrate the importance of those bonds, teachers tell about their honors alumni. *"I for instance got an email a few weeks ago from a student who was in my first honors class. She's working at the Franklin Institute now. I get frequently that students write me after they graduate."* (Alexander)

Several times the teachers told about organizing field trips, visiting museums and organizing conferences as examples to get all parties involved in such a way that they become open to bonding. *"I do a conference every year in the fall and the students are expected to come to the conference from eight in the morning until eight at night. The presenters are faculty from the whole campus. They really love that mix with the students, they live for that annual convention. That event is the highlight of campus life, where the faculty get to show who they are and get to know the students on a personal level"* (Rosalie).

5.4.2 Enhancing academic competence

Enhancing academic competence plays a pivotal role in teaching in honors. However, also in regular programs it is the core business to engender academic competence among the students. Still, teachers indicate there is a clear difference between engendering academic competence in regular classes or in honors classes. According to the honors teachers it may be the intensity of the class, the higher-level thinking and the quality of the output that makes the difference.

During the content analysis of the interviews with American honors teachers, the researchers identified 68 fragments related to enhancing academic competence in honors classes. Three main themes emerged:

- Stimulate critical and independent thinking and reach out for high quality (22 fragments).
- Foster a research attitude and academic depth (23 fragments).
- Set learning tasks that are challenging and aim at a high level of engagement (14 fragments).

Nine fragments could not be allocated to any of these themes. It is illuminating to explore the third theme. Setting difficult or otherwise challenging learning tasks relative to the honors student's level of ability is a strategy that clearly belongs to the approach of enhancing academic competence. However, when teachers talk about challenging assignments and learning tasks, they couple these with autonomy, students' personal interest and offering freedom. This combination or overlap of a high quality of academic work and students' personal interest produces engaged learning.

During the interviews many teachers stressed the significance of teaching and learning critical and independent thinking for the honors students' academic progress and their progress in moral reasoning. Critical thinking is an intellectually disciplined process that questions assumptions. Teachers use the term easily, as they do the term independent thinking. *"I think that my aims are to make sure that students really develop their critical thinking skills, that they tear apart issues and problems and get into in-depth reading of the sources that they read. Also for them to see that history is really relevant to their lives and that who they are is just a link in the chain, tying them to the past"* (Alexander). He continues: *"I want them to think critically. Especially when teaching history classes, you want them to read different stories, different views, until they get to the point where they are very critical of the readings they are doing. So I want them to take that skill and use it when they read Time Magazine or a newspaper article. When they read a statement I want them to ask themselves how the author proves his point, to be critical"* (Alexander). Another teacher makes the link between critical thinking and personal reflection: *"To be able to take the socially scripted consciousness and force it into visibility and into critical reflection so that you can then take up a position towards how your own identity and values were constructed, given the social institutions into which you were born. So broadly said, critical consciousness and the trust in the capacities to express in written and oral form your insights, while you try to draw yourself and your time into a critical perspective"* (Walter).

As may be expected in an interview setting, the teachers did not define what exactly they meant by terms such as critical thinking, higher-order thinking skills, independent thinking or creative thinking. Many teachers combined the concepts, indicating that they strive for both critical and analytical rigor and independent or creative thinking with their honors students. *"I think it's critical that we move beyond just knowing about and even beyond the why – to analyzing something and then to the student generating a new interpretation, instead of memorizing things. I think that for teachers it's important to get students to apply higher-level thinking, critical thinking, and creative thinking. So it is in a way making the material more of their own, so in a sense autonomy has to do with that as well"* (Ann). Many teachers stress that honors education should aim at a level beyond analytical skills. *"In good quality work we want them to be able to analyze, to be able to synthesize their version and draw connections from the culture or history or literature"* (Patrick).

The teachers take it for granted that honors students meet the prerequisites for developing their academic competence. *"Honors students will have more background, more critical thinking skills, more confidence in their ability and, often, more leadership skills and a greater ability to work successfully in groups"* (Martin). But they also mention that teacher engagement is required to trigger this potential and help them develop their thinking skills. *"I think you can be very demanding to honors students if they think you care and if they think you are accessible. So I can get things out of a freshman honors class that I'm not able to get out of a junior regular class, but to do that I have to let them know, they can call me at any time, email me at any time and I will answer"* (Moses).

Particular teaching strategies are needed in order to stimulate higher-order thinking in the class. Teachers should allow students to *"… be relatively more self-directed and independent in their academic work. Further, they should be able to integrate methods and concepts from different disciplines in dealing with complex questions"* (John). Higher-order learning will occur when teachers set the conditions for *"… independent thinking, a taste for adventure and willingness to try what's unfamiliar, the ability to discover and pleasure of discovery, and a deep curiosity – along with perspective on themselves and others in the world"* (Betty). Several teachers indicate that honors students will feel more challenged to develop their thinking skills when they are confronted with complex problems that involve multiple perspectives and academic disciplines. *"Thus, for example, the student with a particular talent in empirical geological research is more creatively challenged, intellectually inspired, and personally enlightened by connecting his or her specialized talent with the aesthetics of landscape, the history of regional culture, the ethics of environmental change. General honors programs, usually configured to cut across various disciplines and encourage connections among content areas, are perhaps better poised to achieve such interdisciplinary enrichment of talent"* (Henry).

The second theme that emerged when analyzing the interview texts allocated to enhancing academic competence as a teaching approach is fostering a research attitude and academic depth. Especially undergraduate research is advocated for honors students' cognitive growth but also for their personal, intellectual and professional development. Most teachers indicate that research – arousing curiosity and enhancing academic competence – is an integral part of honors. *"Everybody in our program has to do a thesis, or what we call a senior project, for the minimum of a year. That's a very close one-on-one relationship in which the feedback process is very constant"* (Rudolf). Sometimes honors programs are differentiated, with research opportunities reserved for more advanced undergraduates with a very high GPA. *"The honors program has got two levels here. There's the general honors program in which the students are allowed to take classes across the university to fulfill an honors certificate, usually in their freshman and sophomore years. In their junior and senior years they are allowed to do upper level honors. To enter you need a GPA of 3.5 and to remain in the program a GPA of 3.0. In addition the main difference is, because it's research oriented, they must do a thesis or a creative project, and they also must do a research class"* (Pierre).

According to the teachers, research stimulates not only students' cognitive and personal growth but also places them in a better position for being selected for graduate school, *"particularly when they have done research or a capstone thesis, or they have other undergraduate research experiences"* (Tim). This conviction is generally shared: *"At our institution, honors degree students must complete a senior honors thesis or similar creative component. This is excellent preparation for graduate school"* (Robert). One of the teachers, who had conducted alumni surveys, states that honors alumni who did undergraduate research *"… perform better and adapt more quickly in a graduate setting. They feel more comfortable undertaking independent research, and considerably more comfortable in focused and prolonged discussion of difficult topics"* (Betty).

A research component in honors can only be successful if honors classes lay the foundation for an 'attitude' towards and skill in research. Teachers mention various strategies to foster such a research attitude. According to Betty, successful honors teachers have *"… a capacity to push students to produce evidence to support their statements, to challenge students, and to in-*

troduce a broad spectrum of questions, drawn from many disciplines, to push students to look for the multiple implications of any important idea or inquiry. Coaching students to ask incisive question is essential" (Betty). Another teacher reports that he tries to get students out of their comfort zone in order to help them develop a research attitude. *"My main goal when teaching honors students is, as crazy as it sounds, to make them uncomfortable so they can learn how to excel. At first they freak out, but somewhere along the line of researching and doing things over and over again, they find out that they finally got it"* (Pierre). There are many ways in which honors teachers can give their students an orientation to research, such as requiring primary data in course papers. *"For example in my "Dissent in America" class, what I might do is, because they have to write a paper on a protest in American history and they have to write another paper on a protest movement that is in existence now in P., they have to go out and maybe go to a meeting, interview people, analyze what their goals are"* (Alexander). As in all their work, feedback is also essential in honors students' research. *"Having a smaller ratio of students to faculty and staff, students receive earlier and more specific feedback on their work and also what steps they should anticipate as they prepare for their exams, their thesis, their study abroad, and their graduation requirements"* (John).

Theme three: give challenging learning tasks

The third theme associated with enhancing academic competence is engagement by learning tasks. Academic competence goes hand in hand not only with research-teaching but also with assignments and challenging learning tasks. Those learning tasks aim at a high level of engagement. Several teachers said that the nature and character of their assignments differ for honors compared to regular classes. *"I usually give more intense assignments. For example, they have to do more papers and I expect a higher level of analysis and a more in-depth analysis"* (Alexander). Pierre says that for him the main difference between honors and non-honors is *"... in the assignments that I give honors vs. non-honors. There's more rote memory in non-honors, there's more testing for the fundamentals. There's more discussion in honors of ideology and philosophy and higher constructs. With non-honors I have to show them the steps to more fundamental types of projects. Honors you can give an assignment and they will do it, without having to deal with the fundamentals. You don't have to specify that on page one you'll have to do this and on page two you'll have to do that. To be honest, that is blissful, because they do ask questions, but they are at least able to get the ball rolling"* (Pierre).

Challenging assignments are seen as a stepping stone to more academic depth. Teachers emphasize that they have to be knowledgeable themselves about the subject matter to make sure the students profit enough. However, the creation of opportunities that enable students' cognitive growth calls for more than scholarship or just some instruments from the didactic honors toolbox. Engaged learning and outstanding performance arise in the combination of academic work and students' personal interest. *"They are intrinsically motivated by that particular focus in music, where they look at a particular composer, a particular time period for example, and they become more knowledgeable about it. The projects reflect their interests"* (Patrick).

In the interviews, teachers report that it is necessary to create a supportive atmosphere or community, as described earlier, in order to make those honors assignments. *"Provide a safe environment so that students may express themselves honestly; open discussions; presentations with PowerPoint, poster board, or models, et cetera and other interactive learning exercises as well as written assignments"* (Janine). Or as another teacher explains, she wants to make sure to *"create an environment in which students are willing to take risk by doing, for example, an assignment they have never done before, by making the situation that students are not afraid to do it, even if they do it badly"* (Aroha).

Teachers say that verbal communication is important during honors classes and that honors students are not only engaged learners but also strong communicators, as was set forth in chapter 4. Teachers' assignments and learning tasks accommodate this, but teachers see a reinforcing relationship. *"Some other major differences are that they are more engaged, they talk more, they are willing to go further. For example, I had a student who was going to fulfill an assignment we had, which was to create a survey, to orchestrate the survey in class and to end up with thirty-five participants. However, she is really interested in the topic and she writes to me asking when we could generalize the results beyond just the class for a large population and she wants to know how to get started. You wouldn't see that in a regular class. A regular student wouldn't willingly go above and beyond what is required for the assignment. When we have events, honors students get into it more"* (Pierre).

5.4.3 Offering freedom

"In the honors program I find that the students can develop an interest on their own. They can choose a free project and a subject they like" (Patrick).

The third teaching approach consists of offering (bounded) freedom as a pedagogical practice. The interview topic list did not include questions specifically about freedom or about possible teaching strategies related to self-regulation. It appears that although teachers give various examples of the importance of flexibility, offering space, scaffolding and innovative teaching, it was less evident to us how we should categorize this third approach. Most examples of offering freedom also include strategies to create community or ways to enhance academic competence. It was decided to categorize those overlapping fragments according to the main aim. Thus, those fragments are categorized either by community or by academic competence but not by offering freedom, as freedom is often seen as an inherent means to achieve a goal. For instance, when teachers talk about independent projects, they emphasize the academic aspect. The fact that students' self-regulation is an integral part of such an independent project is then mentioned as a means. Those fragments are allocated to the teaching approach of enhancing academic competence. Another example of overlapping teaching approaches emerges from the teachers' stories about community. For instance, teachers say they let students take a lead in what happens in class or on campus. Teachers give students the space and freedom to take responsibility for building a community. This responsibility, in turn, gives the students a sense of ownership. Such fragments are categorized under the approach of creating community, while the approach of offering freedom is taken for granted.

Still, 35 fragments did include straightforward remarks about tuning in to students' personal interest, granting responsibility, or teaching students to make their own decisions. Of those fragments, 32 could be allocated to three themes.

- Give students responsibility for their learning, and offer trust and guidance (12 fragments).
- Allow students to make choices in line with their personal academic interest and allow innovation (9 fragments).

- Take the interests and initiatives of students seriously, and thereby help them to create an independent learning strategy (11 fragments).

Theme one: granting responsibility

The interviews illustrate that offering freedom goes hand in hand with trusting. A specific kind of student guidance is needed, both to help the students operate in that freedom and to monitor their performance. During the interviews, teachers told us that it is important to give space to students. So doing, the students get an opportunity to make their own judgments and choices. As a result of the teachers' trust and guidance, students can learn to take responsibility for their own development. The teachers themselves have to be flexible and open-minded in order to foster students' personal development and maturity.

"*Students take ownership. We let them. We have to make a decision if we can trust them; if we can't, we have failed. We have to trust them, have to assume they will do a good job. We have to take the risk that they will screw up, but that's an important risk to take. How else do you develop maturity, responsibility et cetera?*" (Orlanda). In order to be able to grant this space to students, teachers should be conscious of being open-minded themselves and not judgmental. As one honors teacher said, you should have "*the ability to be flexible in recognizing that student growth may occur in a variety of different venues which are, themselves, potentially different from the route or values held by [me]*" (Samuel).

Teachers give examples of the flexible pedagogical practices they engage in during honors classes as well as during one-to-one encounters. One-to-one encounters are highly valued and are seen as an opportunity for interpersonal relations. "*Students meet with their individual instructors usually once a week to work on a project. A benefit of it is that our faculty members can find out what our students are interested in and help them to find out what their opportunities are. Many students don't know what their opportunities are and they tend to think that they don't have that many opportunities. You have to get to know the student to help them. (.....) What we typically try to find for them is something that relates to what they are going to do after they leave college. It may be an internship, it may be study abroad, it may be voluntary work, it may be extra coursework, research experience, it entirely depends on the individual student"* (Ann).

It was noteworthy that several teachers talked about the strong influence parents can have. Maybe this is the case because American undergraduates under 21 years of age are legally minors. *"In teaching I'm really interested in competences. However, with reference to autonomy, it is really important for students to do what they want to do, instead of doing what their parents want them to do or what is guaranteed to make money"* (Ann).

Teachers stress the importance of granting students responsibility and offering them freedom in order for them to gain maturity and learn to make their own choices. The rationale lies partly in the recognition of the societal pressure and high expectations (or pampering in the past) that the students endure.

For instance, in one of the focus groups, Kate says, *"And sometimes academically they seem to have it all under control, but it's the personal issues and basically how to grow up. Sometimes it's life issues that they don't know how to handle. They had their hands held by their parents, teachers and counselors for basically their whole life and then they get to college and don't know what to do"* (Kate). However, as (Lillian) adds, *"(...) but when they have questions, we encourage them to be proactive and go find the answers".*

Theme two: encouraging choice; following personal interest

In the interviews, the teachers reported that freedom for students to follow their personal and academic interests is inherent to honors education. As said earlier, allowing choices is often seen as a means to achieve goals such as engagement, academic depth or bonding.

Teachers express joy and excitement when they talk about honors classes as a 'playground' for the students but also for themselves. It is not only the students who are encouraged to make choices in their academic life and to follow their personal interests. Teachers too have the freedom to follow their personal academic interests. This may be manifest in the choice of a specific book or assignment. Their freedom can also enhance the use of innovative teaching strategies and the use of the classroom as an educational laboratory.

"For the faculty, the honors program can serve as what I call a curricular laboratory. They have the opportunity to develop classes for their department

and they have the students to try their ideas out. For a student, the most important benefit is an enhanced career development. You have the opportunity to have an advisor not only in your academic department, but also an honors advisor. You can do a wide range of experiences through honors" (Nancy).

The theme of stimulating students to follow their own interests is closely related to academic competence, as explained above. Independent projects or capstone courses are particularly gratifying to honors teachers when the students follow their own personal interests because this engagement intensifies the learning process. Fragments cited earlier under enhancing academic competence illustrate this reciprocal relation. For instance, when Patrick talked about the music projects he offered his students, he reported that those projects not only reflect the students' interests but that through the projects the students also become more knowledgeable about their own interests.

This freedom may also partly explain the difference between honors assignments and non-honors assignments. As Walter said, *"When I assign a paper, the (honors) students decide what topic they want to address out of the topics, books and documentaries we discussed and viewed in class".*

Teachers ascribe their own involvement and the student's engagement to all being members of the learning community, to a reciprocity engendered in part by this honors freedom. For instance, a teacher said that *"The students choose the upper classes together with the faculty, so everybody has mutually agreed on the stuff they want to be engaged in"* (Rosalie). So it appears that offering freedom has much to do with the teachers' personality and involvement in the honors community.

Theme three: helping creating independent learning strategies

During the interviews, the teachers said that they take the students seriously. Teachers intend to share responsibility with students, although the teacher remains in charge. As a result of this attitude, students can create an independent learning strategy. *"There can be a high level of autonomy, depending on how the subject matter is presented. When the student is allowed to discover the material, there is freedom"* (Ann).

Offering the students freedom in class implies providing scaffolding. For instance, this would entail giving honors students some support at the beginning of a lesson but gradually requiring them to operate independently;

scaffolding requires class preparation and scholarship. When Peter was asked which qualities are needed to be successful as an honors teacher, he answered, *"Giving guidance, but not too much, and finding ways to involve students in the process of "discovery" in the teacher's discipline"* (Peter).

During the interviews, teachers spoke of 'bounded' freedom. This means that the teachers have to monitor the amount of freedom students get or take.

"I'm teaching a twelve-person seminar this semester and their final project is open-ended. I give them the guidelines, but their job is to demonstrate these objectives; and they can use video or audio and they can use different things, but they have a presentation and a written paper. So I don't meet with them one-on-one, but I answer questions and that kind of things" (Patrick).

In the same vein, teachers gave examples of situations whereby they have to frame issues, lead the discussion and then *"keep quiet so that students engage in their own deliberation with a minimum of "expertise" flowing from the instructor"* (Betty).

5.5   Conclusions

This chapter gives an impression of the teaching approaches in honors education. Honors teachers were asked about teaching strategies in honors programs and about the appropriate teaching qualities in the form of ranking questions and 24 statements in a survey. In this way, the three teaching approaches that stand out as essential in honors education, according to the literature, are explored through questionnaires and interviews. The interviews provided considerable additional details, examples and insights.

The findings from the survey and the interviews are much in line with each other. The teachers concur that the three teaching approaches – namely creating community, enhancing academic competence and offering freedom – are appropriate to honors education.

Enhancing academic competence plays a pivotal role in honors and non-honors education. The teachers, however, indicate that there is a clear difference between engendering academic competence in honors classes and in regular classes. The difference lies, in part, in the high quality of the output from higher-level learning and research. Furthermore, the learning tasks are challenging and there is strong involvement. Teachers make connections between the students' cognitive growth and their personal development.

The findings from the survey suggest that teachers employ different teaching strategies for honors courses than for regular courses. With honors, they place more emphasis on community and freedom. Interactive teaching is seen as appropriate to honors. Research teaching and interdisciplinary teaching are strategies related to enhancing academic competence in honors. The empirical analysis suggests that teachers consider structured teaching as more suitable for regular classes.

The interviews provided more insight and more detailed information. It became clear that the conceptual and theoretical foundation as laid out in chapter 2 resonates with the experiences of the teachers. The teachers perceive creating community to be important. The teachers and students together create a supportive atmosphere. Teachers offer students opportunities to take initiative. Inside the classroom but also outside, teachers support their students, and students are also receptive to their advice.

During the interviews the teachers indicated that offering freedom is often a precondition for student engagement. Teachers give students responsibility for their learning and offer them their trust and guidance. They allow students to make choices in line with their personal and academic interests.

In the perception of the American honors teachers, the three teaching approaches may be considered the pillars of their honors pedagogy.

6 Dutch honors teachers – questionnaire results and comparisons

6.1 Introduction

In 2007 the questionnaire for this research project was distributed among a total of 768 Dutch university teachers who were currently active as teachers in an honors program at one of the eleven Dutch research universities that by that time had initiated such programs. The response rate was 41%: 313 teachers returned the questionnaire (see chapter 3). The results allowed to assemble quantitative information about their teaching orientation, motivation for teaching honors, perception of (honors) students, and about how they envision honors teaching. The survey results regarding the American teachers have been discussed in the two preceding chapters. Chapters 4 and 5 dealt with honors education more generally (teaching conceptions, motivation, opinion about students) and honors teaching (approaches, strategies) respectively. Both chapters were enriched with the vignettes selected from the interviews that were conducted with thirty American honors teachers. This chapter will present an analysis of all the topics covered by the questionnaire survey in the Netherlands: teaching orientation (6.2), motivation for teaching honors (6.3), perceptions of honors students (6.4), and honors teaching in practice (6.5). Each section includes a brief comparison with the outcomes for the American honors teachers, since this study seeks to make a baseline comparison between U.S. and Dutch teachers.

The findings will deepen the understanding and expand the scope of the key components of honors pedagogy by adding European (Dutch) outcomes to those from the American context. The findings will also indicate some areas of difference in perceptions and practices between Dutch and American honors teachers. Such differences are salient when considering what Europe can learn from the more established American honors tradition and practice.

6.2 Conceptions of teaching and learning

6.2.1 Dutch honors teachers

The findings for the Dutch honors teachers with regard to their teaching and learning orientations are presented in the same way as was done for the American respondents in chapter 4 (see table 6.1). As explained earlier, an abbreviated version of Denessen's instrument was made for describing such orientations (teacher-content orientation and student-learning orientation). Twelve Likert-scale items (five-point scale) were used: six for each orientation, in pairs, for the three components of the orientations (educational goal, pedagogical relation, instructional emphasis – see chapters 2 and 3).

The Dutch respondents score higher on the statements related to student-learning orientation than on those related to teacher-content orientation. This is particularly evident on items that refer to the component of instructional emphasis: scores on items about collaborative learning are high (student-learning orientation), whereas scores on items about grading and competition are relatively low (teacher-content orientation). With regard to educational goals, the teachers' responses were evenly distributed over the more instrumental career concerns (teacher-content orientation) and concerns with personal and social development (student-learning orientation). For the pedagogical component, the teachers are more inclined towards open student-teacher relationships (student-learning orientation) than towards a more formal and hierarchical relation (teacher-content orientation).

The questionnaire contained five statements that refer explicitly to a general characterization of honors education (five-point Likert scale with its anchors defined as 1 = completely disagree, 5 = completely agree). The findings are depicted in table 6.2.

Table 6.1 – Teaching orientation scores, by pairs of related statements, Dutch teachers (n=313)

	Statement	Mean Score	SD
	TEACHER-CONTENT ORIENTATION		
Educational goal	If students want to achieve something later in their life, they have to learn a lot at the university.	3.8	1.0
	A good education is the key to success in society.	4.0	0.9
Pedagogical relation	Order and discipline are important at the university.	3.2	1.0
	I consider it important that students behave well at university.	3.7	0.9
Instructional emphasis	Grading is a good boost for the studying of students.	3.7	0.8
	For optimal learning results at the university, I find competition among students important.	3.0	1.1
	STUDENT-LEARNING ORIENTATION		
Educational goal	It is the job of the university to educate students to become critical citizens.	4.4	0.8
	It is the job of the university to pass on values and standards.	3.7	1.0
Pedagogical relation	Involvement of the students in the university is important.	3.8	0.8
	It is important that the university takes the wishes and interests of the students into account.	3.9	0.7
Instructional emphasis	Students can learn a lot from each other too.	4.3	0.7
	I find it important that students at the university can cooperate.	4.2	0.7

Table 6.2 – General characterizations of honors education – questionnaire items, Dutch teachers (n=313)

Item	Statement	Mean	SD
24	I think that taking risk should be at the center of honors education.	3.1	1.14
25	I think that honors education should be focused on evoking excellence.	4.1	0.89
32	Honors education is more focused on the development of talent than my regular education.	3.5	1.15
37	I consider it important that an honors student belongs to the top 10% of the student population with regard to grade average.	3.6	1.15
43	I use honors as an 'educational innovation room'; I try out different education methods and tests.	3.3	1.19

The findings show that honors teachers mainly see honors as programs that aim at evoking excellence from top-performing students. The notions of risk-taking and educational innovation are less commonly seen as key ingredients of honors (mean scores of 3.1 and 3.3 respectively). The results also reveal that honors teachers are not homogeneous in their opinions about honors (see standard deviations). In 2007 most honors programs were still in an early phase of development. 'Talent development' and 'excellence' were key words in the national discourse about honors. Most respondents did not have a long experience in teaching honors, which suggests that the innovative and experimental (involving risk) potential of honors teaching had not yet been fully 'discovered'. These conditions are inherent to the Dutch setting and may explain the teachers' reactions to the five statements.

6.2.2 Comparison

Although both groups are primarily student-learning oriented, the Dutch honors teachers have a stronger component of teacher-content orientation in their views compared to American honors teachers. Specifically, Dutch teachers give more importance to grading and competition as incentives to learn than their American colleagues. In spite of contextual differences between the American institutions, which range from community colleges to research universities, and the Dutch institutions (only research universities) included in the survey, the teachers are remarkably similar in their orientation towards teaching and learning.

As was the case with the American findings, the Dutch responses to teacher-content orientation items showed more internal consistency (Cronbach's Alpha 0.62) than responses to student-learning orientation items (Cronbach's Alpha 0.54).

Both in the American and in the Dutch survey the responses to the five general disposition questions about honors education show scalar consistency (Alpha 0.61 for the Netherlands and 0.59 for the U.S.A.). When we look at the results at face value, without further statistical analysis, we see that U.S. teachers and Dutch teachers fully agree on one point, a fairly evident one, namely that honors education should be focused on evoking excellence. The Dutch teachers' views differ most from those of their American colleagues with respect to risk-taking as the center of honors and with respect to honors as a space for educational innovation; in both cases the Dutch mean scores are substantially (0.8) lower than those of the American respondents.

6.3 Motivation

The findings of the Dutch survey for the seven items that indicate motivation and self-determination are presented in table 6.3. The seven items have sufficient internal consistency (Cronbach's Alpha 0.69) to be deemed reliable. Although the seven items are an abbreviated and slightly modified version of the Intrinsic Motivation Inventory (see chapter 4), they serve jointly as an acceptable scale for intrinsic motivation.

Intrinsic motivation for teaching honors is high, with an overall mean score of 3.9 based on a five-point scale. A high level of motivation was expected though, given the fact that Dutch honors education, which was still in a very early stage of development in 2007, might attract teachers who like to be pioneers in a new endeavor. There is one item, though, with a relatively low average score (3.3): 'My honors education makes me think of matters I had never thought of before'. This seems to fit in with the results presented in the previous section: the Dutch teachers score relatively low on perceptions of honors education as inherently innovative and experimental (risk-taking).

Table 6.3 – Dutch teachers' intrinsic motivation for honors teaching (n=313)

Statement	Mean	SD
I have the feeling that I can decide for myself how I organize my honors education.	4.1	0.9
I am extremely motivated to teach in honors.	3.9	0.9
My honors education makes me think of matters I had never thought of before.	3.3	1.1
My honors course fits, with respect to content, my personal interests.	4.2	0.8
I think that, in comparison with other teachers, I teach well.	3.8	0.7
I want to be one of the best of my work associates.	3.8	1.0
I find it important to be challenged to get the most out of myself.	4.0	0.9
Score of motivation scale	*3.9*	*0.54*

The intrinsic motivation of Dutch teachers may be high, but it is significantly lower than the remarkably high level of intrinsic motivation measured among American honors teachers (chapter 4) as an independent samples t-test (t[393]= 5.874, p<.001) shows. The variation in scores on the seven items suggests several explanations. Indeed, the one item about being challenged by honors (*'makes me think of matters I never thought of before'*) (M 3.3; SD 1.1) had a far lower mean score than that of the Americans (M 4.2; SD 0.9; Mean difference 0.9). The second largest gap in mean scores, for the item '*I want to be one of the best of my work associates*', may be explained by cultural differences between the two national contexts. In the Netherlands it is considered socially less acceptable to say that one wants to be 'one of the best'. Also, the Dutch teachers teach at research universities which may also explain some differences. On this item, the American honors teachers had a mean score of 4.4, the Dutch 3.8. The Dutch respondents also scored noticeably lower (0.4 lower in mean average) than the American teachers on the importance of feeling challenged and on being 'extremely motivated' for honors. In the latter case, it may again be the Dutch cultural reflex to refrain from expressing oneself in positive superlatives or a lower self efficacy as honors education was relatively new.

6.4 Students

6.4.1 Dutch honors teachers

The Dutch teachers believe that qualities of particular importance for honors students are the following: they should be motivated, prepared to invest effort in their studies, think creatively, show initiative and act upon that, and be curious. These are the five items most frequently included among the top-five qualities (chosen from a list of fifteen such qualities) considered important for honors students. Table 6.4 gives the full results for questionnaire items 67 and 68: the two multiple-choice/ranking items that asked teachers to choose those qualities considered of most importance for honors students (item 67) and for students in regular courses (item 68). The order of qualities, from top to bottom, differs from that in table 4.4, where the results for the American respondents are presented. The sequence is dictated by the order of percentage scores for the honors top-five. The five most frequently chosen qualities for both top-fives, for honors students as well as students in regular programs, are presented in bold.

Table 6.4 – Qualities considered most important for honors students and regular students, Dutch teachers (n=313)

Student quality	% in Honors Top-5	% in Regular Top-5	Kappa
Is motivated in his/her courses	**71.6**	**80.5**	0.237
Is prepared to invest considerable time in his/her courses	**64.9**	**61.7**	0.135
Thinks in a creative way	**63.9**	34.2	0.278
Shows initiative and also carries it out	**63.3**	**42.8**	0.249
Is curious	**60.4**	**63.9**	0.302
Has a passion for research	30.4	5.8	0.089
Obtains good results in his/her courses	29.7	**40.9**	0.303
Stimulates other students within the education program	16.3	16.9	0.354
Is involved in the academic community	13.7	10.9	0.276
Is prepared to take risks in his/her academic career	11.2	3.2	0.088
Is not behind with his or her studies	9.3	20.4	0.100
Can keep an appointment	7.7	26.8	0.180
Values my knowledge about a given subject	6.4	11.2	0.386
Behaves well in class	3.2	16.0	0.155
Other	2.9	2.2	0.231
Is easy to get along with	1.3	4.5	0.433

The Dutch teachers constructed almost the same top-five for students in regular programs as they did for honors students. For students in regular courses they consider it particularly important to be motivated, prepared to invest effort in their studies, to be curious, to show initiative and act upon that, and to obtain good results in their courses. The differentiation between the two groups of students is quite limited for the top-prioritized qualities. Creative thinking was chosen in the honors top-five, not in the top-five for regular students. And obtaining good results (which is perhaps taken for granted for honors students) showed up in the top-five for regular students but not for honors students. The Kappa scores show slight to poor similarity in most cases, indicating that the Dutch teachers have ranked the qualities independently for the two contexts (honors and regular). Only for two qualities – '*is easy to get along with*' and '*values my knowledge about a given subject*' – are the Kappa values relatively high.

Another way of considering the data presented in table 6.4 is to look at the difference in frequency of inclusion in each of the top-fives for the individual qualities. From this perspective, Dutch teachers see the following three qualities as most distinctive for honors students:

- They think in a creative way (difference in frequency of inclusion: 29.7%);
- They have a passion for research (24.6%);
- They show initiative and carry it out (20.5%).

The mirror image – qualities chosen more frequently for regular students than for honors students – is less pronounced, but what discriminates most is that regular students:

- Can keep an appointment (difference in frequency of inclusion: 19.1%);
- Behave well in class (12.8%);
- Obtain good results in their courses (11.2%) and are not behind with their studies (11.1%).

All in all, the Dutch teachers believe that motivation, effort, and curiosity are very important for both honors and regular students. What distinguishes honors students most from regular students, in terms of qualities perceived as important by teachers, is creativity, a passion for research, and initiative.

6.4.2 Comparison

Chapter 4 showed that the American teachers included the following student qualities most frequently in their top-five for honors students: they should be enterprising in the sense of taking initiatives (71%), intellectually curious (69%), think creatively (63%), be motivated in their courses (57%), and invest effort in their studies (52%). The Dutch respondents gave priority to exactly the same five qualities for honors students (out of the list of fifteen options) but in a different order. They included motivation most frequently (77%), followed by effort (65%) and creative thinking (64%). A Chi-square test has shown that among these five qualities there are only significant differences in perception between American and Dutch teachers for motivation and effort: the Dutch teachers consider these two qualities more important for honors students (see table 6.5). This might be explained by the fact that at the time of the survey the Dutch discourse about honors was very much about offering something 'extra' on top of the regular curriculum for very motivated and hard-working students, whereas in the United State the conversation did not revolve around issues of students' willingness to take on additional academic endeavors because honors courses are embedded in the regular program. There is a distinct preference in American honors programs to focus on different rather than more work as a means of challenging students' learning.

It is more interesting to consider where the major significant differences occur between American and Dutch honors teachers in their perceptions of qualities that they see as important for honors students. The American teachers attach significantly higher importance to the qualities of risk-taking, involvement in the academic community, and stimulating fellow students within the study program (see table 6.5). It became evident in the interviews with American teachers that risk-taking is perceived as undertaking new, original, out-of-the-box, and open-ended learning tasks within honors. Risk-taking in this sense is related to the teaching approach of offering a degree of freedom to students within honors. The other two qualities – involvement in the academic community and stimulating fellow students – are clearly linked to honors as a learning community and to the teaching approach of creating such a community. Given this outcome, it may be expected that American honors teachers have a stronger focus on creating community and offering freedom than Dutch honors teachers; this difference will be discussed later in this chapter. Table 6.5 also shows that the qualities of risk-taking and involvement in the academic community are considered significantly more important by American teachers for all students, both honors and regular, although the importance is far more pronounced for honors students. Possibly the notions of risk (venturing into something new and open-ended as a study task) and community are more embedded and have other, more academically oriented connotations in American academic culture than in the teaching and learning practice in Dutch higher education.

Table 6.5 – Teachers' perceptions of qualities important for honors and regular students, comparison and Chi-square scores

Student quality	% in honors top-5 U.S.A.	% in honors top-5 NL	Chi-square score	% in regular top-5 U.S.A.	% in regular top-5 NL	Chi-square score
Shows initiative and also carries it out	70.9	63.3	2.31	49.6	42.8	1.69
Is curious	68.5	60.4	2.55	66.1	63.9	0.20
Thinks in a creative way	63.0	63.9	0.03	25.2	34.2	3.38
Is motivated in his/her courses	56.7	71.6	9.08**	73.2	80.5	2.83
Is prepared to invest considerable time in his/her courses	51.2	64.9	7.10**	63.8	61.7	0.17
Is prepared to take risks in his/her academic career	47.2	11.2	69.40***	16.5	3.2	24.55***
Is involved in the academic community	34.6	13.7	24.90***	21.3	10.9	8.18**
Stimulates other students within the education program	31.5	16.3	12.73***	12.6	16.9	1.28
Has a passion for research	16.5	30.4	8.88**	3.9	5.8	0.60
Obtains good results in his/her courses	8.7	29.7	22.18***	26.0	40.9	8.66**
Values my knowledge about a given subject	8.7	6.4	0.71	22.0	11.2	8.69**
Is not behind with his or her studies	4.7	9.3	2.54	44.1	20.4	25.47***
Is easy to get along with	1.6	1.3	0.06	5.5	4.5	0.22
Behaves well in class	0.8	3.2	2.15	15.7	16.0	0.00
Can keep an appointment	0.8	7.7	7.98**	11.0	26.8	13.05***

*(Note: **p<.01, ***p<.001) (U.S.A. n=127; Netherlands n=313)*

Dutch honors teachers place significantly more emphasis on obtaining good grades and having a passion for research, as key qualities of an honors student, than their American colleagues. With regard to the importance of good grades, Dutch teachers are more inclined to see this as essential for all students, both regular and honors, than the American teachers. The explanation might be that a substantial share of the Dutch student population, at the time of the survey, could get away with their weak commitment (and weak grades) without risking expulsion or probation (the rules have changed considerably since 2006-2007). It may be that obtaining good results is therefore more of an issue in the Dutch context. Overall, though, the Dutch teachers place more emphasis than American teachers on the following qualities: inclination towards research – motivation –   effort – good grades. This cluster has clear links to notions of academic competence. It is reasonable to expect, therefore, that Dutch honors teachers consider the teaching approach of enhancing academic competence as more central to honors than their American colleagues. This will also be discussed further down in the chapter.

The other significant differences in perception of students (between American and Dutch respondents) that are shown in table 6.5 seem less relevant to our topic of discussion. For their students in regular classes, the American teachers stress the importance of not falling behind with their studies (significantly more so than the Dutch teachers). This may relate to the fact that it is costly for American students to fall behind, or to the tradition of graduating as a cohort. Dutch teachers value reliability in all students ('can keep an appointment') significantly more than American teachers do. Again, this may relate to the option of non-commitment by students that was inherent in Dutch higher education, although conditions have been changing rapidly over the last years.

6.5   Honors teaching

6.5.1 Dutch honors teachers

As their American colleagues, the Dutch honors teachers filled in a number of questionnaire items about teaching strategies in honors classes and regular classes: they were asked to choose a top-three of the most important strategies (out of a list of ten) for *any* teacher, separately for honors teaching and for regular classes; and they choose which five of their *own* teaching qualities (out of a list of seventeen) they consider most important for success in their teaching, again separately for honors and regular classes. Chapter 3 explained how the items to choose from relate to the three teaching approaches: creating community, enhancing academic competence, and offering freedom. The findings for the Dutch respondents are shown in tables 6.6 and 6.7.

Table 6.6 – Top-three teaching strategies for honors programs and for regular programs, Dutch teachers (n=313)

Strategies	Honors top-three (%)	Regular top-three (%)	Kappa
Invites students to actively participate	**62.8**	**44.7**	0.280
Makes connections with other areas of study	**45.5**	14.1	0.177
Places different points of view opposite to each other	**42.9**	18.6	0.310
Appreciates questions and remarks	35.3	25.7	0.400
Makes the course exciting and has confidence	34.0	37.0	0.264
Enjoys teaching	29.8	38.9	0.506
Is available for his/her students and is easily accessible	24.0	24.1	0.297
Is interested in students as individuals	21.2	10,6	0.306
Offers well-organized subject matter	10.9	**52.7**	0.137
Formulates clear and shared goals for the class	6.1	**39.9**	0.101

What strategies do the Dutch teachers see as most important for any honors teacher to employ in honors classes and in their regular classes? Table 6.6 shows that the following three approaches are considered the most important for honors classes: inviting students to participate actively (63%), making connections to other areas of study (45%), and placing different points of view opposite to each other (43%). The last two scores indicate that Dutch teachers see breadth, context and perspective as important for enhancing academic competence in honors classes. The Dutch teachers also place the strategy to '*invite students to participate actively*' in their top-three for teaching regular classes (45%). But the other two strategies in the top-three for regular classes are radically different from what we see in the honors top-three. For regular courses, teachers give priority to offering well-organized subject matter (53%) and formulating clear learning goals (40%). Breadth and context are seen as distinctive for honors classes, whereas structure is considered distinctive for regular classes. The low Kappa values indicate that there is no similarity in the teachers' opinion about which strategies are essential for honors teaching and which for teaching regular classes. Only two items have a Kappa of 0.4 or higher.

Table 6.7 – Respondents' personal top-five teaching strategies: honors teaching and regular teaching, Dutch teachers (n=313)

Strategies	Honors top-five (%)	Regular top-five (%)	Kappa
I challenge students	**60.3**	35.6	0.243
I inspire students	**53.5**	**44.9**	0.523
I give students room for their own choices	**41.3**	14.7	0.175
I give useful feedback	**40.1**	**53.5**	0.330
I am prepared to deviate from traditional educational methods	**38.8**	10.3	0.259
I give the students new ideas	36.4	20.5	0.238
I grant students much responsibility	34.6	12.5	0.292
I know a subject well	30.1	**45.5**	0.632
I am demanding	27.2	15.1	0.304
I explain well	27.2	**67.3**	0.230
I understand quickly what a student asks or remarks	17.0	24.0	0.317
I am clear about my expectations of students	14.7	**41.7**	0.143
I am friendly	11.2	19.6	0.344
I correct work quickly	6.1	10.3	0.384
I make sure that students keep appointments and deadlines	5,1	15.7	0.183
I discuss course subject matter at a fast pace	4.2	2.4	0.204
I am good at keeping discipline	1.0	1.6	0.210

With respect to their personal qualities, the Dutch teachers place two items in both the honors top-five and the regular top-five: their ability to inspire students (resp. 53% and 45%) and to give students useful feedback (resp. 40% and 53%); both have a relatively high Kappa (See table 6.7). This indicates that teachers consider these qualities to be generically important, i.e., regardless of the context. For the rest of the items, the top-fives are very different. The other personal qualities considered most important for honors teaching are as follows: to challenge students (60%); to offer room for students' own choices (41%); and to be prepared to deviate from traditional educational methods (39%). For successful teaching in regular classes they see it as most essential that they can explain well (67%), know their subject well (45%), and are clear about their expectations of students (42%). This confirms that the teachers see structure as very important in regular classes, whereas they are open to freedom and experimentation in an honors context. Also in the case of table 6.7, the low Kappa values (with two exceptions) indicate that the teachers see the two teaching contexts – honors and regular – as different.

Table 6.8 indicates the distribution of all items included in the top-three and top-five columns of tables 6.6 and 6.7 across the teaching approaches: creating community, enhancing academic competence, and offering freedom /structure. As set forth in chapter 5, there are two kinds of items in the section of the questionnaire that refer to the teaching approach of offering freedom. One kind stresses freedom directly and positively (e.g., 'give students room for their own choices'). The other kind stresses structure (e.g., 'formulate clear goals'). Just like the table in chapter 5, table 6.8 also presents the two dimensions separately.

Table 6.8 – Importance of community, competence, and freedom / structure for honors and regular education, Dutch teachers (n=313)

| Approaches | Number of items chosen | | | |
| | within honors programs | | within regular programs | |
	abs.	%	abs.	%
Community	826	34.8	768	33.2
Competence	684	28.8	724	31.4
Freedom	745	31.4	339	14.7
Structure	118	5.0	479	20.7
Total	2373	100.0	2310	100.0

For the teaching approach of creating community, the Dutch teachers do not differentiate much between honors teaching and teaching regular classes. The difference is not strong when we look beyond the percentages and examine which individual items were chosen. Engaging students in the learning process is seen of importance in both contexts, although stronger in honors. For instance appreciating questions and remarks is more often chosen for honors; giving useful feedback is more chosen for regular programs (see table 6.7). There are minor differences for some items, such as the quality of being 'interested in students as individuals' (see table 6.6). Nonetheless, creating a sense of community is not seen as specific to honors teaching. Similarly, for the approach of enhancing academic competence, the percentages in table 6.8

do not suggest differentiation between honors teaching and regular teaching. But in this case, the aggregate results (percentages) mask a difference at the item level where teachers do distinguish between honors and regular classes with respect to enhancing academic competence. For honors education, they clearly favor academic challenge, looking across the borders of any academic discipline, and application of multiple perspectives within their classes. In regular classes the focus is on providing a solid knowledge base and giving feedback. The major distinction in table 6.8 can be seen for the freedom / structure component. The Dutch teachers have included far more freedom-related items in their top-three and top-five for honors teaching than for regular teaching. For regular teaching, the teachers chose far more structure-related items. Although in the eyes of the Dutch teachers experimentation is not one of the highlights of honors education (see 6.2.1), room for experimentation, space for students' own initiative and questions, and a generally more open learning setting seem to characterize their honors teaching. They believe that their regular students need clear goals, a clear class structure, and well-explained subject matter.

6.5.2 Comparison

Both the American and the Dutch honors teachers were asked to choose their top-three most important teaching strategies for any honors teacher, out of a list of ten items, for honors classes and for regular classes. They were also asked to reflect on their own personal qualities as teachers and to choose the five (out of a list of seventeen options) that they see as most important for successful honors teaching and for successful regular teaching. The full set of comparative results is included as an appendix 2b and 2c in two subsequent tables. Those tables include the results of a Chi-square test for significant differences between the American and the Dutch teachers' responses. The main findings of the comparison will now be discussed.

Striking similarity between the two groups

In each of the two top-threes (for honors and regular classes) and each of the two top-fives (also honors and regular) there is only one difference between the American and Dutch teachers. The rest of the items are the same. For honors teaching, both groups give priority to two strategies: inviting students to participate actively in class; and making connections with other areas of study. For regular classes, both groups acknowledge the overriding importance of formulating clear goals and offering well-organized subject matter. With regard to the personal qualities they deem essential for honors teaching, both groups give priority to the teachers' ability to challenge and inspire students, giving students room for their own choices and being prepared to deviate from established teaching methods. They also agree on which personal qualities are essential for teaching regular classes: to explain well, be clear about expectations, know the subject well, and give useful feedback. At the level of individual strategies and qualities, there are very few significant differences between the American and Dutch teachers, as will be discussed further down.

A more pronounced idea about honors teaching among American teachers

The answers of the Dutch teachers about honors teaching strategies are slightly more diverse and less pronounced than those of their American colleagues. 82% of the Americans included the strategy of inviting students to participate actively among their top-three, versus 63% of their Dutch colleagues; 79% selected 'I challenge students' as one of their top-five, versus 60% of the Dutch teachers. Six of the eight items in the honors top-three plus top-five lists are the same for the two groups (see previous point). Four of those, however, are chosen significantly more by the American teachers (see appendix 2b and 2c). Such strong agreement is not found among the Dutch honors teachers.

The few differences in the priority assigned to the teaching strategies for honors between the two groups show a bias towards freedom strategies among American teachers and academic competence strategies among Dutch teachers

'I grant students much responsibility': this item was included in the U.S. top-five but not in the Dutch (significant difference). This may reflect a higher priority in an American setting for strategies that enhance freedom, risk-taking and experimentation. The Dutch teachers included the item about placing 'different points of view opposite to each other' in their top-three significantly more often than their American colleagues. This may be an indication of a more content-oriented approach to honors (multiple perspectives, academic context) in the Dutch setting. But it could also mean that American teachers shied away from the adversarial phrasing ('opposite to each other' – they might rather say 'confront various perspectives') and therefore chose the option less frequently.

There are also various significant differences in priority among the strategies for teaching regular classes. These can be read from the tables in appendix 2b and 2c and will not be elaborated here.

6.5.3 Teaching approaches

Part 2 of the questionnaire contained 24 comparative items about teaching strategies in honors/regular classes. These items relate to the three teaching approaches that were identified in chapter 2 as essential for honors education: creating a sense of community, enhancing academic competence, and offering freedom. In chapter 5, section 5.3 we discussed the findings for the American respondents. It was possible to create two internally consistent scales: one for creating community (a five-item scale) and one for enhancing academic competence (an eight-item scale). Regarding freedom, the items showed insufficient consistency to warrant constructing a 'freedom scale'. The importance of these two multi-item scales lies in serving as an instrument to demonstrate empirically that the honors teachers do indeed see the teaching approaches as vital for honors teaching.

The 313 Dutch teachers also filled in part 2 of the questionnaire. With the Dutch data too, the community scale was sufficiently coherent (Cronbach's Alpha 0.75). The same holds for the academic competence scale (Cronbach's Alpha 0.76). For both approaches, and similar to the American findings, Anova analysis showed no significant effect of average class size on the importance given by teachers to community or academic competence. And also for both approaches, we found that teachers' intrinsic motivation does have a significant effect on the importance they attach to the two teaching approaches (creating community and enhancing academic competence) (see appendix 2d).

Tables 6.9 – 6.11 specify the findings for the Dutch respondents. Asterisks indicate significant differences from the American findings. As in section 5.3, the findings are presented for those items included in the two (i.e., community and academic competence) scales and for all individual items designed as indicators of 'freedom'. For community two individual items will be discussed as well.

Overall, the Dutch teachers attach significantly less value to the teaching approach of creating community for honors than American teachers do (independent t-test: t(388)=2.766; p<.01). At the item level, there are no significant differences. Dutch teachers think they know their students well enough to report that they think that honors students are more active in the academic community than regular students (M 3.8; SD 1.0). 45% of the Dutch teachers indicated that they know all their honors students by name (score 5; completely agree); only 14% of the Dutch teachers indicated to know all their regular students by name (score 5; completely agree). The American teachers reported differently (55% respectively 41%). The Dutch teachers are only slightly more inclined to active learning and activating teaching in honors classes than in regular classes (3.2) and to take the students' personal interests into account more in honors classes than they would in regular classes (3.3). Dutch teachers are neutral about whether honors students will be the leaders of the future (3.0). Also, the item about stimulating honors students 'to think about personal goals and wishes' gets an almost neutral response (2.8).

Table 6.9 - Creating community as a teaching approach, Dutch teachers (n=313)

Item	Mean NL	SD NL
I stimulate honors students more than regular students to think about personal wishes and goals.	2.8	1.17
I think honors students are more active in the academic community than regular students are.	3.8	1.00
I think that honors students will be our leaders of the future rather than regular students.	3.0	1.11
My approach to honors education has more active teaching and learning methods than my approaches in regular class.	3.2	1.29
The personal interest of a student plays a bigger role in my honors education than it does in my regular education	3.3	1.22
Score of community scale	*3.3***	*0.76*

**p<.01

Table 6.10 - Enhancing academic competence as a teaching approach, Dutch teachers (n=313)

Item	Mean NL	SD NL
I assign more challenging assignments to honors students than to regular students.	3.7**	1.16
I assign more time-consuming assignments to honors students than to regular students.	3.5	1.22
I assess students in the honors program differently than I assess students in the regular program.	3.4	1.21
My methods to evaluate honors education are different from my methods to evaluate regular education.	2.9*	1.28
I teach my honors students more fundamental content knowledge than my regular students.	3.2***	1.32
I teach my honors students more often than my regular students how they can apply their knowledge in real situations.	2.6	1.11
I find it more important that honors students, rather than regular students, are intensively involved in research early in their education	3.5	1.30
I teach my honors students more about different points of view than I teach my regular students.	3.4	1.22
Score of academic competence scale	*3.3*	*0.79*

*p<.05, **p<.01, ***p<.001

Table 6.11 – Items related to the teaching approach of offering freedom, Dutch respondents (n=313)

Statements	Mean NL	SD NL
I find it hard to teach students smarter than me.	1.7	0.91
I give honors students more freedom (with respect to choosing topics and time management) than regular students.	3.6*	1.17
I give feedback to my honors students as if they are junior colleagues.	3.0	1.15
I have more fun with my regular students than with my honors students.	2.1*	0.96
I refer students to experts when their questions or interests are beyond my area of expertise.	4.2	0.84
I use honors also as an ‚educational innovation room'; I try out different education methods and tests.	3.3***	1.18

*p<.05, **p<.01, ***p<.001*

For the domain of enhancing academic competence (see table 6.10), two items have scores that differ significantly from the American data (at p<.01 level at least). Dutch teachers find it significantly more important than American teachers to teach honors students more fundamental content knowledge than regular students. This reflects the stronger subject-matter orientation that Dutch teachers associate with honors, a difference that is visible throughout the findings. American teachers have a significantly higher score for giving more challenging assignments to their honors students. But the Dutch teachers also have a high score for challenging assignments (M 3.7; SD 1.2), followed by a score of 3.5 for larger assignments and more research involvement (in comparison with regular classes). Applying academic knowledge and skills in real-life contexts is not seen as specific to honors education (M 2.9; significantly higher at p<.05 level in the U.S.A.).

For reasons explained in chapter 5, the statements that refer to 'freedom' do not serve as a consistent scale. It is interesting to see a high score for referring honors students to experts (M 4.2; SD 0.8; for U.S. data M 4.4; SD 0.7). This suggests an attitude of openness. It should be noted that the statement does not specifically refer to honors students. Relatively high scores were also found for giving honors students more freedom (M 3.6; SD 1.2) and using the honors class as an innovation space (M 3.3; SD 1.2), although in both cases the American data show significantly higher scores (M 3.9; SD 1.1; M 4.1; SD 0.80).

6.6   Conclusion

The 313 Dutch honors teachers who filled in the questionnaire in 2007 were mostly pioneers in young honors programs. Most of their American counterparts were experienced honors teachers who worked in a setting where honors programs had existed for a long time. Yet we found many similarities between the two groups. The Dutch teachers were inclined towards a student-learning orientation, like the American teachers. Both groups demonstrated a high level of intrinsic motivation, although American teachers reported even higher motivation for teaching in general and for honors teaching in particular. The Dutch teachers see honors education as a means to evoke academic excellence among top-performing students. They have lower scores than the American teachers for honors as a risk-taking venture and as a source of educational innovation. The qualities that they find important in honors students include being motivated, creative, hard-working, curious and resourceful. Although they see many similarities in the teaching strategies required for honors classes and regular classes, they also distinguish between the two settings. Academic challenge and multi-disciplinary approaches are seen as more important for honors classes; structure is seen as vital for regular classes. The scales that were constructed for the teaching approaches of creating community and enhancing academic competence on the basis of the American data also apply to the Dutch context. Overall, Dutch honors teachers appear to place less emphasis on teaching strategies that help to create a sense of community. Strategies for offering freedom – for taking risk, for experimentation – are seen as important by the Dutch teachers but are not given as much prominence as in the American setting. The strategies for enhancing academic competence – both in terms of depth and in the sense of academic breadth – are predominant in the Dutch teachers' perceptions of honors. The findings give the distinct impression that the mix of the three approaches that are essential for honors – creating community, enhancing academic competence, offering freedom – is more balanced in the American honors context.

7 Conclusions and discussion

7.1 Introduction

The overarching research question for this study was formulated as follows: What are the key components of honors pedagogy and how do these translate into honors teaching practice? The reasons for asking this question were twofold. First, few empirical studies have been conducted on honors teaching within higher education with the aim to systematically uncover, analyze and describe honors pedagogies (see, for instance, Clark & Zubizarreta 2008; Cosgrove 2004; Rinn 2007; Shushok 2002). This is why the research question has academic relevance, since the present study is one of the first attempts to systematically investigate which teaching approaches are appropriate for honors education. Secondly, the question serves a practical need. Honors education is a relatively new phenomenon in Europe. Specifically in the Netherlands, most research universities and universities of applied sciences have started honors experiments and honors programs over the last ten to fifteen years, with a major boost in the past five years. This has created a need for empirical research on honors pedagogies, the outcomes of which may be used in faculty development, training and coaching of honors teachers.

Honors programs are specially designed for gifted and motivated students who are willing and able to do more than they could in a regular program. In the search for *key components of honors pedagogy*, the first step was to explore relevant bodies of literature: the practical and often case-based descriptive literature about teaching practices in American honors programs; the empirical and theoretical literature about giftedness, with a specific focus on implications for teaching; and an important strand of theoretical and empirical work in motivational theory – self-determination theory – which can be linked to honors education because of the above-average motivation of honors students and the importance of understanding teaching and learning strategies that support and build upon such high motivation. By doing so, honors pedagogies were analyzed through the lenses of three relevant fields of knowledge.

On the basis of this literature review, the author hypothesized that at least three dimensions of honors education are important: *creating a sense of community within honors programs; enhancing academic competence; and offering freedom* to honors students in their learning. The completion of the literature review, which was reported in chapter 2, enabled to specify the research question for the empirical part of the study in the following way: *To what extent do honors teachers approach their teaching differently – with regard to creating community, enhancing academic competence and offering freedom – with honors students compared to regular students?*

Data were collected from honors teachers from multiple institutions that work with different models for their honors programs. This diversity allowed us to develop a rich empirical basis on which to describe honors pedagogies in terms of these three teaching approaches: creating community, enhancing academic competence and offering freedom.

In the present study, the three approaches were studied from the perspectives of various informants. Using a mixed methodology, questionnaires were distributed among honors teachers in the United States of America (n=127) and in the Netherlands (n=313), and interviews and focus groups were conducted with honors teachers in the U.S.A. (n=30). The questionnaire was used to survey both American and Dutch university honors teachers to make a baseline comparison between American and Dutch honors teachers with respect to their teaching strategies and their underlying attitudes and beliefs about (honors) teaching and students.

The survey research among American and Dutch honors teachers gave evidence that the three teaching approaches – creating community, enhancing academic competence and offering freedom – are indeed according to the teachers, more relevant in honors settings than in regular higher education. The interviews with American honors teachers provided a wealth of additional information about the concrete teaching strategies and forms of behavior that teachers say they apply in order to create the conditions of community, enhanced academic competence, and freedom.

The answers to the research questions are discussed in the next section. Section 7.3 discusses the findings of this study, with special attention to its limitations, questions for further research, and the practical implications and applicability of the outcomes.

7.2 Conclusions

7.2.1 Key components of honors pedagogy

The author's approach to the body of literature was a mix of induction and deduction. Having read the potentially relevant honors literature, it was clear that most of the teaching practices treated there could be classified under three headings: 'community', 'academic competence' and 'freedom'. These three concepts were then used for organizing the literature review.

First, the author examined the American literature on honors in higher education. There is a substantial body of well-documented reports on good practice. While the number of empirically grounded publications is growing, these empirical studies rarely deal with teaching practices. Indeed, most honors studies are descriptive, based on experience and the examination of a single institution.

The next step was to analyze the literature on giftedness, a field with a solid theoretical basis and ample empirical output. Publications in this field contain not only definitions of concepts such as excellence but also extensive studies on instructional models. Furthermore, the giftedness literature queries whether it is legitimate to differentiate between teaching strategies for honors and regular students, mainly at the level of pre-university education. Studies reveal that gifted students, on the whole, have different characteristics than regular students in the same age range and need distinct learning opportunities. According to several state-of-the-art publications, relatively few studies have dealt with the teacher qualifications and teaching approaches for working with gifted students in higher education. Nevertheless, the outcomes of giftedness research could be linked to the teaching approaches that were identified in the literature and were subsequently adopted as the three dimensions of honors teaching: creating community, enhancing academic competence, and offering freedom.

Teachers of the gifted should have knowledge about gifted students that engenders effective teacher-student relationships. This corresponds to the dimension of creating community. To be successful with gifted learners, teachers must be scholars, offer enrichment, have a passion for their discipline and be able to support complex learning by offering escalating opportunities. Altogether, this profile resembles the dimension of enhancing academic competence. Gifted learners bloom through independent projects. Accordingly, teachers of the academically gifted need to take flexible approaches to providing content and encouraging learning. This requirement echoes the dimension of offering freedom.

Thirdly, motivational theory was included, specifically self-determination theory, for further theoretical underpinning of the three teaching approaches of honors teaching. Self-determination theory has proven useful in explaining the variation in students' learning strategies, performance and persistence, even though self-determination theory was not specifically developed with (university) education or honors teaching in mind. The theory indicates that the degree to which teachers support students' motivation is positively associated with strong student performance. According to self-determination theory, three basic psychological needs should be supported: relatedness, competence and autonomy. If a student's need for all three is not satisfied, one's self-motivation, self-determination and wellbeing will be jeopardized. The need for relatedness, or feeling connected with significant others, resonates with the notion of a sense of community. The need for competence refers to the desire for increasing mastery and for a sense of satisfaction in exercising and extending one's capabilities. As such, it resembles our dimension of enhancing academic competence. Feelings of competence, however, will not increase one's intrinsic motivation unless a student perceives the educational context as being supportive of autonomy. This motivating effect could arise, for instance, by being allowed more space to self-organize one's studies or choose one's subject. Clearly, this is related to the research dimension of offering freedom.

Thus the literature survey brought to light three dimensions, hence teaching approaches of honors pedagogies: creating community, enhancing academic competence and offering freedom. It was a deductive step to coordinate each dimension with a teaching approach. Each approach was assigned a cluster of teaching strategies to put it into practice. Those three teaching approaches, and the clusters of teaching strategies related to them, partly overlap and interconnect. It was a deliberate decision to define teaching strategies very broadly. There is wide variation among the teaching strategies needed for honors classes. Indeed, as the literature suggests, and our research data confirm, honors teaching is not just about formal didactic activities (for example, giving feedback). It is equally about behavior that reflects the teacher's personality (for example, being friendly, accessible or enthusiastic). As this study shows, experienced honors teachers apply strategies as part of a more comprehensive practice: they try to create conditions that are in their perception conducive to optimal learning for their honors students.

The framework for an honors pedagogy that is presented in this study appears to resonate with the daily practice of honors teachers, notwithstanding the differences in their backgrounds. Whether they are experienced honors teachers or novices; coming from different learning environments such as community colleges or research universities; or coming from an American or European context –all make a clear distinction between honors teaching and regular teaching. Are there signature procedures for teaching and learning within honors, like one's name written in one's own handwriting? That are conducted in similar ways, by all honors teachers and from one institution to the next? The answer is yes. Broadly speaking, teachers agree on the teaching strategies related to three dimensions of honors teaching: creating community, enhancing academic competence and offering freedom. On that basis, we can now turn to a discussion in more detail of the outcomes of the study, in the order of these three key pedagogical concepts.

7.2.2 Creating community

The three bodies of academic literature that were used in chapter 2 allow to formulate three specific clusters of teaching strategies and forms of teacher behavior under the broader approach of creating community. These three clusters, which were labeled with various words instead of one key term, are the following:

- *Interaction, (peer) feedback, active learning*: strategies for building an effective relationship between teacher and honors students and among honors students.
- *Encouragement, joy, inspiration*: strategies and forms of teacher behavior that create a positive and supportive spirit.

- *Availability, interest in students, commitment*: strategies and forms of teacher behavior that make the teacher part of the community in a practical and a personal sense.

The three teaching clusters related to the approach of 'creating community' formed the basis for constructing questionnaire items about this specific teaching approach. According to the survey findings, the American honors teachers apply community-enhancing teaching strategies significantly more often with their honors students than in their regular classes. They believe it is crucial to invite honors students to participate actively in class and that it is important for a teacher to be interested in honors students as individuals. The five-item community scale (chapters 5 and 6) revealed a significant difference between honors and regular teaching practices, and not only among the American teachers. Dutch honors teachers, however, are less inclined towards community-enhancing teaching strategies and forms of behavior than American honors teachers.

The interviewers did not explicitly ask about creating community as a teaching approach, since this would limit the opportunities to get an impression of what teachers themselves will come up with. Even so, 24 of the 30 American teachers spontaneously brought up the topic of creating community. They stressed the importance of their own engagement, and that of other honors teachers, in jointly creating a supportive atmosphere. Thanks to the reciprocal relationships between teachers and students, both parties can learn from and stimulate each other. Teachers think they know their honors students well enough to encourage them to follow their own path. Teachers consider it important that students know them well enough to ask for advice and support. Furthermore, teachers foster initiative by offering all kinds of opportunities for students to stand up and develop leadership skills. In short, teachers give students the opportunity to play their own role in the process of collaborative learning and creating an honors community.

Moreover teachers stress the importance of institutional conditions that support the creation of an honors community. For instance, a supportive board, well trained honors staff, and a physical honors space are considered necessary.

7.2.3 Enhancing academic competence

Three clusters of teaching strategies related to the dimension of academic competence emerged from the review of the literature:

- *Multi- and interdisciplinary thinking, multiple perspectives*: strategies for providing context, both academic and societal, and supporting connective thinking.
- *Scholarly teaching, academic depth, involvement in research*: strategies that support the development of in-depth analytical thinking and of research skills.
- *Challenging learning tasks, difficulty, and acceleration*: the range of strategies that create challenge, both in quality (difficulty, complexity) and in quantity (pacing, size of tasks).

Honors teachers, from the U.S.A. as well as from the Netherlands, show a slight inclination to apply strategies for enhancing academic competence to a greater extent in honors classes than in regular classes. But overall, the analyses imply that enhancing academic competence is important for honors as well as for regular education. However, the findings reveal that the related teaching strategies to do so differ for honors and for regular teaching. Crossing traditional educational borders, offering interdisciplinary content and assigning undergraduate research are important strategies within honors. Teachers see breadth, context and perspective as important for enhancing academic competence in honors classes. Also, within honors classes, academic competence can be displayed through undergraduate research and challenging assignments. For regular classes it is considered relatively more important for a teacher, in order to enhance academic competence among students, to know his or her subject well and to explain it well.

The American teachers tell in the interviews that their assumption that honors students can think at higher levels may be paramount to productive honors classes. Classroom activities that stimulate critical and independent thinking as well as creative thinking are considered especially important. During the interviews, the American teachers also mentioned that assignments and other learning tasks should be challenging, since this leads to engagement and a richer and deeper conversation in honors classes. Independent projects, capstone projects and thesis work are seen as essential within honors. Research teaching and undergraduate honors research are described as important vehicles for students' cognitive growth as well as for their personal and professional development. In light of these findings, there is good reason to add a fourth cluster of teaching strategies that promote critical, independent and creative thinking.

7.2.4 Offering freedom

Also for the dimension of offering freedom, three clusters of teaching strategies were distilled from the literature survey:

- *Flexibility, allowing for self-regulation, openness*: strategies that create space for students' questions, choices, and initiatives, scaffolding
- *Innovative teaching, experimentation, fun*: strategies that foster the sense and excitement of experimentation
- *Professionalism, novice relationship, challenge*: strategies that treat honors students as 'junior colleagues' in research and education (activities).

The findings of the survey reveal that for honors teachers, both from the U.S.A. and from the Netherlands, offering freedom distinguishes their honors teaching from their regular teaching. The teachers included far more freedom-related items in their top-three and top-five lists for honors teaching compared to regular teaching. By splitting the results into freedom and structure, we discerned a distinct difference between honors teaching and regular reaching. Indeed, the teachers do not consider freedom an appropriate approach for regular classes. Instead, they consider offering structure as appropriate. This entails, for instance, offering well-organized subject matter and being clear about their expectations.

Granting responsibility to honors students and allowing them freedom in choosing which topics to study and in their time management are considered appropriate teaching strategies in honors programs. Leaving room for experimentation, creating space for the students' own initiative and encouraging questions seem to characterize honors education. In sum, they believe that a greater tailoring of honors programs to students' needs within a strong framework of community would be appropriate.

The list of topics covered in the interviews did not explicitly include freedom. It was left out so that the interviewers could get an unbiased impression of how teachers deal with their honors students. However, the teachers did speak readily about the importance of freedom. Their teaching is student-centered and offers a high degree of flexibility to honors students. Teachers allow room for student choice, subject focus and time-management and grant them responsibility for themselves. It appears as well that the teachers often see teaching strategies related to offering freedom as a means to another end. For instance, the development of an honors student's capacity for self-regulation (means) is seen as an integral part of a capstone project (end). Encouraging choices is often seen as a means to achieve goals such as engagement, academic depth or bonding. It appears that the way teachers apply strategies related to offering freedom has much to do with the teachers' personality and involvement in the honors community. The interviews illustrate that offering freedom goes hand in hand with trusting the students and taking them seriously. Teachers grant honors students responsibility, not only so that they can learn to make choices and reflect on them but also to put the students in a position to create their own independent learning strategy.

Furthermore, the teachers talked about their own freedom in teaching. Honors teachers use the honors class as an educational innovation room. This was also borne out by the survey, showing that this is more common in the American setting than in the Dutch context. When the survey was conducted, honors programs were relatively new in the Netherlands. Only 3% of all Dutch teachers had more than ten years of teaching experience in honors, whereas 40% of the American teachers had. Honors education was an experiment in itself in the Dutch situation, while it was a long-standing tradition in the American context.

7.2.5 The honors teachers

Honors teaching cannot be studied in isolation. It was assumed that attributes such as the teachers' conception of teaching and learning, their motivation and feeling of self-determination, and their perception of students all have an impact on teaching practice in general and also on practices in honors teaching.

The outcomes about those attributes and their relationships with teaching will be discussed in this section, starting with the teachers' conceptions of honors teaching and learning in higher education.

The findings give the overall impression that honors teachers are more inclined towards a student-learning orientation than a teacher-content orientation, particularly in how they organize their classes (instructional emphasis). Moreover, the findings show that American teachers see their honors classes as a laboratory for educational innovation, which may involve some risk – for teachers as well as students. The Dutch honors teachers do not perceive the notions of risk-taking and educational innovation as key ingredients of honors education. Dutch teachers also give more importance to learning products, such as grading.

During the interviews, the American teachers reflected spontaneously on what they believe to be the core of honors education. Their reactions led to the identification of several main themes: outstanding performance, with a strong focus on the process of learning more than on its outcomes; the notion of high expectations of a fairly homogeneous group of students with strong motivation and academic potential; and the notion of honors as being strategically important for their institution in the sense of attracting good faculty as well as students.

Intrinsic motivation and self-determination are high among Dutch teachers and even significantly higher among American teachers. Does motivation make a difference for teachers' teaching approach? The answer is yes, it does. If teachers are more motivated, they subscribe to the importance of creating community or enhancing academic competence within honors. The effect of motivation on offering freedom could not be measured.

From the teachers' point of view as they said in the interviews, it is both motivating and pleasurable to work with honors students and help them to fulfill their potential. Teachers are enthusiastic about being able to share in depth much of their academic field of interest with the students. It seems as if their motivation supports them to act in a relaxed and authentic style which helps to create an informal, relaxed yet demanding class atmosphere – and the other way around. Many American teachers perceive honors teaching as a challenge, which they find inherently exciting and rewarding.

The interviews with American teachers also illuminated their concerns about some of their honors students: various teachers reported that honors students may be over-competitive or over-committed. This may result in losing track of the honors learning experience while focusing on the output instead of on the process. Furthermore, the American teachers experience honors students as engaged and both academically and personally more mature than students in regular programs. They perceive their honors students as young people who are willing to work harder than students in regular programs. Honors students are seen as people who approach learning differently than regular students and are generally stronger communicators, often skilled in debate and other forms of verbal communication. Both American and Dutch teachers believe that their regular students need clear goals, clear class structure and well-explained subject matter.

American and Dutch teachers include in the survey the same five qualities in their top-five for honors students (although in a different order): enterprising in the sense of taking initiatives, curiousness, creative thinking, motivation and willingness to invest effort in their studies. Compared to their Dutch colleagues, the American teachers attach significantly higher importance to the following qualities of honors students: risk-taking, involvement in the academic community and being stimulating for fellow students. Risk-taking is perceived as engagement in original, out-of-the-box and open-ended tasks; as such it is related to the teaching approach of offering freedom. Student qualities of involvement and stimulating fellow students are linked to the teaching approach of creating community. This is in line with the finding that both approaches are important in American honors education. Dutch teachers place significantly more emphasis on qualities of honors students that reflect academic competence: a passion for research and getting good grades.

7.3 Discussion

7.3.1 Limitations of this study

It was the ambition of this research to examine reported strategies in honors education systematically, also in contrast to teaching strategies in regular classes, on the basis of a conceptual framework that draws upon multiple perspectives (honors literature, giftedness research, self-determination theory) and multi-institutional survey data from two countries, supplemented by qualitative interview data from experienced U.S. honors teachers. Some limitations of the conceptual and methodological choices that were made in this study have come to light and will be discussed below.

Conceptually, the author made a choice to focus on the three teaching approaches that have been labeled 'creating community', 'enhancing academic competence' and 'offering freedom'. It was an inductive step to distil three theoretical dimensions from the most prominent themes in the honors literature, then it was a deductive step to study giftedness research and motivational and self-determination theory. Then, these same phrases were used as labels for the three most important teaching approaches to operationalize them as teaching strategies.

Giftedness research is mainly about children in primary and secondary school; moreover, studies in this field dealing with teaching strategies are few and far between. Self-determination theory is about human motivation and the basic conditions for it; not all self-determination theory research is about education. Although the conceptual framework of the three teaching approaches can be seen as solid, it is admittedly somewhat eclectic. The conceptual framework could be made more robust by incorporating other perspectives from learning theory, instructional research and higher education research. One might argue that the strong focus on the three teaching approaches leaves some other aspects underexposed. In this regard, the author sees it as reassuring that most of the points made by experienced honors teachers during the interviews reflect the core importance of the three teaching approaches, although these were not explicitly introduced into the topiclist of the interviews.

In hindsight, the survey design could have been more transparent. Some of the survey items use a five-point Likert scale; others use ranking and selection (top-three or top-five questions). Technically it is not possible to combine the two types of items in the construction of one composite variable or scale (such as the scales for the approaches of creating community and enhancing academic competence). This limited the options for scale construction. Even though the survey was pre-tested, some items were poorly understood, making them not usable in the construction of composite variables. Regarding survey items on 'offering freedom', more items with greater differentiation could have been used. That would have allowed for the construction of a scale for the approach of freedom during the analysis. Even though some issues that arose during the analysis concerning 'structure versus freedom' (see chapters 5 and 6) could have been resolved in the design phase, their open-ended nature eventually allowed them to be properly identified.

From a methodological perspective, one might argue that an exploration of honors teaching strategies on the basis of practices reported by teachers is one-sided. While that critique is valid, for the sake of feasibility, the project had to focus on what teachers say they do. This also contributed to the relatively large number of respondents in the surveys, compared to a possible alternative methodological approach of classroom observations. The author believes that the rich yield of relevant and valuable data justifies the choice of methods. It is hard to imagine why teachers would give biased answers in the survey and the interviews, or why they would report teaching practices untruthfully. It is obvious that studies of actual teaching practices (classroom observations) and of students' perceptions of teaching practices in honors would enrich the picture (Pascarella & Terenzini 2005). Some of these issues will be discussed in the following section.

7.3.2 Implications

The findings presented in this study have several implications for both practice and future research activities. First and foremost, the findings can contribute to the fostering of faculty development initiatives for honors. The findings reveal that teaching in honors is deemed different from teaching in regular classes; in short, a teacher can make the difference. The extent to which teachers in higher education are equipped to facilitate the creation of this kind of honors environment is a topic that certainly requires further debate and analysis. However, as more students and teachers become involved in honors programs it is important to invest specifically in this area of faculty development. Yair (2008) is right: the scholarship of teaching is not simply amenable to transfer or distribution, but steps can be taken to encourage the proliferation of good teaching practice in honors. This should already start with teacher education. Having said that, this study showed striking similarities between American and Dutch honors teachers in their perception of honors teaching. These shared understandings allow for an international exchange of honors teachers and international collaboration among institutes.

It should be noted however, that educational contexts differ between Europe and the U.S.A., so obviously that must be taken into account.

Second, the outcomes from the interviews suggest that institutional conditions for creating an honors community and support for teachers are crucial. The outcomes reveal that teachers are motivated and committed to their students, and such honors teachers may function as role models for an institution's faculty. Institutions should therefore cherish and nurture their motivation and commitment. Honors education can thrive in the right institutional conditions and, vice versa, institutions can mirror the honors experience by building an academic environment that stimulates personal relations, personal and professional growth and passion for teaching amongst all faculty.

With respect to future research activities, the implications of the present thesis are numerous. Three avenues for further research are described in the next section.

7.3.3 Avenues for further research

This thesis has attempted to substantiate key components of honors pedagogies, based on an extensive literature review and empirical research among honors teachers. Three main avenues for further research could build on the findings of this study as some reasons for debate and reflection.

The study reveals that teaching strategies that are generally seen as essential in honors education fall under the three main teaching approaches, creating community, enhancing academic competence and offering freedom. Those three approaches stand out as essential in honors teaching and were explored through teachers' self-reported teaching practices.

These findings could be used as a basis for further research into what teachers actually do in their daily practice in honors classes, for example by conducting classroom observations. The validity of the three approaches could then be further tested and possibly enriched by referring to actual practices. This could lead to practice-based honors course descriptions focused on effective honors teaching strategies, in line with the work of, for instance, Dixon et al. (2004) and Wiegant, Scager & Boonstra (2011). The findings of this study reveal the importance of offering freedom within honors pedagogies. Teachers' practices related to offering freedom and structure within honors and regular courses could be further investigated. An understanding of the unique dynamic between freedom and structure could lead to new methods for eliciting excellence within higher education. Examples of research into actual teaching practices include conducting a comparative content analysis of course syllabi of honors courses and courses in the regular curriculum on the same subject matter, and classroom observations on teacher-student interactions comparing honors and regular courses. These types of research allow for a further analysis of the three approaches that were developed in this thesis, based on actual classroom practices.

Another avenue for further research would take the students' perspectives into account. After all, the single most important difference between teaching honors and regular classes is made by the students. This study did not include student perceptions of honors teachers or courses. It would be interesting to discover the students' opinion of their teachers' approaches and strategies (see, for instance, Shaunessy & McHatton 2009; Van der Valk, Grunefeld & Pilot 2010). Doing so could indicate if the three approaches of creating community, enhancing academic competence and offering freedom also remain essential in the light of students' needs and wishes and those of alumni. For instance, this could be investigated by conducting interviews among students in honors programs versus students in regular programs who are being educated by the same teachers.

It is known that data for learning outcomes assessment may suffer from low validity and may fail to capture the complete essence of the complex field of honors education (Carnicom & Snyder 2010). Yet new insights may come from research on the effectiveness of honors teaching whereby students' learning outcomes are analyzed. While most of the teachers who participated in this study agree that honors education should be focused on eliciting excellence, we do not know whether the proposed strategies are effective in reaching this goal, as the students' outcomes were not included in this study. To take this research further, it would be interesting to investigate the effect of honors teaching strategies on students' outcomes, perceived wellbeing and mindset (Dweck 2000). Research on honors alumni should then be included.

This study reveals a distinct set of teaching practices facilitating the mastery of the honors experience, envisioning the 'signature pedagogy' (Shulman 2005a, 2005b) evolved by honors. Although this study offers a rich basis for faculty development in honors, it would be good to undertake further study on the effectiveness of such initiatives. This is the third avenue for further research that the author envisions. The role of teachers is pivotal, certainly for highly talented and motivated students, in creating community, scaffolding, and balancing freedom and structure. However, faculty development for honors is in its initial phase in the Netherlands. It is largely absent in teacher education, which is a hiatus. As noted by Segers & Hoogeveen (2012), there is a need for research on the quality of faculty development for honors. Specifically, further research is needed into the design and the effects of faculty development (Van Veen, Zwart & Meirink 2012). Honors programs have been shown to serve as laboratories for innovation (Denisson 2008), so faculty development should cover effective ways to integrate room for experimentation by honors teachers. With regard to the effects, we need more insight into the relation between faculty development interventions and the effectiveness of honors teachers' strategies as well as students' outcomes.

Besides these three avenues for further empirical research described above, the outcomes of this study warrant a conversation about ethical issues concerning honors education, reflecting on its purposes and on education policies.

What should be our goal with honors education and how are we to reach it? Do teachers have a special responsibility to inspire honors student to respect other humans, disciplines and cultures through genuine conversations, interactive learning and international exchange? Do honors students have specific moral and ethical sensitivities (Tirri & Nokelainen 2011) that honors programs should address? And why would this be true for students in honors programs more than for students in regular programs?

The purpose of education must be to enhance, not compromise, human difference and dignity (Sacks 2007). Education in a democratic society must provide all students with opportunities to develop their talents, taking into account all of the differences between them. This requires differentiation among students, implying the allocation of resources specifically for talented and motivated students as a means to elicit excellence. Reflection on why and how to evoke excellence from these students, and whether we succeed to sufficiently address their moral and ethical questions is crucial. In honors courses, one of the important questions should be, what makes a life well-lived? The answers have everything to do with moral principles and values that give continuity and dignity to life. The answers relate education to contribution, fulfillment and happiness. Teachers should be educating critical and creative young people to develop the desire, capacity and confidence to make a difference in society and science. Reflection is needed to provide direction for the design of social and ethical themes in honors programs and higher education. Further research could explore how teachers provide such an education.

Reference list

Achterberg, C. (2004). Honors in research: Twenty years later. *Journal of the NCHC, 5*(1), 33-36.

Achterberg, C. (2005). What is an honors student? *Journal of the NCHC, 6*(1), 75-83.

Anderson, L. W., & Krathwohl, D. R. (Eds.). (2001). *A taxonomy for learning, teaching, and assessing: A revision of Bloom's taxonomy of educational objectives.* Complete edition. New York, NY: Longman.

Anderson, R., Manoogian, S. T., & Reznick, J. S. (1976). The undermining and enhancing of intrinsic motivation in preschool children. *Journal of Personality and Social Psychology, 34*, 915-922.

Andrews, L. (2011). The wisdom of our elders: Honors discussions in *The Superior Student, Journal of the NCHC, 12*(2), 17-45.

Austin, C.G. (1986). Orientation to honors education. In P. G. Friedman, & R. C. Jenkins-Friedman (Eds.), *Fostering academic excellence through honors programs* (pp. 5-16). San Francisco, CA: Jossey-Bass.

Austin, C.G. (1991). *Honors programs: Development, review and revitalization.* Radford, VA: NCHC.

Aydelotte, F. (1944). *Breaking the academic lock step. The development of honors work in American colleges & universities.* New York, NY: Harper & Brothers Publishers.

Baldwin, A. Y., Vialle, W., & Clarke, C. (2002). Global professionalism and perceptions of teachers of the gifted. In K. Heller, F. Mönks, R. Sternberg, & F. Subotnik (Eds.), *International handbook of giftedness and talent* (pp. 565-572). Oxford, UK: Elsevier Science Ltd.

Bastedo, M. N., & Gumport, P. J. (2003). Access to what? Mission differentiation and academic stratification in U.S. public higher education. *Higher Education, 46*, 341-359.

Bennett, R.J. (2009). Legal history meets the honors program. *Journal of Legal Studies Education, 26*(1), 211-239.

Biggs, J.B., & Tang, C. (2007). *Teaching for quality learning at university: what the student does* (3rd ed.). Maidenhead, UK: Society for Research into Higher Education & Open University Press.

Bishop, W. E. (1968). Successful teachers of the gifted. *Exceptional Children, 34,* 317-325.

Blalock, H.M. (1979). *Social statistics* (revised 2nd ed.). Tokyo, Japan: McGraw-Hill Kogakusha.

Bok, D. (2008). *Our underachieving colleges: a candid look at how much students learn and why they should be learning more* (8th printing with a new afterword). Princeton, NJ: Princeton University Press.

Breen, R.L. (2006). A practical guide to focus-group research. *Journal of Geography in Higher Education, 30*(3), 463-475.

Brekelmans, M., Wubbels, T., & Van Tartwijk, J. (2005). Teacher-student relationships across the teaching career. *International Journal of Educational Research, 43*(1-2), 55-71.

Brown, E.B. Jr. (2001). Level differentiation in the United States. Part I: A brief history of honors. *The National Honors Report, 22,* 48-54.

Brown, E.B. Jr. (2002). Level differentiation in the United States. Part II: Level differentiations and honors programs. *The National Honors Report, 22,* 35-44.

Bryman, A. (2004). *Social research methods* (3rd ed.). New York, NY: Oxford University Press.

Bunting, C.E. (1985). Dimensionality of teacher educational beliefs: a validation study. *Journal of Experimental Education, 4,* 188-192.

Byrt, T. (1996). How good is that agreement? *Epidemiology, 7*(5), 561-561.

Cambia, J.M., & Engel, R.S. (Eds). (2004). *Innovations in undergraduate research and honors education proceedings of the second schreyer national conference.* Lincoln, NE: NCHC.

Carnicom, S., & Snyder, Ch. A. (2010). Learning outcomes assessment in honors: An appropriate practice? *Journal of the NCHC, 11*(1), 69-82.

Chan, D.W. (2011). Characteristics and competencies of teachers of gifted learners: The Hong Kong student perspective. *Roeper Review, 33*(3), 160-169.

Charmaz, K. (2006). *Constructing grounded theory: A practical guide through qualitative analysis.* London, UK: Sage.

Cheung, H. Y., & Hui, S.K.F. (2011). Competencies and characteristics for teaching gifted students: A comparative study of Beijing and Hong Kong teachers. *Gifted Child Quarterly, 55*(2), 139-148.

Clark, L. (2002). A review of the research on personality characteristics of academically talented college students. In Ch. Fuiks, & L. Clark (Eds.), *Teaching and learning in honors* (pp. 7-20). Lincoln, NE: NCHC.

Clark, L. (2008). Motivational issues in the education of academically talented college students. In L. Clark, & J. Zubizarreta (Eds.), *Inspiring exemplary teaching and learning: perspectives on teaching academically talented college student,* (pp. 65-106). Lincoln, NE: NCHC.

Clark, L., & Zubizarreta, J. (Eds.). (2008). *Inspiring exemplary teaching and learning: perspectives on teaching academically talented college students.* Lincoln, NE: NCHC.

Cohen, J. (1960). A coefficient of agreement for nominal scales, *Educational and Psychological Measurement, (201)*1, 37-46.

Cohen, J. W. (Ed.). (1966). *The superior student in American higher education.* New York, NY: McGraw-Hill Book Company.

Colangelo, N., & Davis, G. (Eds.). (2003). *Handbook of gifted education* (3rd ed.). Boston, MA: Pearson Education.

Cole, M., John-Steiner, V., Scribner, S., & Souberman, E. (Eds.). (1978). *L. S. Vygotsky – Mind in society. The development of higher psychological processes.* Cambridge, MA: Harvard University Press.

Commissie Ruim Baan voor Talent (2007). *Wegen voor Talent.* Eindrapport 2007. Den Haag.

Copenhaver, R., & Intyre, D. (1992). Teachers' perception of gifted students. *Roeper Review, 14,* 151-153.

Corbalan, G., Kester, L., & Van Merriënboer, J. (2009). Dynamic task selection: Effects of feedback and learner control on efficiency and motivation. *Learning and Instruction, 19*(6), 455-465.

Corley, C.R., & Zubizarreta, J. (2012). The power and utility of reflective learning portfolios in honors. *Journal of the NCHC, 13*(1), 63-76.

Cosgrove, J.R. (2004). The impact of honors programs on undergraduate academic performance, retention, and graduation, *Journal of the NCHC, 5*(2), 45-53.

Cotton, S. R., & Wilson, B. (2006). Student-faculty interactions: Dynamics and determinants. *Higher Education, 51,* 487-519.

Creswell, J.W. (2009). *Research design: Qualitative, quantitative and mixed methods approaches* (3rd ed.). Los Angeles, CA: Sage.

Croft, L.J. (2003). Teachers of the gifted: gifted teachers. In N. Colangelo, & G. Davis (Eds.), *Handbook of gifted education* (pp. 558-571). Boston, MA: Pearson Education.

Cronbach, L.J. (1951). Coefficient Alpha and the internal structure of tests. *Psychometrika, 16*(3), 197-334.

Csikszentmihalyi, M. (1996). *Creativity. Flow and the psychology of discovery and invention.* New York, NY: Harper Collings Publishers.

Csikszentmihalyi, M., Rathunde, K., & Whalen, S. (1997). *Talented teenagers: The roots of success and failure.* Cambridge, UK: Cambridge University Press.

Cummings, R.J. (1994). Basic characteristics of a fully-developed honors program and how they grew: a brief history of honors evaluation in NCHC. *The National Honors Report, 15,* 27-31.

Dai, D.Y., Swanson, J.A., & Cheng, H. (2011). State of research on giftedness and gifted education: A survey of empirical studies published during 1998-2010. *Gifted Child Quarterly, 55*(2), 126-138.

Deci, E.L., Eghrari, H., Patrick, B.C., & Leone, D.R. (1994). Facilitating internaliza-tion: The self-determination theory perspective. *Journal of Personality, 62*(1), 119-142.

Deci, E. L., & Ryan, R.M. (1985). *Intrinsic motivation and self-determination in human behaviour.* New York, NY: Plenum.

Deci, E., & Ryan, R. (1991). A motivational approach to self: Integration in personal-ity. In R. Dienstbier (Ed.), *Nebraska symposium on motivation: Vol. 38. Perspectives on motivation* (pp. 237-288). Lincoln: University of Nebraska Press.

Deci, E. L., & Ryan, R.M. (1995). Human autonomy: The basis for true self-esteem. In M. Kernis (Ed.), *Efficacy, agency, and self-esteem* (pp. 31-49). New York, NY: Plenum.

Deci, E., & Ryan, R. (Eds.), (2002). *Handbook of self-determination research.* Roches-ter, NY: University of Rochester Press.

Deci, E., Vallerand, R., Pelletier, L., & Ryan, R. (1991). Motivation and education: The self-determination perspective. *Educational Psychologist, 26*(3&4), 325-346.

Denessen, E. (1999). *Opvattingen over onderwijs. Leerstof- en leerlinggerichtheid in Nederland.* Doctoral dissertation, Radboud Universiteit Nijmegen. Apeldoorn, Netherlands: Garant uitgevers.

Denisson, G.M. (2008). Honors education and the prospects for academic reform, *Innovative Higher Education, 33,* 159-168.

De Vocht, A. (2009). *Basishandboek SPSS 17. SPSS.* Utrecht: Bijleveld Press.

Dewey, J. (1921). *Democracy and education: an introduction to the philosophy of educa-tion.* New York, NY: MacMillan.

Digby, J. (Ed.) (2005). *Smart choices: Peterson's honors programs & colleges* (4rd ed.). Lawrenceville, NJ: Thomson-Peterson's.

Dixon, F.A., Prater, K.A., Vine, H.M., Wark, M.J., Williams, T., Hanchon, T., & Shobe, C. (2004). Teaching to their thinking: A strategy to meet the critical-thinking needs of gifted students. *Journal for the Education of the Gifted, 28*(1), 56-76.

Doornenbal, J. (2007). *Ploegen & bouwen. De brede school als open leergemeenschap.* Lectorale rede installatie lectoraat Integraal jeugdbeleid, Hanzehogeschool Gron-ingen, the Netherlands, May 15, 2007.

Draper, S., Hazelton, N., McNamara, J., & Kahn, R. (1999). The mentor/talented stu-dents honors program at SUNY Rockland. *Paper presented at the Annual Meeting of the American Association of Community Colleges.* Nashville, TN, April 7-10, 1999.

Dweck, C. S. (2000). *Self-theories: Their role in motivation, personality and develop-ment.* Philadelphia, PA: Psychology Press.

Eccles, J. S., & Wigfield, A. (2002). Motivational beliefs, values and goals. *Annual Re-view of Psychology, 53*(1), 109-132.

England, R. (2010). Honors programs in four-year institutions in the northeast: A preliminary survey toward a national inventory of honors. *Journal of the NCHC, 11*(2), 71-82.

Entwistle, N. (1991). Approaches to learning and perceptions of the learning environment. Introduction to the special issue. *Higher Education, 22,* 201-204.

Feldhusen, J. F. (1997). Educating teachers for work with talented youth. In N. Colangelo, & G. A. Davis (Eds.), *Handbook of gifted education* (2nd ed.) pp. 547–552. Boston, MA: Allyn & Bacon.

Fenollar, P., Román, S., & Cuestas, P.J. (2007). University students' academic performance: An integrative conceptual framework and empirical analysis. *British Journal of Educational Psychology, 77,* 873-891.

Field, A. (2009). *Discovering statistics using SPSS (and sex and drugs and rock 'n' roll)* (3rd rev. ed.). London, UK: Sage.

Fortier, M. S., Vallerand, R. J., & Guay, F. (1995). Academic motivation and school performance: toward a structural model. *Contemporary Educational Psychology, 20,* 257-274.

Freeman, J. (1999). Teaching gifted pupils. *Journal of Biological Education, 30*(4), 185-291.

Freyman, J. (2005). What is an honors student? *Journal of the NCHC, 6*(1), 75-83.

Friedman, P. G., & Jenkins-Friedman, R. C. (Eds.). (1986). *Fostering academic excellence through honors programs.* San Francisco, CA: Jossey-Bass.

Fuiks, C., & Clark, L. (Eds). (2002). *Teaching and learning in honors.* Lincoln, NE: NCHC.

Fuiks, C., & Gillison, L. R. (2002). A review of pedagogy in honors courses. In C. Fuiks & L. Clark. (Eds.), *Teaching and learning in honors* (pp. 93-102). Lincoln, NE: NCHC.

Gagné, F. (1995). From giftedness to talent: A developmental model and its impact on the language of the field. *Roeper Review, 18*(2), 103-120.

Garcia, T., & Pintrich, P. (1996). The effects of autonomy on motivation and performance in the college classroom. *Contemporary Educational Psychology, 21,* 477-486.

Gentry, M., Rizza, M., & Owen, S. (2002). Examining perceptions of challenge and choice in classrooms: The relationship between teachers and their students and comparisons between gifted students and other students. *Gifted Child Quarterly, 46*(2), 145-155.

Gerrity, D.A., Lawrence, J.F., & Sedlacek, W.E. (1993). Honors and non-honors freshmen: demographics, attitudes, interests, and behaviors. *NACADA Journal,* 43-52.

Gibbs, G., & Coffey, M. (2004). The impact of training of university teachers on their teaching skills, their approach to teaching and the approach to learning of their students. *Active Learning in Higher Education, 5*(1), 87-100.

Gottfried, A.E., & Gottfried, A.W. (2004). Toward the development of a conceptualization of gifted motivation. *Gifted Child Quarterly, 48*(2), 121-132.

Graffam, B. (2006). A case study of teachers of gifted learners: Moving from prescribed practice to described practitioners. *Gifted Child Quarterly, 50*(2), 119–131.

Gravetter F.J., & Walnau, L.B. (2011). *Essentials for the statistics for the behavioral sciences* (7th ed.). Belmont, TN: Wadsworth.

Groothengel, C., & Van Eijl, P. (2008). Honoursprogramma's in het HBO - Inventarisatie 2007 (deel I) met een nadere verkenning (deel II). *IVLOS mededelingenreeks nr 85.* Universiteit Utrecht.

Gross, M.U.M. (2003). *Exceptionally gifted children* (2nd ed.). London, UK: Routledge Falmer.

Gross, M., & Van Vliet, H. (2005). Radical acceleration and early entry to college: A review of the research. *Gifted Child Quarterly, 49*(2), 154-171.

Gruber, H., & Mandl, H. (2002). Instructional psychology and the gifted. In K. Heller, F. Mönks, R. Sternberg, & F. Subotnik (Eds.), *International handbook of giftedness and talent* (pp. 383-396). Oxford, UK: Elsevier Science Ltd.

Guest, G., Bunce, A., & Johnson, L. (2006). How many interviews are enough? An experiment with data saturation and variability. *Field Methods, 18*(1), 59-82.

Guzy, A. (2003). *Honors composition; historical perspectives and contemporary practices.* Ames, IA: NCHC.

Guzy, A. (2008). Honors culture clash: The high achieving student meets the gifted professor. *Journal of the NCHC, 9*(1), 31-34.

Hansen, J.B., & Feldhusen, J.F. (1994). Comparison of trained and untrained teachers of gifted students. *Gifted Child Quarterly, 38*(3), 115-121.

Hattie, J. (2009). *Visible learning, a synthesis of over 800 meta-analyses relating to achievement.* New York, NY: Routledge.

Haynes, C. (2006). The integrated student: Fostering holistic development in advance learning. *About campus, 10*(6), 17-23.

Hébert, T.P., & Mcbee, M.T. (2007). The impact of an undergraduate honors program on gifted university students. *Gifted Child Quarterly, 51*(2), 136-151.

Heller, K.A. (2007). Scientific ability and creativity. *High Ability Studies, 18*(2), 209-234.

Heller, K., Mönks, F., Sternberg, R., & Subotnik, F. (Eds.). (2002). *International handbook of giftedness and talent* (2nd ed.). Oxford, UK: Elsevier Science Ltd.

Heller, K., Perleth, C., & Lim, T. (2005). The Munich model of giftedness designed to identify and promote gifted students. In R. Sternberg, & J. Davidson. (Eds.), *Conceptions of giftedness* (pp. 147-170). New York, NY: Cambridge University Press.

Hoekman, K., McCormick, J., & Gross, M.U.M. (1999). The optimal context for gifted students: A preliminary exploration of motivational and affective considerations. *Gifted Child Quarterly, 43*(3), 170-193.

Holman, D. (2007). *Annotated bibliography honors research library.* Denver, CO: NCHC Conference.

Holman, D.K., & Banning, J.H. (2012). Honors dissertation abstracts: A bounded qualitative meta-study. *Journal of the NCHC, 13*(1), 41-61.

Hrabowski, F. A. (2009). Expanding access for America's future. In G. A. Olsona, & J. W. Presley (Eds.), *The future of higher education. Perspectives from America's academic leaders* (pp. 151-161). Colorado: Paradigm Publicer.

Hultgren, H. W., & Seeley, K. R. (1982). *Training teachers of the gifted: A research monograph on teacher competencies.* Denver, CO: University of Denver, School of Education.

Jamieson, S. (2004). Likert scales: how to (ab)use them. *Medical Education, 38,* 1212-1218.

Jeter, J., & Chauvin, J. (1982). Individualized instruction: Implications for the gifted. *Roeper Review, 5*(1), 2-3.

Kaczvinksy, D.P. (2007). What is an honors student? A Noel-Levitz survey. *Journal of the NCHC, 8*(2), 87-95.

Karnes, F.A., & Bean, S.M. (Eds.). (2001). *Methods and materials for teaching the gifted.* Waco, TX: Prufrock Press.

Kember, D. (1997). A reconceptualisation of the research into university academics' conceptions of teaching. *Learning and instruction, 7*(3), 255-275.

Kember, D., & Gow, L. (1994). Orientations to teaching and their effect on the quality of student learning. *Journal of Higher Education, 65*(1), 58–74.

Kember, D., & Kwan, K.-P. (2000). Lecturers' approaches to teaching and their relationship to conceptions of good teaching. *Instructional Science, 28*(5-62), 469-490.

Kezar, A. (2001). Theory of multiple intelligences: Implications for higher education. *Innovative Higher Education, 26*(2), 141-154.

Kiley, M., Boud, D., Manathunga, C., & Cantwell, R. (2011). Honouring the incomparable: honours in Australian universities. *Higher Education, 62,* 619-633.

Kitagaki, I., & Li, D. (2008). On training excellent students in China and the United States. *Journal of the NCHC, 9*(2), 45-54.

Krueger, R. A. (1994). *Focus groups: A practical guide for applied research* (2nd ed.). Thousand Oaks, CA: Sage Publications.

Kuh, G., Kinzie, J., Schuh, J., & Whitt, E. (2005). *Student success in college. Creating conditions that matter.* San Francisco, CA: Jossey-Bass.

Lambert, R., & Butler, N. (2006). *The future of European universities. Renaissance or decay?* London, UK: Centre for European Reform.

Lanier, G. (2008). Towards reliable honors assessment. *Journal of the NCHC, 9*(1), 81-149.

Leikin, R. (2011). Teaching the mathematically gifted: Featuring a teacher. *Canadian Journal of Science, Mathematics and Technology Education, 11*(1), 78-89.

Levesque, C., Zuehlke, A. N., Stanek, L. R., & Ryan, R. M. (2004). Autonomy and competence in German and American university students: a comparative study based on self-determination theory. *Journal of Educational Psychology, 96*(1), 68-84.

Light, G., & Calkins, S. (2008). The experience of faculty development: patterns of variation in conceptions of teaching. *International Journal for Academic Development, 13*(1), 27-40.

Light, G., Cox, R., & Calkins, S. (2009). Learning and teaching in higher education: the reflective professional (2nd ed.). London, UK: Sage Publications ltd.

Lockwood, P., & Kunda, Z. (1997). Superstars and me: Predicting the impact of role models on the self. *Journal of Personality and Social Psychology, 73*(1), 91-103.

Long, B.T. (2002). *Attracting the best: the use of honors programs to compete for students.* Report for the Harvard Graduate School of Education. Chicago, IL: Spencer Foundation (ERIC Document Reproduction Service No. Ed465355).

Long, E.C.J., & Lange, S. (2002). An exploratory study: A comparison of honors and nonhonors students. *The National Honors Report, 23*(1), 20-30.

Lòpez-Chávez, C., & Shepherd, U.L. (2010). What is expected of twenty-first-century honors students: An analysis of an integrative learning experience. *Journal of the NCHC, 11*(2), 57-70.

Mack, M. (1996). These things called honors programs. *Liberal Education, 82*(2), 34-39.

MacQueen, K.M., McLellan, E., Kay, K., & Milstein, B. (1998). Codebook development for team-based qualitative analysis. *CAM: The Cultural Anthropology Methods Journal, 10*(2), 31-36.

Markland, D., & Hardy, L. (1997). On the factorial and construct validity of the intrinsic motivation inventory: Conceptual and operational concerns. *Research Quarterly for Exercise and Sport*, 20-32.

Martens, R., & Boekaerts, M. (2007). *Motiveren van studenten in het hoger onderwijs.* Groningen, Netherlands: Wolters-Noordhoff.

Martens, R., & Kirschner, P. (2004). *How many factors predict intrinsic motivation?* Paper presented at ORD conference, Utrecht University.

Mathiasen, R. E. (1985). Characteristics of the college honors student. *Journal of College Student Personnel, 26*(2), 171-173.

Mathijsen, I. (2006). *Denken en handelen van docenten.* Doctoral dissertation, Universiteit Utrecht.

Mills, C.J. (2003). Characteristics of effective teachers of gifted students: Teacher background and personality styles of students. *Gifted Child Quarterly, 47*(4), 272–281.

Mönks, F., Heller, K., & Passow, A. (2002). The study of giftedness: Reflections on where we are and where we are going. In K. Heller, F. Mönks, R. Sternberg, & R. Subotnik (Eds.), *International handbook of giftedness and talent* (pp. 839-869). Oxford, UK: Elsevier.

Mooij, T., & Fettelaar, D. (2010). *Naar excellente scholen, leraren, leerlingen en studenten*. ITS, Radboud Universiteit Nijmegen.

Moore, S., & Kuol, N. (2007). Retrospective insights on teaching: exploring teaching excellence through the eyes of alumni. *Journal of Further and Higher Education, 31*(2), 133-143.

National Collegiate Honours Council (2012). *Honors course design*. Retrieved from http://nchchonors.org/faculty-directors/honors-course-design/.

Niemiec, C., & Ryan, R. (2009). Autonomy, competence, and relatedness in the classroom: Applying self-determination theory to educational practice. *Theory and Research in Education, 7*(2), 133-144.

Nunnally, J. C. (1978). *Psychometric Theory* (2nd ed.) (pp. 225-255). New York, NY: McGraw-Hill Book Company.

Okpala, C. O., Smith, F., & Jones, E. (2000). A clear link between school and teacher characteristics, student demographics, and student achievement. *Education, 120*(3), 487-494.

Olszewski-Kubilius, P. (2003). Special summer and Saturday programs for gifted students. In N. Colangelo, & G. Davis (Eds.), *Handbook of gifted education* (pp. 219-228). Boston, MA: Pearson Education.

Otero, R., & Spurrier, R. (Eds.). (2005). *Assessing and evaluating honors programs and honors colleges. A practical handbook*. Lincoln, NE: NCHC.

Pajares, M.F. (1992). Teachers' beliefs and educational research: Cleaning up a messy construct. *Review of Educational Research, 62*(3), 307-332.

Park, I. (2005). Teacher commitment and its effects on student achievement in American high schools. *Educational Research and Evaluation, 11*(5), 461-485.

Park, S., & Oliver, J. S. (2009). The translation of teachers' understanding of gifted students into instructional strategies for teaching science. *Journal Science Teacher Education, 20*, 333-351.

Pascarella, E.T., & Terenzini, P.T. (2005). *How college affects students: A third decade of research* (Vol. 2). San Francisco, CA: Jossey-Bass.

Pelletier, L., Séquin-Lévesque C., & Legault, L. (2002). Pressure from above and pressure from below as determinants of teachers' motivation and teaching behaviors. *Journal of Educational Psychology*, 186-196.

Pennock, J.R. (1953). The Swarthmore honors system. *The Journal of Higher Education, 24*(2), 57-63+106.

Philips, N., & Lindsay, G. (2006). Motivation in gifted students. *High Ability Studies, 17*(1), 57-73.

Pleiss, M.K., & Feldhusen, J.F. (1995). Mentors, role models, and heroes in the lives of gifted children. *Educational Psychologist, 30*(3), 159-169.

Postareff, L., Lindblom-Ylänne, S., & Nevgi, A. (2007). The effect of pedagogical training on teaching in higher education. *Teaching and teacher education, 23*, 557-571.

Pratt, D.D. (1992). Conceptions of teaching. *Adult Education Quarterly, 42*(4), 203-220.

Prosser, M., & Trigwell, K. (1999). *Understanding learning and teaching: The experience in higher education*. Buckingham, UK: Society for Research into Higher Education and Open University Press.

Rea, D.W. (2000). Optimal motivation for talent development. *Journal for the Education of the Gifted, 23*(2), 187-216.

Reeve, J., Bolt, E., & Chai, Y. (1999). Autonomy-supportive teachers; how they teach and motivate students. *Journal of Educational Psychology, 91*(3), 537-548.

Reis, S.M., & Renzulli, J.S. (2004). Current research on the social and emotional development of gifted and talented students: good news and future possibilities. *Psychology in the Schools, 41*(1), 119-130.

Reis, S.M., & Renzulli, J. S. (2010). Is there still a need for gifted education? An examination of current research. *Learning and Individual Differences, 20*, 308-317.

Renzulli, J. (1968). Identitying key features in programs for the gifted. *Exceptional Children, 35*, 217-221.

Renzulli, J. (1986). The three-ring conception of giftedness: A developmental model for creative productivity. In R. Sternberg, & J. Davidson (Eds.), *Conceptions of giftedness* (pp. 53-92). New York, NY: Cambridge University Press.

Renzulli, J. (2003). Conception of giftedness and its relationship to the development of social capital. In N. Colangelo, & G. Davis.(Eds.), *Handbook of gifted education* (pp. 75-87). Boston, MA: Pearson Education.

Renzulli, J. (2005). Applying gifted education pedagogy to total talent development for all students. *Theory into Practice, 44*(2), 80-89.

Renzulli, J. (2008). *Redefining the role of gifted education for the twenty-first century*. Vancouver, Canada: Keynote address World Conference World Council for gifted and talented children.

Renzulli, J., & Purcell, J. (1996). Gifted education; a look around and a look ahead. *Roeper Review, 18*(3), 173-178.

Rijksoverheid (2011). Naar de top: de hoofdlijnen van het nieuwe bedrijfsleven beleid. *Brief aan de Tweede Kamer*, 04-02-2011.

Rinn, A. (2005). Trends among honors college students: An analysis by year in school. *Journal of Advanced Academics, 16*(4), 157-167.

Rinn, A.N. (2006). Major forerunners to honors education at the collegiate level. *Journal of the NCHC, 7*(2), 63-84.

Rinn, A.N. (2007). Effects of programmatic selectivity on the academic achievement, academic self-concepts, and aspirations of gifted college students. *Gifted Child Quarterly, 51*(3), 232-245.

Rinn, A. (2008). Pre-college experiences and characteristics of gifted students. In L. Clark, & J. Zubizarreta (Eds.), *Inspiring exemplary teaching and learning: perspec-*

tives on teaching academically talented college students (pp. 9-17). Lincoln, NE: NCHC.

Rinn, A., & Cobane, T. (2009). Elitism misunderstood: In defense of equal opportunity. *Journal of the NCHC, 10*(1), 53-56.

Rinn, A., & Plucker, J. (2004). We recruit them, but then what? The educational and psychological experiences of academically talented undergraduates. *Gifted Child Quarterly, 48*(1), 54-67.

Robinson, A. (1996). Caught on fire: Motivation and giftedness. *Gifted Child Quarterly, 40*, 177-178.

Robinson, N.M. (1997). The role of universities and colleges in educating gifted undergraduates. *Peabody Journal of Education*, 217-236.

Rogers, K.B. (2002). *Re-forming gifted education: Matching the program to the child.* Scottsdale, AZ: Great Potential Press.

Rogers, K.B. (2007). Lessons learned about educating the gifted and talented: a synthesis of the research on education practice. *Gifted Child Quarterly, 51*(4), 382-396.

Romney, A.K., Weller S.C., & Batchelder, W.H. (1986). Culture as consensus: A theory of culture and informant accuracy. *American Antropologist, 88*(22), 313-338.

Rosenthal, R., & Jacobson, L. (1992). *Pygmalion in the classroom. Teacher expectations and pupils' intellectual development* (newly expanded edition). Wales, UK: Crown House Publishing Limited.

Roulston, K., deMarrais, K., & Lewis, J.B. (2003). Learning to interview in the social sciences. *Qualitative Inquiry, 9*(4), 643-668.

Rostan, M., & Vaira, M. (Eds.) (2011). *Questioning excellence in higher education. Policies, experiences and challenges in national and comparative perspective.* Rotterdam, Netherlands: Senge Publications.

Rubie-Davies, C.M. (2010). Teacher expectations and perceptions of student attributes: Is there a relationship? *British Journal of Educational Psychology*, 121-135.

Ryan, R.M. (1982). Control and information in the intrapersonal sphere: An extension of cognitive evaluation theory. *Journal of Personality and Social Psychology, 43*(3), 450-461.

Ryan, R.M., & Deci, E.L. (2000). Self-determination theory and the facilitation of intrinsic motivation, social development, and well-being. *American Psychologist, 55*(1), 68-78.

Ryan, R., & Grolnick, W.S. (1986). Origins and pawns in the classroom: Self-report and projective assessments of individual differences in children's perceptions. *Journal of Personality and Social Psychology, 5*(2), 550-558.

Sacks, J. (2007). *The dignity of difference. How to avoid the clash of civilizations.* Londen, UK: Continuum.

Sansone, C., & Harackiewicz, J. (2000). *Intrinsic and extrinsic motivation. The search for optimal motivation and performance.* San Diego, CA: Academic Press.

Scager, K., Akkerman, S.F., Keesen, F., Mainhard, M.T., Pilot, A., & Wubbels, T. (2012). Do honors students have more potential for excellence in their professional lives? *Higher Education, 64,* 19-39.

Schaeper, T.J., & Schaeper, K. (1998). *Cowboys into gentlemen: Rhodes scholars, Oxford, and the creation of an American elite.* New York, NY: Berghahn Books.

Schuman, S. (2005). Teaching honors. *Journal of the NCHC, 6*(2), 31-35.

Sederberg, P. (Ed.). (2008). *The Honors college phenomenon.* Lincoln, NE: NCHC.

Segers, E., & Hoogeveen, L. (2012). *Programmeringsstudie. Excellentieonderzoek in primair, voortgezet en hoger onderwijs.* Behavioural Science Institute & Centrum voor Begaafdheidsonderzoek, Radboud Universiteit Nijmegen. Retrieved from http://www.nwo.nl/files.nsf/pages/NWOP_8SRC2K_Eng/$file/PROO%20Excellentie%20Programmeringsstudie.pdf.

Shaunessy, E., & McHatton, P.A. (2009). Urban students' perceptions of teachers: views of students in general, special, and honors education. *Urban Rev, 41,* 486-503.

Shepherd, G., & Shepherd G. (1996). War attitudes and ideological orientations of honors directors in American higher education. *The Journal of Higher Education, 67*(3), 298-321.

Shore, B., Cornell, D., Robinson, A., & Ward, V. (1991). *Recommended practices in gifted education: A critical analysis.* New York, NY: Teacher College Press.

Shulman, L. (2005a). Pedagogies of uncertainty. *Liberal Education, 91*(2), 18-25.

Shulman, L. (2005b). Signature pedagogies in the professions. *Daedalus, 134*(3), 52-59.

Shushok, F. Jr. (2002). *Educating the best and brightest: Collegiate honors programs and the intellectual, social and psychological development of students.* Dissertation, University of Maryland. College Park.

Sim, J., & Wright, C.C. (2005). The kappa statistic in reliability studies: use, interpretation, and sample size requirements. *Physical Therapy, 85*(3), 257-268.

Sirius Programma (2012). *Sirius programma: Excellentie in het hoger onderwijs.* Retrieved from http://www.siriusprogramma.nl/.

Sisk, D. (1987). *Creative teaching of the gifted.* New York, NY: McGraw-Hill.

Sosniak, L. (2003). Developing talent: Time, task and context. In N. Colangelo, & G. Davis, (Eds.), *Handbook of gifted education* (pp. 247-253). Boston, MA: Pearson Education.

Spangler, L.J. (1985). *The development of a scheme for staff development in gifted education.* Dissertation, University of Virginia.

Stake, R. (2002) Teachers conceptualizing student achievement. *Teachers and Teaching: Theory and Practice, 8*(3-4), 303-312.

Sternberg, R. (2001). Giftedness as developing expertise: a theory of the interface between high abilities and achieved excellence. *High Ability Studies, 12*(2), 159-179.

Sternberg, R. (2002). Giftedness as developing expertise. In K. Heller, F. Mönks, R. Sternberg, & F. Subotnik (Eds.), *International handbook of giftedness and talent* (pp. 55-66). Oxford, UK: Elsevier Science Ltd.

Sternberg, R. (2003). WICS as a model of giftedness. *High Ability Studies, 14*(2), 109-137.

Sternberg, R., & Davidson, J. (Eds.). (2005). *Conceptions of giftedness* (revised 2nd ed.). New York, NY: Cambridge University Press.

Sternberg, R., & Grigorenko, E. (2007). *Teaching for successful intelligence. To increase student learning and achievement.* California: Corwin Press.

Stes, A., Coertjens, L., & Van Petegem, P. (2010). Instructional development for teachers in higher education: impact on teaching approach. *Higher Education, 60,* 187-204.

Stopper, M. (2000). *Meeting the social and emotional needs of gifted and talented children.* London, UK: David Fulton Publishers.

Strauss A., & Corbin, J.M. (1990). *Basics of qualitative research: Grounded theory procedures and techniques.* Newbury Park, CA: Sage.

Strong, P. (2008). The prairie home companion honors program. *Journal of the NCHC, 9*(1), 35-40.

Swarthmore College Faculty (1941). *An adventure in education. Swarthmore College under Frank Aydelotte.* New York, NY: The Macmillan Company.

Tashakkori, A., & Creswell, J.W. (2007). Exploring the nature of research questions in mixed methods research. *Journal of Mixed Methods Research, 1*(3), 207-211.

Taylor, W. (2002). Promoting critical thinking through classroom discussion. In C. Fuiks & L. Clark. (Eds.), *Teaching and learning in honors* (pp. 77-83). Lincoln, NE: NCHC.

Taylor, I.M., Ntoumanis, N., & Smith, B. (2009). The social context as a determinant of teacher motivational strategies in physical education. *Psychology of Sport and Exercise, 10,* 235-243.

Teddlie, C., & Tashakkori, A. (2009). *Foundations of mixed method research. Integrating quantitative and qualitative approaches in the social and behavioural sciences.* Thousand Oaks, CA: Sage Publications.

Tirri, K., & Nokelainen, P. (2011). *Measuring multiple intelligences and moral sensitivities in education.* Rotterdam, Netherlands: Sense Publishers.

Trigwell, K., Prosser, M., & Taylor, P. (1994). Qualitative differences in approaches to teaching first year university science. *Higher Education, 27,* 75-84.

Trigwell, K., Prosser, M., & Waterhouse, F. (1999). Relations between teachers' approaches to teaching and students' approaches to learning. *Higher Education, 37,* 57-70.

Trost, G. (2002). Prediction of excellence in school, higher education, and work. In K. Heller, F. Mönks, R. Sternberg, & F. Subotnik (Eds.), *International handbook of giftedness and talent* (pp. 317-327). Oxford, UK: Elsevier Science Ltd.

Tsui, L. (1999). Courses and instruction affecting critical thinking. *Research in Higher Education, 40*(2), 185-200.

Tuckman, B.W. (1972). *Conducting educational research.* New York, NY: Hartcourt, Brace, Jovanovich.

Van den Doel, W. (2007). De stille onderwijsrevolutie. In P. Van Eijl, M. Wolfensberger, L. Schreve-Brinkman & A. Pilot, *Honors, tool for promoting excellence* (pp. 5-7). Universiteit Utrecht: IVLOS.

Van der Valk, A.E., Grunefeld, H., & Pilot, A. (2010). Empowerment en leerresultaten bij getalenteerde bètaleerlingen in een verrijkte onderwijsleeromgeving. *Pedagogische Studien, 88,* 73-89.

Van Eijl, P., Pilot, A., & Wolfensberger, M. (Eds.) (2010). *Talent voor morgen. Ontwikkeling van talent in het hoger onderwijs.* Groningen, Netherlands: Noordhoff Uitgevers.

Van Eijl, P., Wientjes, H., Wolfensberger, M., & Pilot, A. (2005). Het uitdagen van talent in onderwijs. In Onderwijsraad (Ed.), *Onderwijs in Thema's* (pp. 117-156). Den Haag, Netherlands: Drukkerij Artoos.

Van Eijl, P.J., Wolfensberger, M.V.C., Cadée, M., Siesling, S., Schreve-Brinkman, E.J., Beer, W.M., Faber, G., & Pilot, A. (2003). *Plusprogramma's als proeftuin, met als bijlage een inventarisatie van plusprogramma's in Nederland.* Utrecht: Universiteit Utrecht (IVLOS-mededeling 69).

Van Eijl, P., Wolfensberger, M., Schreve-Brinkman, L., & Pilot, A. (2007). *Honors, tool for promoting excellence.* Universiteit Utrecht: IVLOS

Vansteenkiste, M., Lens, W., & Deci, E.L. (2006). Intrinsic versus extrinsic goal contents in self-determination theory: another look at the quality of academic motivation. *Educational Psychologist, 41*(1), 19-31.

Vansteenkiste, M., Sierens, E., Goossens, L., Soenens, B., Dochy, F., Mouratidis, A., Aelterman, N., Haerens, L., & Beyers, W. (2012). Identifying configurations of perceived teacher autonomy support and structure: Associations with self-regulated learning, motivation and problem behavior. *Learning and Instruction* (in press).

VanTassel-Baska, J. (2002). Theory and research on curriculum development for the gifted. In K. Heller, F. Mönks, R. Sternberg, & F. Subotnik (Eds.), *International handbook of giftedness and talent* (pp. 345-365). Oxford, UK: Elsevier Science Ltd.

VanTassel-Baska, J., & Stambaugh, T. (2005). Challenges and possibilities for serving gifted learners. *Theory into Practice 44*(3), 211-217.

Van Veen, K., Zwart, R., & Meirink, J. (2012). What makes teacher professional development effective? A literature review. In: M. Kooy, & K. Van Veen (Eds.), *Teacher learning that matters: International perspectives* (pp. 3-21). New York, NY: Routledge.

Veerman, C.P., Berdahl, R.M., Bormans, M.J.G., Geven, K.M., Hazelkorn, E., & Rinnooy Kan, A.H.G. (2010). *Differentiëren in drievoud omwille van kwaliteit en ver-*

scheidenheid in het hoger onderwijs. Advies van de Commissie Toekomstbestendig Hoger Onderwijs Stelsel. Ministerie OCW, Den Haag.

Vialle, W. (2001). Acceleration: a coat of many colours. *Roeper Review, 24*(1), 14-20.

Vialle, W., & Tischler, K. (2004). Teachers of the gifted: a comparison of students' perspectives in Australia, Austria and the United States. *Gifted Education International, 19*(2), 173-181.

Viera, A.J., & Garrett, J.M. (2005). Understanding interobserver agreement: The Kappa statistic. *Family Medicine, 37*(5), 360-363.

Weiner, N. (2009). Honors is elitist, and what's wrong with that? *Journal of the NCHC, 10*(1), 19-24.

Weinstein, R.S. (2002). *Reaching higher: the power of expectations in schooling.* Cambridge, MA: Harvard University Press.

Whitlock, M.S., & DuCette, J.P. (1989). Outstanding and average teachers of the gifted: a comparative study. *Gifted Child Quarterly, 33*(1), 15-21.

Wiegant, F., Scager, K., & Boonstra, J. (2011). An undergraduate course to bridge the gap between textbooks and scientific research. *CBE Life Sciences Education, 10*(1), 83-94.

Wolfensberger, M. (2004). Qualities honours students look for in faculty and courses. *Journal of the NCHC, 5*(2), 55-66.

Wolfensberger, M. (2008). Six habits of highly effective honors teachers. In L. Clark, & J. Zubizarreta (Eds.), *Inspiring exemplary teaching and learning: perspectives on teaching academically talented college students* (pp. 107-112). Lincoln, NE: NCHC.

Wolfensberger, M., De Jong, N., & Drayer, L. (2012). *Leren excelleren. Excellentieprogramma's in het HBO: een overzicht.* Groningen, Netherlands: Hanzehogeschool Groningen.

Wolfensberger, M.V.C., Van Eijl, P., & Pilot, A. (2004). Honours programmes as laboratories of innovation: A perspective from the Netherlands. *Journal of the NCHC, 5*(1), 115-142.

Wolfensberger, M., & Van Gorp, B. (2008). De Geocase. Talentontwikkeling door honours. *Onderzoek van Onderwijs, 37*(4), 82-87.

Yair, G. (2008). Can we administer the scholarship of teaching? Lessons from outstanding professors in higher education. *Higher Education, 55*, 447-459.

Zeegers, M., & Barron, D. (2009). Honours: a taken-for-granted pathway to research? *Higher Education, 57*, 567-575.

Ziegler, A., & Raul, T. (2000). Myth and reality: A review of empirical studies on giftedness. *High Ability Studies, 11*(2), 113-136.

Zubizarreta, J. (2008a). The learning portfolio for improvement and assessment of significant student learing. In L. Clark, & J. Zubizarreta (Eds.), *Inspiring exemplary teaching and learning: perspectives on teaching academically talented college students* (pp. 121-136). Lincoln, NE: NCHC.

Zubizarreta, J. (2008b). The importance of class size in teaching and learning for higher-level achievement. In L. Clark, & J. Zubizarreta (Eds.), *Inspiring exemplary teaching and learning: perspectives on teaching academically talented college student*, (pp. 147-161). Lincoln, NE: NCHC.

Zuckerman, M., Porac, J., Lathin, D., Smith, R., & Deci, E. L. (1978). On the importance of self-determination for intrinsically motivated behavior. *Personality and Social Psychology Bulletin, 4*(3), 443-446.

Summary

Introduction

From the start of honors education at the beginning of the 20th century, it has been assumed that honors education is appropriate for students with an intellectual hunger, greater maturity, higher motivation and higher level of abilities, because other content and 'different methods' for a specific peer group are involved (Pennock 1953). Furthermore, the key to a successful honors program is said "not [to be] the intelligence of the student or the subject matter of the course, but the attitude and approach of the instructor" (NCHC website). Rather than assigning extra work, these teachers are said to provide a 'different' focus – which entails risk-taking, additional challenges and transformative learning experiences for high-ability students – in order to elicit excellence (see for instance Clark and Zubizarreta 2008; Friedman and Jenkins-Friedman 1986; Robinson 1996). As a researcher who is active in the development of honors programs in Dutch higher education, this profile sparked my curiosity. I was eager to find out more about those 'different' teaching methods for honors courses compared to regular courses and to learn more about the teacher's attitude and teaching approach specific to honors courses.

Have characteristic forms of teaching and learning been developed within honors, like the name of a person written in his own handwriting, that are similar from one honors teacher to the next and across institutions? This query led to the overarching research question for this study: What are the key components of honors pedagogy and how do these translate into honors teaching practice?

The objective of this thesis was twofold. The first aim was to conceptualize and operationalize honors pedagogy using a dimensional approach. Thus, a theoretical and conceptual framework for honors pedagogy was developed. The second aim was to extend the state of knowledge on honors teaching by assessing this framework by means of empirical research.

The relevance of this study is also twofold: academic and practical. First, research on honors education within higher education is bounded and specifically limited with regard to systematically uncovering and describing honors pedagogies (Achterberg 2005; Cosgrove 2004; Holman 2007; Long and Lange 2002; Rinn and Plucker 2004; Rinn 2007; Shepherd and Shepherd 1996; Shushok 2002). That is why this inquiry has academic relevance. Secondly, my quest serves a practical purpose. Honors education is spreading around the globe and drawing more interest. In the Netherlands, for instance, most research universities and universities of applied sciences have started honors experiments and honors programs over the last ten to fifteen years (Wolfensberger, De Jong and Drayer 2012). This expansion has created a need for evidence-based teaching approaches that may be used in the training and coaching of honors teachers.

Overview of the subsequent chapters

The introductory chapter provides a brief overview of honors education around the globe, including the debate about equal access, admissions and assessment of honors. The prime focus of the present study is on honors teaching in the United States, in view of its longstanding tradition of honors education. However, to discover if lessons can be learned from the American practice for the European context, particularly for the Netherlands, a baseline comparison was made between American and Dutch honors education. Chapter 2 presents the theoretical framework used for the research design. Three different strands of academic work were explored: honors literature, publications about giftedness and studies about motivation, specifically self-determination theory. This literature survey brought to light three pillars of honors pedagogy: creating community, enhancing academic competence and offering freedom. Teaching strategies do not exist in isolation; they are influenced by the teachers' personal context. Therefore a brief survey of the literature on teachers' conceptions of honors teaching and learning in higher education, their motivation to work in higher education and their perception of (honors) students was carried out.

Chapter 3 presents the research design and explains the use of a mixed methodology, combining a questionnaire survey among honors teachers in the U.S.A. and the Netherlands with interviews conducted with American honors teachers. Chapter 4 investigates the American honors teachers' conceptions of (honors) teaching and learning, their motivation and their perceptions of (honors) students. Chapter 5 extends the scope of the previous chapter by examining the questionnaires about honors teaching and the interviews conducted with experienced honors teachers in the U.S.A. about their honors teaching approaches. Chapter 6 shows, on the basis of questionnaires, whether the three dimensions of teaching approaches are also applicable to honors teachers in the Netherlands and includes a systematic comparison with the core findings from the American setting. Chapter 7 presents the conclusions and a discussion as well as some comments on the limitations of the study and avenues for further research.

Issues addressed in this thesis

Conceptual and theoretical foundation for honors pedagogies; Pillars of Honors Pedagogy

First, the author examined the literature on honors education focusing on higher education. There is a substantial body of well documented good practices and essays, and the number of empirically based studies is growing. However, literature with a focus on faculty members or their teaching is scanty (e.g., Achterberg 2005; Cosgrove 2004; Holman and Banning 2012; Rinn and Plucker 2004). Many honors studies are descriptive and consist of single-institution research. Through an inductive literature survey, three commonalities were found concerning three dimensions of teaching approaches within honors education: (1) the ability to create a sense of community; (2) enhancing academic competence; and (3) the power to offer students an effective degree of freedom.

Secondly, the author drew on the insights from scholarship on the education of gifted students. That is a field where research and its theoretical underpinning have been called rigorous by some (cf. Heller et al. 2002). Research has been done on teachers and teaching approaches (Chan 2011; Dai, Swanson and Cheng 2011; Heller et al. 2002; Leikin 2011; Ziegler and Raul 2000).

Various authors point out that gifted students, as a group, show different characteristics compared to regular students in the same age range and therefore need distinct learning opportunities (Croft 2003; Colangelo and Davis 2003; Gagné 1995; Karnes and Bean 2001; Leikin 2011; Rogers 2007; Park and Oliver 2009; Olszewski-Kubilius 2003; Sternberg and Davidson 2005). The field of giftedness research offers empirical evidence for the effectiveness of the three teaching approaches, although most studies on giftedness, including those on programming for and the development of giftedness, concentrate primarily on children below the age of 18, so on pre-university contexts (e.g., Colangelo and Davis 2003; Heller et al. 2002, Sternberg 2002) .

Thirdly, the author turned to motivational theories, selecting self-determination theory (Ryan and Deci 2000) as a guiding framework. The motivational theories offered further validation of the importance of the three dimensions of honors approaches (creating community, enhancing academic competence and offering freedom). Self-determination theory has proven useful in explaining the variation in students' learning strategies, performance and persistence (Vansteenkiste, Lens and Deci 2006). This theory indicates that the degree to which teachers support students' motivation is positively associated with strong student performance (Eccles and Wigfield 2002; Ryan and Deci 2000; Sansone and Harackiewicz 2000). According to self-determination theory, three basic psychological needs should be supported: relatedness, competence and autonomy. If a student's need in all three areas is not satisfied, that individual's self-motivation, self-determination and well-being will become problematic (see, for example, Ryan and Deci 2000). Relatedness, which concerns feeling connected with significant others, resonates with a notion put forth in this thesis, namely a 'sense of community'. The need for competence – defined as the need to increase one's mastery and to experience satisfaction in exercising and extending one's capabilities – echoes a dimension at the core of this thesis, namely 'enhancing academic competence'. Feelings of competence, however, will not enhance one's intrinsic motivation unless the students perceive their educational context as supportive of autonomy, for instance by being allowed more space to self-organize their studies or choose their subject (Levesque et al. 2004). Offering freedom, the third dimension in this thesis, resonates with autonomy-supportive teaching approaches. However, self-determination theory was not specially developed with education or honors teaching in mind. Little is known about the impact of relatedness in higher education (Martens and Boekaerts 2007) or about the effects of competence on the satisfaction of needs (Levesque et al. 2004).

In line with the above, it is expected that teachers take a different approach for honors courses than for regular courses. The research question was refined to read as follows:

To what extent do honors teachers approach their teaching differently – with regard to creating community, enhancing academic competence and offering freedom – with honors students compared to regular students, and what are the beliefs, attitudes and expectations on which they base such differences in their approach?

Research design

This study combines questionnaires circulated among American and Dutch honors teachers with interviews held with American honors teachers. Given the longstanding honors tradition in the U.S.A., the interviews were conducted only with American honors teachers in order to draw lessons from the American practice for European honors education. In this context it is important to know to what extent American and Dutch honors teachers have similar or different approaches and dispositions in their honors teaching. The requisite baseline comparison was facilitated by the questionnaires.

The design of the survey, the set-up of the actual questionnaires and the methods used for the analysis of the resulting data are described in Chapter 3. There, similar aspects are also described for the interviews conducted among American honors teachers. Data collection in the U.S.A. took place in 2006 during an annual conference of the National Collegiate Honors Council. In all, 127 honors teachers filled in the questionnaire, and 30 interviews were conducted with American honors teachers. In total, we know that at least 75 American higher educational institutions are represented in this study. In the Netherlands, data collection took place in 2007. At that time, eleven research universities offered honors programs (Van Eijl et al. 2003; Van Eijl, Wientjes, Wolfensberger and Pilot 2005). All honors teachers (N = 768) involved in those honors programs received a digital questionnaire; 313 teachers returned it completed. It should be noted that universities of applied sciences were not included in the survey as they did not yet have fully established honors programs at that time (Groothengel & Van Eijl 2008).

When teachers employ their teaching strategies, they do so on the basis of an underlying structure for teaching and learning. This implicit structure has been described by Shulman (2005b) as a moral dimension that comprises a set of beliefs about attitudes, values and dispositions. Chapter 4 explores the American honors teachers' conceptions of teaching and learning in higher education, their motivation to teach honors and their perceptions of students. The use of mixed methods allowed the author to present factual conclusions but also to elaborate in detail and offer an interpretation. Knowledge on those issues could provide better understanding and a more differentiated view of what exactly constitutes honors pedagogy. American honors teachers are oriented towards the learning of students. They see honors education as a setting for outstanding performance by a select group of students, as a setting that allows for educational innovations. Honors teachers show high intrinsic motivation and self-determination. They ascribe their orientation – at least partially – to certain conditions: the pleasure and fun of working with able and motivated students; the possibility to go deeper into their academic subject; and the challenges that come with teaching honors students. They perceive honors students as engaged and dedicated to learning and as strong communicators, eager to converse. They also consider honors students to be more advanced than their peers, both academically and personally. The teachers may be concerned about honors students being too competitive and over-committed. Some of the most important qualities they see in honors students are initiative, curiosity and creativity. The greatest differences between their honors students and their regular students lie in remaining on schedule with coursework (which is more important for regular students) and to creativity and a readiness to take risk (which is more important for honors students).

American honors teachers: approaches in honors education

Teachers make a clear distinction between honors teaching and regular teaching. They perceive the three approaches – namely creating community, enhancing academic competence and offering freedom – as the pillars of honors pedagogies. Within honors, they put more emphasis on creating community and on offering bounded freedom as means to academic growth and personal development. The empirical analysis suggests that teachers consider structured teaching as more suitable for regular classes. And whereas enhancing academic competence plays a pivotal role in both types of education, the teachers clearly differentiate between the two in the way this is accomplished. For instance, higher-level learning, research activities and making interdisciplinary links are seen as more appropriate in honors classes.

In sum, while it is important to challenge all students, the way to do so differs for honors and regular students. Interactive teaching, research teaching and interdisciplinary teaching are also seen as appropriate for honors. In that setting, these strategies are viewed as means to enhance academic competence. Teachers offer their honors students all kinds of opportunities to take initiative. Many consider offering freedom to honors students as a precondition for student engagement.

The interviews allow us to elaborate in more detail. We distilled three themes that capture the teaching strategies related to the approach of creating community. The first is to create, together with the students, a strong social network by showing genuine interest in students and supportive feedback from both teachers and peers. The second is to offer students ample opportunity to take initiative so they can develop their leadership skills. And the third is to coach students in improving their intellectual and personal development.

In order to enhance academic competence, honors teachers say they employ various strategies. First, they stimulate critical, independent and creative thinking and reach out for high-quality products. Secondly, they foster a research attitude and academic depth. And thirdly, they set challenging learning tasks that need a high level of engagement.

Offering freedom is often seen as an inherent means to achieve a goal. This goal may be involvement, commitment or motivation, each of which in turn is necessary to obtain outstanding performance. Teachers indicate that they tune in to students' personal interests and take students' initiatives seriously, coaching them to reflect while making decisions and creating an independent learning strategy. Secondly, they allow students to make choices in line with their personal academic interests. And thirdly, they grant students responsibility for their learning, while offering them their trust.

Dutch and American honors teachers fully agree that honors education should be focused on evoking excellence. Honors teachers in the Netherlands consider the following teaching strategies as effective for honors teaching: inviting students to actively participate; making connections with other areas of study; juxtaposing different points of view; challenging students; inspiring students; and giving students room to make their own choices. For regular classes the Dutch teachers make a somewhat different list: offering well-organized subject matter; formulating clear and shared goals for the class; inviting students to actively participate; explaining well; giving useful feedback; and knowing a subject well. All three teaching approaches – creating community, enhancing academic competence and offering freedom – are perceived as important within honors education. Compared to regular education, the most striking difference is that offering freedom is seen as important for honors classes while not for regular classes. Structure is important for regular classes while it is rarely mentioned for honors education. Furthermore, enhancing academic competence is important for both regular and honors education.

There are some striking similarities between Dutch and American honors teachers with regard to teaching approaches and strategies. For honors teaching, both groups give priority to the same strategies. With regard to the personal qualities they deem essential for honors teaching, both groups give priority to the teachers' ability to challenge and inspire students, giving students room for their own choices and being prepared to deviate from established teaching methods. For regular classes, both groups acknowledge the overriding importance of formulating clear goals and offering well-organized subject matter. They also agree on which personal qualities are essential for teaching regular classes: to explain well; be clear about expectations; know the subject well; and give useful feedback.

Furthermore, both groups are primarily oriented towards student learning. However, Dutch honors teachers assign more importance to grading and competition as incentives to learn than their American colleagues. The latter prefer to cultivate the innovative and experimental (involving risk) potential of honors teaching. While the intrinsic motivation of the Dutch teachers may be high, it is significantly lower than the remarkably high level measured among American honors teachers.

Teachers' perceptions and expectations of students can influence their approaches to teaching. It is salient that the Dutch and American honors teachers give priority to the same five qualities for honors students (out of our list of fifteen options) but in a different order: they should be enterprising in the sense of taking initiative; be intellectually curious; think creatively; be motivated for their courses; and invest effort in their studies. What distinguishes honors students most from regular students, in terms of the qualities considered important by all teachers, is the combination of creativity and initiative. For the American honors students, this pair is supplemented by taking risks in the academic career; for the Dutch honors students, the third quality is a passion for research.

It is interesting to consider the major differences between American and Dutch honors teachers in the qualities they look for in honors students. The American teachers attach greater importance to risk-taking, involvement in the academic community and stimulating fellow students within the study program. Dutch honors teachers place significantly more emphasis on obtaining good grades and having a passion for research, as key qualities of an honors student, than their American colleagues. This is in line with another outcome: that Dutch honors teachers consider the teaching approach of enhancing academic competence as more central to honors than their American colleagues.

Teaching for excellence

This study reveals the three pillars of an honors pedagogy. Teachers from the United States and the Netherlands perceive the following teaching approaches as appropriate for honors education: creating community, enhancing academic competence and offering freedom.

The teaching strategies related to this pedagogy are explored, and a different cluster is presented for each approach.

Three clusters of teaching behavior are related to creating community: 1) fostering social relatedness between the teacher and honors students and among honors students through interaction; 2) creating a positive and supportive atmosphere through encouragement; 3) becoming part of the community through interest and commitment. According to additional information from the interviews, teachers believe that institutional support for honors is needed to be able to create an honors community.

Three clusters of teaching strategies are related to enhancing academic competence: 1) offering an academic and societal context and stimulating connective thinking by tackling issues from an interdisciplinary angle; 2) stimulating analytical thinking and research skills by taking part in research; 3) presenting a quantitative and qualitative challenge, for instance by giving challenging assignments.

In the interviews, the teachers stressed the importance of fostering creative, critical and independent thinking for honors students.

Finally, three clusters of teaching strategies are related to offering freedom: 1) teaching behavior that offers space for students' questions, choices and initiatives, like allowing self-regulation; 2) stimulating enthusiasm and experimentation by surprising the students; 3) encouraging students to behave professionally (in teaching, learning and research), for instance through a master – apprentice relationship.

In the interviews, teachers said that offering freedom is possible thanks to the mutual trust and respect. Giving responsibility to students, coaching them to reflect, and presuming that they will take ownership of their learning are strategies related to offering freedom. Teachers see offering freedom as a means to foster student involvement and outstanding performance.

This study has some limitations. The theoretical framework could have been strengthened by including a more diverse range of learning theories in the literature review. In this regard, it is considered reassuring that most of the points made by the teachers during the interviews reflect the core importance of the three teaching approaches, although these were not explicitly introduced during the interviews. Another limitation of the research is the missing voice of honors and regular students. It is advisable to do research among students to reveal their perceptions of honors and regular education. Furthermore, studies of actual teaching practices would obviously enrich the picture.

Creating community, enhancing academic competence and offering freedom are links in a complex chain of approaches. These links are self-reinforcing because they create favorable results such as high-quality articles, good evaluations and, hopefully, happy students. As a teacher, you need community to know your students. And only if you know your students can you focus on higher-order thinking tasks, conversations and reflection; only then can a teacher embrace the Vygotskain notion of the zone of proximal development. When offered freedom and confidence, students will speak out, which in turn will create community. While discovering who they are, and by expressing what they want, they will study because they want to. That motivation will give them the fuel to strive for outstanding academic performance.

Samenvatting (Summary in Dutch)

Deze studie gaat over de didactiek die ten grondslag ligt aan honoursonderwijs. Het creëren van gemeenschap, het stimuleren van academische competenties en het bieden van vrijheid zijn doceerbenaderingen die zowel Amerikaanse als Nederlandse docenten als essentieel ervaren binnen hun honoursonderwijs.

In hoofdstuk 1 is beschreven dat honoursonderwijs het volledig potentieel wil aanspreken van studenten. Honoursonderwijs is speciaal ontworpen voor getalenteerde en gemotiveerde studenten in het hoger onderwijs die meer willen en kunnen dan het reguliere onderwijs hen kan bieden. Het aanbod binnen honoursonderwijs is gericht op intellectuele ontwikkeling die verbonden is met professionele en persoonlijke groei. Honoursonderwijs verschilt met regulier onderwijs niet zozeer doordat het veelomvattender is, maar veeleer doordat het accent anders ligt. De honoursdocent, als katalysator van talentontwikkeling, speelt daarbij een belangrijke rol. Wat zijn de hoofdpijlers van de honoursdidactiek en hoe zijn deze te vertalen naar de honours onderwijs praktijk? Dit is de vraag die centraal staat in deze studie. Het doel van de studie is tweeledig. In de eerste plaats wil het een theoretisch en conceptueel raamwerk bieden voor het doceren in honoursonderwijs. Ten tweede voorziet deze studie in een empirische onderbouwing van dit raamwerk, gebaseerd op gehouden enquêtes onder en interviews met honoursdocenten in de Verenigde Staten en in Nederland. De studie wil met dit conceptuele raamwerk de kennis over honoursdidactiek vergroten.

Er blijkt, zoals beschreven in hoofdstuk 2, verrassend weinig onderzoeksliteratuur te bestaan over honoursonderwijs, al komt daar sinds deze eeuw wel verandering in. Honoursonderwijs heeft zich sinds de jaren twintig van de vorige eeuw verspreid, eerst vooral in Amerika en na de Tweede Wereldoorlog ook daarbuiten. Er is sinds die tijd veel geschreven over honoursonderwijs, zeker ook in publicaties van de Amerikaanse National Collegiate Honours Council. Dit betreft vooral casusbeschrijvingen waarbij de focus ligt op honoursstudenten. Toch is uit deze literatuur een beeld gerezen van succesvolle en veel gebruikte onderwijsbenaderingen. De steeds terugkerende sleutelbegrippen hierbinnen zijn gemeenschap, academische competenties en vrijheid. Nader literatuuronderzoek binnen het 'gifted and talented' domein, dat zich met name richt op zeer jonge kinderen tot leerlingen aan het einde van de middelbare school, laat zien dat voor de pre-universitaire periode dezelfde drie benaderingen belangrijk zijn voor het leerproces van begaafde jonge mensen. Wanneer het gaat om het komen tot uitmuntende prestaties en (intellectuele) groei worden dezelfde sleutelbegrippen in het onderwijs cruciaal genoemd. Onderzoek in het veld van de motivatie en in het bijzonder de 'self determination theory' ondersteunt deze bevindingen. Deze motivatiestudies laten zien dat het nodig is om drie specifieke behoeften, namelijk sociale verbondenheid, competentie en autonomie, te ondersteunen. Dit zorgt er voor dat mensen intrinsiek gemotiveerd zijn, zich goed voelen en goed kunnen presteren.

Ondanks dat er nog niet veel over het specifieke onderwerp van honoursdidactiek is geschreven, levert de literatuurverkenning wel belangrijke aanknopingspunten op. Die zijn te vertalen naar drie pijlers voor honoursdidactiek: het creëren van gemeenschap, het stimuleren van academische competenties en het bieden van vrijheid. Honoursdidactiek in de vorm van deze pijlers leidt echter niet tot kant-en-klare doceerstrategieën. Daarvoor zijn ook andere aspecten van belang, zoals wat docenten belangrijk vinden in het onderwijs, hoe ze tegen hun studenten aankijken en of ze gemotiveerd zijn om les te geven. Dit speelt allemaal mee in hun percepties en gedrag en zijn daarom meegenomen in deze studie.

De drie dimensies, 'creëren van community', 'stimuleren van academische competenties' en 'bieden van vrijheid' vormen de basis van het conceptuele raamwerk en voor de verdere studie naar de strategieën die ervaren docenten hanteren in hun honoursonderwijs. Zoals genoemd is er beperkt literatuur over honoursdidactiek beschikbaar, wat deze studie academisch relevant maakt. Het aantal honoursstudenten is groeiend in de VS en ook in Europa, in het bijzonder in Nederland, waardoor de maatschappelijke behoefte aan gefundeerde kennis over honoursdidactiek toeneemt.

Als onderzoeker die ook betrokken is bij honoursontwikkelingen in het Nederlandse hoger onderwijs, was de auteur geïnteresseerd welke lessen geleerd kunnen worden van de Amerikaanse honourspraktijk. In die context is het belangrijk om te weten of Amerikaanse en Nederlandse honoursdocenten hun honoursonderwijs gelijk of juist anders benaderen. Deze kennis is ook bruikbaar bij de verdere ontwikkeling van docentenprofessionalisering op het gebied van honoursonderwijs. Er is nog maar een beperkt aanbod aan professionaliseringstrajecten die zich specifiek richten op honoursonderwijs waarbij het gaat om doceren om te excelleren. Deze studie wil daarom ook handvatten voor deze professionaliseringstrajecten bieden.

Zou het geschetste theoretisch raamwerk van drie doceerbenaderingen resoneren met gerelateerde doceerstrategieën uit de honoursonderwijspraktijk van ervaren honoursdocenten? Om dat te onderzoeken is een vragenlijst en een interviewschema opgesteld. Deze mix van methoden geeft de mogelijkheid van generaliseerbaarheid en tegelijkertijd van verdieping, zoals verder uitgewerkt in hoofdstuk 3. De auteur wilde inzicht in meningen en ervaringen van ervaren honoursdocenten van verschillende hoger onderwijsinstellingen in Amerika omdat daar immers een lange honourstraditie bestaat. De interviews zijn daarom alleen in Amerika afgenomen en bieden meer details, diepte en aanvullingen doordat niet direct naar de drie doceerbenaderingen is gevraagd. In Nederland zijn wel dezelfde enquêtes afgenomen als in Amerika om zo een vergelijking mogelijk te maken tussen de twee landen wat betreft de doceerstrategieën en houding die docenten rapporteren in honours- en regulier onderwijs.

De enquête is afgenomen tijdens de jaarlijkse conferentie van de National Collegiate Honours Council in 2006 te Philadelphia, wat 127 bruikbare vragenlijsten opleverde. Er zijn ook interviews met 30 ervaren Amerikaanse honoursdocenten – inclusief focusgroepen – gehouden. Docenten van ten minste 75 Amerikaanse hoger onderwijsinstellingen zijn betrokken bij het onderzoek.

In 2006 waren, voor zover bekend, 768 docenten in Nederland actief in honoursonderwijs. Zij hebben allen een vragenlijst per mail toegezonden gekregen, wat 313 bruikbare vragenlijsten opleverde vanuit alle 11 universiteiten waar honoursprogramma's of colleges werden aangeboden. Honoursdocenten werkzaam in het HBO zijn niet betrokken in dit onderzoek omdat daar toen nog nauwelijks honoursprogramma's bestonden.

De enquêtes en de interviews zijn geanalyseerd om antwoord te kunnen geven op de onderzoeksvraag hoe honoursdocenten zeggen te doceren in hun honoursonderwijs – en of de aanpak verschilt met de wijze waarop zij hun reguliere studenten benaderen? Daarbij wordt specifiek ingegaan op de rol van de drie pijlers van honoursonderwijs: het creëren van gemeenschap, het stimuleren van academische competenties en het bieden van vrijheid, alsmede op de vraag of docenten deze pijlers herkennen en toepassen. De studie richt zich verder op de onderwijsvisie en beleving van honoursonderwijs door honoursdocenten, hun motivatie om les te geven en hun percepties van honoursstudenten. Het gaat dus om gerapporteerde strategieën - en niet om het ter plekke observeren van honoursonderwijs - omdat zo een beeld gekregen wordt van wat van docent tot docent en van instelling tot instelling belangrijk wordt gevonden binnen het honoursonderwijs.

Hoofdstuk 4 schetst een beeld van de Amerikaanse honoursdocent. De Amerikaanse honoursdocent gelooft dat uitmuntende prestaties een belangrijk onderdeel zijn van het honoursonderwijs, maar hecht meer belang aan de weg daarnaartoe. Honoursdocenten zijn dus meer gericht op het leerproces van de student dan op de uitkomsten. De docenten zeggen in de interviews dat een aparte groep voor honoursonderwijs belangrijk is; deze groepsvorming is stimulerend voor zowel de studenten onderling als voor de docenten die lesgeven. Honoursonderwijs heeft volgens de docenten een goede naam waardoor ze zich er graag aan verbinden. De honoursdocenten zijn - zoals blijkt uit zowel de enquêteresultaten als uit de interviews- zeer gemotiveerd om honoursonderwijs te geven. Ze zijn enthousiast door de inhoudelijke klik die ze kunnen hebben met studenten. Het geeft hen plezier en voldoening om studenten te helpen hun volle potentieel te ontwikkelen. Honoursonderwijs daagt de docenten op verschillende vlakken uit en dat doet hen, ondanks het extra harde werken dat ook nodig is, goed.

Ondernemendheid, nieuwsgierigheid en creativiteit zijn kwaliteiten die Amerikaanse honoursdocenten belangrijk vinden voor hun honoursstudenten. Belangrijke kwaliteiten voor hun reguliere studenten zijn motivatie voor de cursus, nieuwsgierigheid en de bereidheid tijd in de cursus te stoppen. Hun honoursstudenten duiden ze in de interviews verder nog als betrokken, hardwerkend en altijd in voor een inhoudelijk gesprek . Docenten zeggen dat ze het belangrijk vinden dat hun honoursstudenten durven te leren, en bijvoorbeeld het risico aangaan van een nieuw type opdracht. Ze zien hierbij ook dat dit lastig kan zijn voor honoursstudenten die veel waarde kunnen hechten aan cijfers en behoorlijk competitief kunnen zijn.

Hoofdstuk 4 laat dus verschillen zien in de beelden die Amerikaanse docenten hebben van zowel honoursstudenten als van reguliere studenten. Hoofdstuk 5 gaat hierop door en toont aan dat de doceerstrategieën binnen het honoursonderwijs verschillen van de strategieën die docenten belangrijk vinden in het reguliere onderwijs. Amerikaanse honoursdocenten vinden het belangrijk om honoursstudenten uit te dagen, hen ruimte te bieden voor eigen keuzes en hen te leren interdisciplinaire connecties te maken. Voor hun reguliere studenten vinden de docenten het belangrijker om het lesaanbod duidelijk te organiseren door structuur te bieden en heldere doelen te formuleren. De resultaten laten ook zien dat de docenten bereid zijn om binnen honours af te wijken van traditionele onderwijsmethoden en studenten uitnodigen actief te participeren. Binnen het reguliere onderwijs vinden de docenten het belangrijk dat ze duidelijk zijn over wat ze verwachten van hun reguliere studenten, dat ze nuttige feedback en duidelijke uitleg geven en dat ze hun reguliere studenten uitdagen.

De docenten vertellen in de interviews wat ze doen om gemeenschap te creëren. Ze bieden bijvoorbeeld een student de mogelijkheid om initiatief te tonen waardoor deze een bepaalde rol kan vervullen binnen de gemeenschap en persoonlijk leiderschap kan ontwikkelen. Academische competenties stimuleren de docenten onder andere door het geven van uitdagende leertaken om hun studenten kritisch en creatief te leren denken. Daarnaast is het ontwikkelen van onderzoeksvaardigheden ook een manier om academische competenties te stimuleren. Het geven van vrijheid aan studenten betekent onder andere het overdragen van verantwoordelijkheden aan studenten, bijvoorbeeld in hun eigen keuzes in cursusthema's, opdrachten en leerstrategieën. Docenten zeggen dat ze de initiatieven en interesses van studenten ondersteunen. De docenten gaan daarbij uit van een 'gebonden vrijheid' waarbij de docent monitort welke vrijheid de student nodig heeft of aankan.

Hoofdstuk 5 laat zien dat de Amerikaanse honoursdocenten het binnen het honoursonderwijs belangrijk vinden om gemeenschap te creëren, academische competenties te stimuleren en vrijheid aan te bieden. Vooral dit laatste aspect krijgt volgens de Amerikaans honoursdocenten meer nadruk in het honoursonderwijs vergeleken met het reguliere onderwijs. Docenten vinden het belangrijk dat in het reguliere onderwijs structuur wordt aangeboden, terwijl dat voor het honoursonderwijs nauwelijks wordt genoemd.

Hoofdstuk 6 bespreekt de doceerbenaderingen van de Nederlandse honoursdocenten om deze vervolgens te vergelijken met die van de Amerikanen. Dit is mogelijk doordat in de VS en in Nederland dezelfde vragenlijst is gebruikt. Nederlandse honoursdocenten zijn, net als de Amerikaanse, gemotiveerd om te doceren in honoursonderwijs. Nederlandse honoursdocenten vinden ook dat honoursonderwijs excellentie moet bevorderen en geloven dat het leerproces van de student daarbij centraal moet staan. De Nederlandse docenten denken ook dat specifieke kwaliteiten belangrijk zijn voor honoursstudenten: initiatief tonen, nieuwsgierig zijn, creatief en gemotiveerd zijn en inzet tonen voor hun studie. Toch zijn er wel verschillen tussen de percepties van de Nederlandse en de Amerikaanse docenten. Zo vinden de Nederlandse docenten motivatie en inzet significant belangrijker voor hun honoursstudenten. Daarnaast vinden Nederlandse honoursdocenten het behalen van goede cijfers en een passie voor onderzoek hebben belangrijker voor hun honoursstudenten dan dat de Amerikaanse docenten dat vinden. De Amerikaanse docenten hechten er significant meer waarde aan dat hun honoursstudenten risico's durven te nemen en betrokken zijn bij de academische gemeenschap en bij hun medestudenten. Uit de interviews blijkt dat Amerikaanse docenten het uitvoeren van originele opdrachten, of nieuwe toetsvormen ook als een risico zien voor studenten.

Het is opvallend hoe gelijksoortig de Nederlandse en Amerikaanse honoursdocenten zeggen hun honoursonderwijs te benaderen. Ook hun keuzes voor doceerstrategieën die ze geschikt vinden voor hun reguliere onderwijs zijn eenduidig. Toch zijn er ook verschillen. De Amerikanen zijn in de vragenlijst over de hele linie meer uitgesproken: ze geven hogere scores op de Likertschalen en ze lijken wat eensgezinder door het vaker maken van dezelfde keuzes. Verder vinden de Amerikanen het geven van vrijheid passender dan dat de Nederlandse docenten dat vinden; de Nederlanders lijken meer te hechten aan het stimuleren van academische competenties dan de Amerikaanse docenten. Het zijn echter accentverschillen in de keuzes voor doceerstrategieën.

Vergeleken met het gestructureerde reguliere onderwijs is voor zowel de Nederlanders als voor de Amerikanen het geven van vrijheid binnen hun honoursonderwijs van belang. Het stimuleren van academische competenties is voor zowel het honours- als voor het reguliere onderwijs belangrijk, al zijn de honoursdoceerstrategieën om dat te bereiken anders, bijvoorbeeld door meer aandacht voor fundamentele kennis en interdisciplinariteit binnen het honours onderwijs.

In hoofdstuk 7 worden de doceerstrategieën geclusterd weergegeven bij de drie pijlers van de honoursdidactiek: creëren van gemeenschap, stimuleren van academische competenties en bieden van vrijheid. Zo passen bij het creëren van gemeenschap drie clusters van strategieën, namelijk doceergedrag:

- dat sociale verbondenheid vormt tussen docent en honoursstudenten en tussen de honoursstudenten onderling, zoals interactie.
- dat een positieve en ondersteunende sfeer creëert, zoals aanmoediging.
- waarmee de docent zichzelf binnen de honoursgemeenschap plaatst, zoals interesse en betrokkenheid.

Een aanvulling vanuit de interviews is het aanbieden van mogelijkheden aan studenten om taken te vervullen, onder andere ten dienste van de gemeenschap. Ook kwam uit de interviews het belang van institutionele ondersteuning van de honoursgemeenschap naar voren.

Drie clusters van doceerstrategieën zijn gerelateerd aan het stimuleren van academische competenties, namelijk doceergedrag dat:

- academische en maatschappelijke context aanbiedt en verbindend denken stimuleert, zoals een interdisciplinaire benadering van vraagstukken.
- analytisch denken en de onderzoeksvaardigheid van studenten bevordert, zoals studenten laten participeren in onderzoek.
- kwalitatieve en kwantitatieve uitdaging creëert, zoals het geven van uitdagende opdrachten.

Uit de interviews komt naar voren dat docenten veel belang hechten aan stimulerende strategieën die creatief, kritisch en zelfstandig denken bevorderen.

194

Drie clusters van strategieën tenslotte zijn gerelateerd aan het geven van vrijheid, namelijk doceergedrag dat:

- ruimte geeft aan de vragen, keuzes en initiatieven van studenten, zoals het toestaan van zelfregulatie.
- opgetogenheid en experimenteren stimuleert, zoals het verrassen van studenten.
- studenten leert zich professioneel te gedragen in onderzoek en onderwijs, zoals in een meester-gezelrelatie.

Uit de interviews komt naar voren dat volgens de docenten deze vrijheid kan bestaan dankzij onderling en wederzijds vertrouwen en respect. Het geven van verantwoordelijkheid, het stimuleren van eigenaarschap en leren reflecteren zijn eveneens onderdeel van een 'gebonden' vrijheid. Docenten spreken ook over het geven van vrijheid als een middel om studentbetrokkenheid te vergroten en goede prestaties te verkrijgen.

De studie kent beperkingen. Zo had het theoretische raamwerk verder versterkt kunnen worden door andere leertheorieën bij de literatuurstudie te betrekken. Nu zijn deze drie doceerbenaderingen misschien overbelicht en andere onderbelicht. Het feit dat docenten echter tijdens de interviews spontaan aansloten bij de drie doceerbenaderingen geeft het kernbelang van deze benaderingen aan. Er is voor gekozen om verschillende type vragen op te nemen in de enquête, zoals stellingen en meerkeuzevragen, waardoor een breder inzicht gekregen kon worden. Hierdoor werd echter het maken van schalen beperkt. En deze studie kent beperkingen in het perspectief omdat het gaat over percepties van docenten, en observaties of studentenperspectief hier dus niet bij betrokken zijn.

De bevindingen van dit proefschrift geven aanleiding om ook andere onderzoekswegen te verkennen. Zo kan de uitvoerbaarheid van de hier voorgestelde benaderingen verkend worden door observaties te doen tijdens activiteiten binnen honours- en regulier onderwijs. Ook is het interessant om te verkennen hoe studenten de voorgestelde honoursdidactiek percipiëren. Onderzoek naar vergelijkingen tussen honours alumni en reguliere alumni zou kunnen bijdragen aan kennis over de effectiviteit van honoursonderwijs.

Drie pijlers van de honoursdidactiek zijn met deze studie geopenbaard: het creëren van gemeenschap, het stimuleren van academische competenties en het bieden van vrijheid. De bevindingen laten zien dat deze honoursdidactiek wordt herkend door honoursdocenten die werkzaam zijn aan een diversiteit van verschillende hoger onderwijsinstellingen verspreid over Amerika en door honoursdocenten werkzaam op Nederlandse universiteiten. Het verdient aanbeveling deze inzichten te gebruiken bij honours docentenprofessionalisering en verder te bouwen aan dit theoretische en conceptuele raamwerk en daarbij ook andere onderzoekswegen in te slaan en op zoek te gaan naar nieuwe perspectieven.

Appendix 1 - Questionnaire

 **Universiteit Utrecht**

IVLOS
Heidelberglaan 8
3584 CS Utrecht

| Mark a box like this: | O O O O O | If possible fill in this form using a ballpoint pen! Do not use red ink. |
| To make a correction: | O O O O O | This form will be processed by machine. |

This research is about teaching within honors. The results of this questionnaire are used for a PhD research in the Netherlands. Answering all questions will take about 15 minutes. Thank you for your effort. You can drop your completed questionnaire into a box at the NCHC table. If you have any questions or remarks about this questionnaire you can contact me at m.wolfensberger@geo.uu.nl

PART 1: FACTUAL COMPONENTS 1 – 15

1 How would you characterize the Honors Program or College in which you participate?
O University Honors Program
O Disciplinary Honors Program organized by a department or faculty
O An Honors College
O Other, namely: _____

_____

_____

2 How are you involved in the Honors Program? (multiple answers possible)
O Teacher of a course
O Coordinator of an Honors Program or Honors College
O Supervisor of research of honors students
O Supervisor of other activities such as: _____
O Other, namely: _____

_____

_____

3 What are the average group sizes of your *honors* courses? (multiple answers possible)
Group sizes honors classes
O 1-5
O 6-10
O 11-25
O 26-50
O 51-100
O More than 100
O Does not apply

4 And what are the average group sizes of your *regular* courses? (multiple answers possible)
Group sizes regular classes
O 1-5
O 6-10
O 11-25
O 26-50
O 51-100
O More than 100
O Does not apply

5 In which department are you currently engaged as a teacher?
O Fine Arts
O Humanities
O Medicine
O Interdisciplinary
O Science, Math & Technology
O Social Science
O Other, namely: _____

6 How many years of experience do you have with teaching *honors* education?
O 0-2 years
O 3-10 years
O 11 years and longer

7 How many years of experience do you have with teaching *regular* education?
O 0-2 years
O 3-10 years
O 11 years and longer

8 Are you a man or a woman?
- ○ man
- ○ woman

9 What is your age?
- ○ 20-30
- ○ 31-40
- ○ 41-50
- ○ 51-60
- ○ Older than 60

10 Are you supported in teaching your honors education? (multiple answers possible)
- ○ Yes, by the feedback of my colleagues
- ○ Yes, by NCHC meetings
- ○ Yes, by practices
- ○ Yes, other, namely: _____
- ○ No

11 Have you been active in the honors program during the last two years? If not, go to question 13.
- ○ Yes
- ○ No

12 Have you assessed honors students during the last two years?
- ○ Yes
- ○ No

13 How often do students ask questions during your *honors* classes, respectively?
- ○ Never
- ○ Now and then
- ○ Now and then Often
- ○ Often
- ○ Really often

14 How often do students ask questions during your *regular* classes, respectively?
- ○ Never
- ○ Now and then
- ○ Now and then Often
- ○ Often
- ○ Really often

15 Report of results. We will send you a summary of the results of this study if you like.
If so, please e-mail me or provide your e-mail address:
_____
_____

16-43

We ask for your opinion about several propositions. Below you will find a number of propositions. We would like to know your opinion about them. Mark the box that reflects your opinion the best. It is not important how other people think about it, but what your own opinion is. Do not think too long about each question. You should give the answer that first comes to your mind.
Scale: 1= completely disagree, 2= disagree, 3= not disagree and not agree, 4= agree, 5= completely agree.

	1	2	3	4	5
16 I teach my honors students more fundamental content knowledge than my regular students.	O	O	O	O	O
17 I teach my honors students more often than my regular students how they can apply their knowledge in real situations.	O	O	O	O	O
18 I find it more important that honors students, rather than regular students, are intensively involved in research early in their education.	O	O	O	O	O
19 My approach to honors education has more active teaching and learning methods than my approaches in regular class.	O	O	O	O	O
20 I teach my honors students more about different points of view than I teach my regular students.	O	O	O	O	O
21 I assess students in the Honors Program differently than I assess students in the regular program.	O	O	O	O	O
22 I consider 'peer feedback' to be more important in regular education than in honors education.	O	O	O	O	O
23 My methods to evaluate honors education are different from my methods to evaluate regular education.	O	O	O	O	O
24 I think that taking risks should be at the centre of honors education.	O	O	O	O	O
25 I think that honors education should be focused on evoking excellence.	O	O	O	O	O
26 My relation with honors students is equal to my relation with regular students.	O	O	O	O	O
27 I find it hard to teach students smarter than me.	O	O	O	O	O
28 The personal interest of a student plays a bigger role in my honors education than it does in my regular eduation.	O	O	O	O	O
29 I assign more challenging assignments to honors students than to regular students.	O	O	O	O	O
30 I assign more time consuming assignments to honors students than to regular students.	O	O	O	O	O
31 I give honors students more freedom (with respect to choosing topics and time-management) than regular students.	O	O	O	O	O
32 Honors education is more focused on the development of talent than my regular education.	O	O	O	O	O
33 I know all my honors students by name.	O	O	O	O	O
34 I know all my regular students by name.	O	O	O	O	O
35 I give feedback to my honors students as if they are junior colleagues.	O	O	O	O	O
36 I have more fun with my regular students than with my honors students.	O	O	O	O	O
37 I consider it important that an honors student belongs to the top 10% of the student population with regards to grade average.	O	O	O	O	O
38 I refer students to experts when their questions or interests are beyond my area of expertise.	O	O	O	O	O
39 I think honors students are more active in the academic community than regular students are.	O	O	O	O	O
40 I think that honors students will be our leaders of the future rather than regular students.	O	O	O	O	O
41 I stimulate honors students more than regular students to think about personal wishes and goals.	O	O	O	O	O
42 I stimulate regular students more than honors students to enjoy their achievements.	O	O	O	O	O
43 I use honors also as a 'educational innovation room'; I try out different education methods and tests.	O	O	O	O	O

44-45

Below you will find *10 characteristics of teachers*. Do you want to indicate which THREE characteristics you find especially important for a teacher of an **honors program**, and which THREE characteristics you find especially important for a teacher of a **regular program**.

44 Three especially important within **honors program**

- O a. places different points of view opposite to each other
- O b. makes connections with other areas of study
- O c. formulates clear and shared goals for the class
- O d. offers well-organized subject matter
- O e. invites students to actively participate
- O f. appreciates questions and remarks
- O g. is available for his/her students and is easily accessible
- O h. is interested in students as individuals
- O i. enjoys teaching
- O j. makes the course exciting and has confidence

45 Three especially important within **regular program**

- O a. places different points of view opposite to each other
- O b. makes connections with other areas of study
- O c. formulates clear and shared goals for the class
- O d. offers well-organized subject matter
- O e. invites students to actively participate
- O f. appreciates questions and remarks
- O g. is available for his/her students and is easily accessible
- O h. is interested in students as individuals
- O i. enjoys teaching
- O j. makes the course exciting and has confidence

46-47

Below you will find *17 qualities of teachers*. Please indicate which FIVE qualities of yourself make you especially appropriate to teach in an **honors program** and which FIVE qualities make you especially appropriate to teach in a **regular program**.

46 Especially appropriate for **honors program**, choose 5 options

- O a. I am demanding
- O b. I am friendly
- O c. I explain well
- O d. I know a subject well
- O e. I inspire students
- O f. I give the students new ideas
- O g. I am clear about my expectations of students
- O h. I give students room for their own choices
- O i. I understand quickly what a student asks or notices
- O j. I challenge students
- O k. I give useful feed-back
- O l. I grant students much responsibility
- O m. I make sure that students keep appointments and deadlines
- O n. I discuss course subject matter at a fast pace
- O o. I am prepared to deviate from traditional education methods
- O p. I correct work quickly
- O q. I am good at keeping discipline
- O r. Other, namely: _____
- _____
- _____
- _____

47 Especially appropriate for **regular program**, choose 5 options

- O a. I am demanding
- O b. I am friendly
- O c. I explain well
- O d. I know a subject well
- O e. I inspire students
- O f. I give the students new ideas
- O g. I am clear about my expectations of students
- O h. I give students room for their own choices
- O i. I understand quickly what a student asks or notices
- O j. I challenge students
- O k. I give useful feed-back
- O l. I grant students much responsibility
- O m. I make sure that students keep appointments and deadlines
- O n. I discuss course subject matter at a fast pace
- O o. I am prepared to deviate from traditional education methods
- O p. I correct work quickly
- O q. I am good at keeping discipline
- O r. Other, namely: _____
- _____
- _____
- _____

PART 3: CONTEXTUAL COMPONENTS 48 – 68
- about teachers' conception of teaching and learning (honors) in higher education (48-59)
- about teachers' motivation to teach (honors) (60-66)
- about teachers' perception of honors and regular students (67, 68)

48-59
Below you will find 12 general propositions about education on university/college. As this is an international survey, we would like to know your opinion about them. Mark the box that reflects your opinion the best. It is not important how other people think about it, but what your own opinion is. Do not think too long about each question. You should give the answer that first comes to your mind.

Scale: 1= completely disagree, 2= disagree, 3= not disagree and not agree, 4= agree, 5= completely agree

	1	2	3	4	5
48 If students want to achieve something later in their life, they have to learn a lot at the university.	O	O	O	O	O
49 Order and discipline are important at the university.	O	O	O	O	O
50 Students can learn a lot from each other too.	O	O	O	O	O
51 Grading is a good boost for the studying of students.	O	O	O	O	O
52 It is the job of the university to educate students to become critical citizens.	O	O	O	O	O
53 I find it important that students at the university can cooperate.	O	O	O	O	O
54 For optimal learning results at the university, I find competition among students important.	O	O	O	O	O
55 Involvement of the students in the university is important.	O	O	O	O	O
56 It is the job of the university to pass on values and standards.	O	O	O	O	O
57 I consider it important that students behave well on the university.	O	O	O	O	O
58 It is important that the university takes the wishes and interests of the students into account.	O	O	O	O	O
59 A good education is the key to success in society.	O	O	O	O	O

60-66
Below are 7 propositions about your profession. Mark the box that reflects your opinion the best. It is not important how other people think about it, but what your own opinion is. Do not think too long about each question. You should give the answer that first come to your mind.

Scale: 1= completely untrue, 2= untrue, 3= not untrue, not true, 4= true, 5= completely true

	1	2	3	4	5
60 I have the feeling that I can decide for myself how I organize my honors education.	O	O	O	O	O
61 I think that, in comparison with other teachers, I teach well.	O	O	O	O	O
62 I am extremely motivated to teach in honors.	O	O	O	O	O
63 I want to be one of the best of my work associates.	O	O	O	O	O
64 I find it important to be challenged to get the most out of myself.	O	O	O	O	O
65 My honors education makes me think of matters, I had never thought before.	O	O	O	O	O
66 My honors course fits, with respect to content, my personal interests.	O	O	O	O	O

Below you will find 15 qualities of *students*. Please indicate which FIVE qualities you find to be the most important in an *honors student*, and which FIVE qualities you find most important in a *regular student*.

67 Five most important qualities **honors student**
- O a. The student can keep an appointment
- O b. The students obtains good results in his/her courses
- O c. The student is motivated in his/her courses
- O d. The student behaves well in class
- O e. The student is easy to get on with
- O f. The student values my knowledge about a given subject
- O g. The student is prepared to invest considerable time in his/her courses
- O h. The student thinks in a creative way
- O i. The student has a passion for research
- O j. The student is curious
- O k. The student shows initiative and also carries it out
- O l. The student is not behind with his or her studies
- O m. The student is prepared to take risks in his/her academic career
- O n. The student stimulates other students within the education program
- O o. The student is involved in the academic community
- O p. Other, namely: _____

68 Five most important qualities **regular student**
- O a. The student can keep an appointment
- O b. The students obtains good results in his/her courses
- O c. The student is motivated in his/her courses
- O d. The student behaves well in class
- O e. The student is easy to get on with
- O f. The student values my knowledge about a given subject
- O g. The student is prepared to invest considerable time in his/her courses
- O h. The student thinks in a creative way
- O i. The student has a passion for research
- O j. The student is curious
- O k. The student shows initiative and also carries it out
- O l. The student is not behind with his or her studies
- O m. The student is prepared to take risks in his/her academic career
- O n. The student stimulates other students within the education program
- O o. The student is involved in the academic community
- O p. Other, namely: _____

69 What are important goals that you want to achieve with your honors teaching?

_____
_____
_____
_____
_____

70 What is an important source of inspiration for you when teaching honors students?

_____
_____
_____
_____
_____

Do you gave any further remarks about teaching within honors or about this questionnaire, please write them down.

_____
_____
_____
_____
_____

Thank you very much for answering. You can drop your completed questionnaire into a box at the NCHC table.

Appendix 2 – Statistical analyses

2a – Correlations with U.S. teacher's motivation

Variable	Correlation	P	n
Community	0.247	0.009	112
Academic competence	0.463	0.000	106

Intrinsic motivation and community and intrinsic motivation and academic competence correlate with each other (p<.01). The bivariate correlations are respectively 0.25 ($r^2 = .06$) and 0.46 ($r^2 = 0.21$).

2b – Chi square tests United States versus Netherlands: three most important strategies of teachers for an honors program and for a regular program (% and Chi-square score)

Strategy	% in Honors Top-3 U.S.A.	% in Honors Top-3 NL	Chi-square score (χ^2)	% in Regular Top-3 U.S.A.	% in Regular Top-3 NL	Chi-square score (χ^2)
Invites students to actively participate (1)	81.9	62.8	15.17***	34.6	44.7	3.74
Makes connections with other areas of study (2)	51.2	45.5	1.64	18.9	14.1	1.55
Makes the course exciting and has confidence (3)	33.1	34.0	0.03	34.6	37.0	0.21
Is interested in students as individuals (4)	32.3	21.2	6.07*	12.6	10.6	0.36
Appreciates questions and remarks (5)	26.0	35.3	3.53	18.9	25.7	2.32
Enjoys teaching (6)	24.4	29.8	1.30	37.8	38.9	0.04
Is available for his/her students and is easily accessible (7)	23.6	24.0	0.01	22.0	24.1	0.22
Places different points of view opposite to each other (8)	19.7	42.9	21.15***	10.2	18.6	4.70*
Formulates clear and shared goals for the class (9)	8.7	6.1	0.94	45.7	39.9	1.25
Offers well-organized subject matter (10)	6.3	10.9	2.21	57.5	52.7	0.82

*Note: *p<.05, **p<.01, ***p<.001*

2c - Chi square tests U.S.A. versus Netherlands: three most important strategies of teachers for an honors program and for a regular program (% and Chi-square score)

Strategy	% in Honors Top-5 U.S.A.	% in Honors Top-5 NL	Chi-square score (χ^2)	% in Regular Top-5 U.S.A.	% in Regular Top-5 NL	Chi-square score (χ^2)
I challenge students (1)	78.7	60.3	13.67***	53.5	35.6	12.07**
I am prepared to deviate from traditional education methods (2)	63.8	38.8	22.71***	21.3	10.3	9.39**
I give students room for their own choices (3)	56.7	41.3	8.56**	17.3	14.7	0.46
I grant students much responsibility (4)	48.8	34.6	7.67**	11.8	12.5	0.04
I inspire students (5)	47.2	53.5	1.43	27.6	44.9	11.29**
I give the students new ideas (6)	39.4	36.5	0.31	23.6	20.5	0.52
I give useful feedback (7)	29.1	40.1	4.63*	55.1	53.5	0.09
I am demanding (8)	24.4	27.2	0.37	25.2	15.1	6.28*
I know a subject well (9)	23.6	30.1	1.89	42.5	45.5	0.33
I am friendly (10)	18.1	11.2	3.74	29.9	19.6	5.56*
I am clear about my expectations of students (11)	15.0	14.7	0.00	58.3	41.7	10.00**
I explain well (12)	9.4	27.2	16.60***	51.2	67.3	10.03**
I understand quickly what a student asks or remarks (13)	6.3	17.0	8.61**	18.1	24.0	1.83
I correct work quickly (14)	4.7	6.1	0.31	13.4	10.3	0.89
Other, namely (x)	3.1	1.3	0.19	2.4	1.3	1.83
I discuss course subject matter at a fast pace (15)	1.6	4.2	1.84	2.4	1.6	0.67
I am good at keeping discipline (16)	1.6	1.0	0.30	3.9	4.8	0.16
I make sure that students keep appointments and deadlines (17)	0.8	5.1	4.57*	3.1	15.7	13.40***

Note: *p<.05, **p<.01, ***p<.001

204

2d– Correlations with Dutch teacher's motivation

Variable	Correlation	P	n
Community	0.300	0.000	267
Academic competence	0.286	0.000	268

Intrinsic motivation and community and intrinsic motivation and academic competence correlate with each other (p<.01). The bivariate correlations are respectively 0.30 ($r^2 = .09$) and 0.29 ($r^2 = .08$).

Acknowledgements

Welk uitzicht is mooier dan staand op de schouders van leermeesters en raadgevers als Gerard Hoekveld, Ria Kloppenburg, Rob van der Vaart en mijn vader Gerrit Wolfensberger. Ik ruik de aarde zoals eens in de glasscherpe vulkaanvelden van Hawaï. Ik zie grazige weiden, wijkende horizonten en een stoet van jonge mensen. Elk van hen heeft het gevoeld: ik ga dit doen, mijn hart klopt omdat ik deze taak volbrengen zal, deze beproeving aanvaard, ik zal niet wanhopen, ik zal bereikbaar zijn, moedig zijn in een poging tot genezing.

Welk begin van de werkdag is beter dan een vrolijke conciërge, vriendelijke gezichten bij de receptie, een welkom van Achive Koçak in de gang, een deur die openzwaait, de telefoon die gaat en de zangerige stem van Norma Adams.

Stevig met je beide benen op de grond - spring je niet ver. Wat een voorrecht omringd te mogen zijn door mensen die jong blijven, die me bij de les houden, me uitdagen die extra sprong te wagen. Kracht ligt ook in de verbijzondering – daarom hier de namen die symbool staan voor al die anderen om daarmee al mijn leerlingen en studenten te danken voor het plezier, de inspiratie en de belofte. In herinnering Nelie Vergouwen – voor de middelbare schoolleerlingen van het Christelijk Gymnasium Utrecht; Maarten Trijsburg omdat geslacht op geslacht elkaar ontmoet; Joost Beunderman & Compaan voor de leerlingen die studenten worden; Jonna Snoek en Daniel Wiegant voor de vrouwen en mannen die het avontuur zoeken; Jorim Schraven voor de mensen die trouw blijven aan hun idealen; Tim Schwanen voor degenen met wetenschappelijke loopbanen; Guillaume Burghouwt die het eerste honours testimonium in ontvangst neemt; Martin Zebracki de eerste bachelor met een undergraduate honours speech; Alissa Zuijdgeest voor de studenten in interdisciplinaire honours projecten; Maarten van der Meiden voor duaal en honours combineren met onderzoek over de grens; Marielle Hoff voor de inzet van student-assistenten; Imre Végh van drs. naar master naar vredevol ondernemer; Henrik Looij voor degene met maatschappelijke carrières; Wouter Schenke voor al de alumni die de cirkel rondmaken; Patrick Witte voor de multitaskende talenten in studie, sport, beeld of muziek; Monique Geerdink voor diegene die opstaan en doorgaan. Douwe Hooijenga en Derk Berends voor de studenten die de gemeenschap dragen in commissies en besturen; Marte Wachter voor de studenten die onderzoek doen naar honours.

Honours is de weg van de meeste weerstand; en zonder wrijving geen glans. Ik noem enkele van de rebellen van de stille revolutie in hoger onderwijsland; Christiaan van den Berg, Bas Derks, Pierre van Eijl, Gerrit Faber, Maarten Hogenstijn, Pieter Hooimeijer, Machiel Keestra, André Schram, Liesbeth Schreven-Brinkman, Sara Steyn, Sanne Tromp, Siu Siu Oen, Leo Paul, Hein Hoitink, Albert Pilot, Marjolijn Vermeulen, Herman Wijffels.

Van een mug een vlinder maken kan makkelijker met collegae die je er aan herinneren dat je soms dromen hebt die je wakker houden totdat je ze uitvoert, maar bovenal die je ook helpen je dromen te leven. Ik voel me een bevoorrecht mens dat ik mag werken bij Sociale Geografie en Planologie, Faculteit Geowetenschappen, Universiteit Utrecht, Europa, de Wereld. Toen honours echt nog niet kon in Nederland – toen kon het daar wel. Ik ben trots op mijn universiteit. Ik noem één naam in herinnering om daarmee al mijn collegae te eren: Han Floor die me aan de Kappa hielp in dit proefschrift.

Share your talent, move the world is het kloppend motto van de Hanzehogeschool Groningen; de plek waar ik mijn vleugels uit mag slaan en als lector een onderzoeksgroep mag leiden. Een zegen. Ik wil de kringleden van toen tot nu danken voor hun inzet voor het honoursonderwijs middels ons onderzoek en noem Pieter Veenstra die in rust ons overzicht maakt. De conferentie Evoking Excellence in Higher Education and Beyond waar ruim 325 mensen uit 12 landen samenkwamen, onderzoek presenteerden en ervaringen uitwisselden is exemplarisch voor de durf en de klasse van de Hanzehogeschool met een CvB dat staat voor excellentie. De voorzitter van de Sirius auditcommissie noemde ons team een gideonsbende met Trijnie Faber als boegbeeld.

"*Ik spijbel alleen als ik buiten school meer kan leren*" (Loesje). Humor, ander perspectief, roze taart, champie, intocht, after-party, tweets, lavendel voor ontspanning, bellen op de fiets, verwennerij, yoga, uitsmijter met wit en bruin brood, 'aangetrouwde' familie, Oorsprongkunst, wachten bij de lift

– ook die in de sneeuw, harde noten, een zachte hand en heel veel vertrouwen, de meisjes in huis. Wat is me veel gegeven door de mensen waardoor ik vertrekken kan van waar ik nu sta. Hoe hun te eren, hoe al hun namen te noemen. Ondoenlijk. Wel de namen die zorgen voor de lichtheid van ons bestaan en de rolletjes waarop ons gezin mag lopen: Magda, Rosa, Tanina, Kunera, Sanne, Willy, Ida, Cathy, Marleen en Ingrid.

'Teachers open the door, but you must enter by yourself.' I want to thank all the teachers who participated in my research and all teachers who are dedicated to their students and to celebrating teaching and learning academically talented college students.

Op reis om te ontdekken of de wereld er nog is! Conferences, international collaboration, making friends, and I say your name - Janine DeWitt. In het hart gegrifte honours ervaringen dankzij de National Collegiate Honors Council. John Zubizarreta, special friend, you are my honors counselor and inspirator.

"For we know we shall find, our own peace of mind" (Andrew Lloyd Weber). Het lijkt simpel en volgens 'Loesje' is dat het ook. Het is ook een kunst om het goede dat gedaan wordt te zien, op je in te laten werken en voort te zetten. Mensen als Roelf Haan, Pieter van Tuinen en Piet Warners gidsen me daarin, net als anderen met hun doelgerichte werk die ik heb mogen ontmoeten in de Kerkenraad, Aardrijkskunde Olympiade, de Glazen Globe, de Jury Excellente School. Mensen in en rondom de Sirius Beoordelingscommissie, de ontmoetingen binnen het Nederlandse Sirius Netwerk en tijdens studiereizen bemoedigen me. Met stip mijn 'small group Outrageous' die me elke keer weer een spiegel weet aan te reiken. Vragen die me weer een hoofdstuk verder brachten.

Marieke van Denderen, Lilian Eggens, Pierre van Eijl, Matte Hartog, Niels van der Kamer, Elles Kazemier, Lucas van der Linden, Ton Markus, Wolter Paans, Albert Pilot, Marin van Rijn, Jan Ritsema van Eck, Margot Stoete, Fred Trappenburg, Judith Vos, Nancy van Weesep hebben ieder op hun eigen wijze vanuit verschillende expertises het feest van mijn proefschrift-tijd versierd. Dank! Nelleke de Jong hielp me de zomer door; Bouke van Gorp is de luis in mijn pels. Welk een voorrecht dat jullie zelfs mijn paranimfen willen zijn! Ik wil mijn leescommissie bedanken voor hun betrokkenheid: Martin Dijst, Jeannette Doornenbal, Orlanda Lie, Jan van Tartwijk, en John Zubizarreta.

Ik wil hier zeker mijn promotor Rob van der Vaart eren en danken; al schieten woorden te kort. Hij heeft me vertrouwd en gesteund; heeft me gedragen en liet zich verrassen; liep voor me uit en stond achter me.

Er zat vuurwerk in jouw ogen dat ik nooit eerder zag. Als jij kijkt en ik kijk dan spatten de vonken over. Kruitdamp. We proefden samen Mount Tongariro's as. Sanne Tromp, loving man, you spark my desires. Door het leven heen ben jij er bij, voed en verrijk je me. Je zei: gun het jezelf. Marekjeliefste-zoon – zo sta je in mijn appeltje – je rake Flyley Focus rapteksten en vrienden doelpunten, je hang naar luxe en into the wild, je oog voor kleur en vorm, waarmee je de aanzet voor de cover gaf. Je brengt me verankering. Mere Mere Meisje, 'Miracle of Love', een schoonheid om rekening mee te houden die weet wat ze wil en mij liefdevol bij de les houdt. Renard kan kijken met zijn hart, Kapla tovertuinen bouwen, sterren bewegen en warm plezier rondstrooien. Je zegt dat je trots bent dat je bestaat en dat geeft me kracht. Ons gezin: Betrokken, actief en mooi, rustpunt en energy-tap.

De Tuinen van Dorr is het mooiste boek dat mijn moeder me voorlas: al ben je alleen en op zoek, je bereikt het toch samen en had je de liefde niet, je zou niets zijn. Vrouwen van 10 tot 86 jaar vierden met elkaar mijn verjaardag. Anne en ik dansten op Patti Smith terwijl ze de liefde van Rembrandt bezong. Mijn vriendschappen en familielijnen gaan tot ver terug – en dankzij ieder van jullie behoud ik mijn evenwicht als ik reik naar idealen en spreek over vergezichten die mij voor ogen blijven. Omdat ik geloof in een betere wereld, omdat ik geloof dat onderwijs en democratie verbonden zijn, omdat ik hoop dat honoursonderwijs bijdraagt aan geluk – omdat eens 'elke laars die dreunend stampt, en elke mantel, in bloed gewenteld, verbrand zal worden, een prooi van het vuur' en eindeloos de vrede.

Curriculum Vitae

Marca Wolfensberger has been active in honors education for the past two decades. She has conducted research on honors education, publishing numerous articles, reports and book chapters on the topic. She was co-editor of a book on 'Talent for tomorrow' (2010). She gives invited talks and workshops at (inter)national conferences. Wolfensberger is an honors teacher and a teacher-trainer in faculty development programs for honors in various settings. She has a dream that opportunities for honors education are available to every student who wants to join.

She is a teacher-researcher and the honors director at the Department of Human Geography and Spatial Planning, Faculty of Geosciences, Utrecht University (1997-present). Wolfensberger co-founded one of the first honors programs in the Netherlands. This program received a grant 'Ruim Baan voor Talent' (2005), and again 'Sirius' (2009) both from the Ministry of Education, Culture and Science. The honors program became part of the interdisciplinary *Honours College Geosciences*. Also, Wolfensberger co-designed the dual learning program (1998-2001) in which she then became a lecturer. As honors teacher, Wolfensberger emphasizes the personal and intellectual growth of honors students.

She also heads the research center for Talent Development in Higher Education and Beyond at the Hanze University of Applied Sciences in Groningen (2009-present). The research group consists of 14 teacher-researchers, among whom two PhD candidates and three visiting fellows. Marca Wolfensberger gives priority to international research collaboration, such as that with the University of Helsinki (Finland). Her research group obtained two grants from the Hanze University: one to conduct research on characteristics of excellent professionals; and one to develop and execute a faculty development program for honors teachers. In 2011, collaborating with Wolfensberger, Marymount University (Va, U.S.A.) won a grant from the State University of New York to create an international online honors course. With her research group Wolfensberger was an organizer of a conference on 'Evoking Excellence in Higher Education and Beyond', with 325 participants from all around the globe (2012).

Recently, the Minister of Education appointed Wolfensberger to a jury to identify 'excellent' primary and secondary schools in the Netherlands (2012-present).

As a member of the Sirius Assessment Committee, she has reviewed proposals for 'excellence' programs from over thirty institutions of higher education on behalf of the Dutch government (2008-2010).

She is chair of the National Collegiate Honors Council Research Committee (2009-present). Her site-visiting experience goes back to 2001, when a group of four individuals committed to talent development in higher education, including Wolfensberger, established the Dutch *Plusnetwerk* (a 'little sister' of NCHC). Since 2008, Marca has held the title of NCHC-Recommended Site Visitor. The issue 'Honors around the Globe' (2012) of the research journal of the National Collegiate Honors Council is dedicated to Wolfensberger.

Wolfensberger has worked as a senior educational consultant on honors programs (2003-2005) at the Institute for Interdisciplinary Studies at the University of Amsterdam. Wolfensberger also does voluntary work. For instance, she was a member of the board of the Geographical Olympiads for secondary schools (1996-2005) and serves on the jury for the *Glazen Globe* (geographical youth books; 1996-present).

At the beginning of her career, Wolfensberger was as co-director of the Media Institute of Churches – specialized in local and regional media. There she learned about the pleasure of working with passionate people. During the same period she worked as a secondary school geography teacher at the Christelijk Gymnasium Utrecht, where she discovered her love for teaching and an exuberant interest in gifted and motivated students.

Wolfensberger started her academic studies at Utrecht University at the Faculty of Geosciences and was awarded her master's (*doctorandus*) degree in Regional Geography cum laude (1991). She continued to study geography, at the University of Applied Sciences Utrecht (teacher certifications with a special interest in gifted education, 1993, 1997). She took also other pathways: her studies of Cultural Anthropology (Utrecht University, propedeutic exam 1987) and Theology (Utrecht University, propedeutic exam 1988; VU Amsterdam).

Wolfensberger received her Gymnasium β school diploma at the Herman Jordan Lyceum in Zeist. During those years she had transformative learning experiences and became convinced that everyone loves learning.

Marca Wolfensberger and her partner Sanne Tromp live with their three children, Marek, Mere and Renard in a 'family & study' house in Utrecht, a listed monument that has now been restored according to the principles of organic architecture.

Marca Wolfensberger was born in Geneva, Switzerland, where her father, Gerrit Wolfensberger, was a vicar working for the World Council of Churches. As director of the *Ruimzicht* foundation, he created convivia – living & learning communities – for students. Her mother, Betty Wolfensberger-van Paassen, worked as a psychiatrist who also taught young nursing aides. Her brother Onno was an entrepreneur. Marca has fond memories of living in the woods. Being part of a boarding-school learning community made an indelible impression: of summertime, with scholars reading books at tables on the green grass, connecting the outside world with intellectual growth. Of white forests with yellow crocus blossoms that announce the arrival of new days.